CITY OF MY HEART

BUFFALO, 1967–2020

• MARK GOLDMAN •

Friends of the Buffalo Story
398 Jersey Street
Buffalo, NY 14213
markgoldman915@gmail.com

Book design by Goulah Design Group, Inc.

ISBN: 978-0-9740702-2-3 (softcover)

Library of Congress control number available upon request.

Printed in the U.S.A.

10 9 8 7 6 5 4 3 2 1

"… seek the welfare of the city where I have sent you …
pray to the Lord for it, for in its welfare you will find your welfare."

Jeremiah, 29:5–7
(*Holy Bible*, English Standard Version, 2001)

• • •

To the children of Buffalo:
Happy are those who love their city.

Contents

Foreword: *by Karen Brady* 1

Introduction: A New York State of Mind 5

CHAPTER 1: A Brand New World – Buffalo, 1967 15

CHAPTER 2: An Italian Hill Town in Buffalo? – How the neighborhood of Black Rock changed my way of thinking about life in the city 33

CHAPTER 3: Into the 'Seventies – How people stared down decline and, with faith in themselves, rolled up their sleeves, went to work and got it done 43

CHAPTER 4: Into the 'Eighties – How a teacher and his students discovered their city ... together 77

CHAPTER 5: Judge John T. Curtin – Struggling with the challenges of a changing city, he helped restore my faith in Buffalo 89

CHAPTER 6: The Calumet Arts Café – The arts as a tonic for an ailing downtown 99

CHAPTER 7: What Would Grandma Rosie Do? – How everyday wisdom brought sanity to downtown development plans 127

CHAPTER 8: The Buffalo Story – History and heritage as the building blocks of community. 147

CHAPTER 9: Next Year in Jerusalem – What? A New Yorker finds his Jewish identity in, where? Buffalo? 171

CHAPTER 10: Discovering the Power of Faith, Family, and Friendship – In South Buffalo, I learned, you are never alone 187

CHAPTER 11: In the End – The enchanted landscape of North Buffalo and Central Park 211

Epilogue: A healing heart: Buffalo, 2020 221

Gratitude: Thanks to the book production team 235

Index 237

Foreword

In the summer of 1967 – as Buffalo's best and brightest were departing their declining city in droves – a 24-year-old Mark Goldman rolled into town. More than half a century later, that then-budding historian is still here, now also an activist, author, educator and entrepreneur who, it is fair to say, has been behind or had a hand in nearly every significant stride made by Buffalo in the interim.

Yes, long before the city's Young Turks of today, there was an earlier Young Turk named Goldman who came here fresh from his native Manhattan – and was undeterred by what many Buffalonians in the 1960s deemed irredeemable urban decay.

What they saw as blight, Goldman saw as opportunity even as city leaders – whose idea of progress left little room for preservation – continued to gut still-glorious pieces of Buffalo's past grandeur, destroying in the process the hallowed Frederick Law Olmsted-designed Humboldt Parkway and prime parts of his Delaware Park, to make way for the Kensington and Scajaquada expressways.

Goldman was not alone in seeing this as a grave error for Buffalo – a city also experiencing the losses of the area's shipping and steel industries, and the myriad jobs associated with them.

But Goldman had an advantage – or three: He was not from Buffalo and therefore enough removed to see the city's larger picture. He was a Manhattanite who had experienced firsthand the harm such travesties as the destruction of New York's old Penn Station had inflicted on the city itself. And he had been exposed to the great urban activist Jane Jacobs who maintained that urban developers of the time "did not respect the needs of city-dwellers."

That wasn't all: Goldman also had something sorely needed in late 1960s Buffalo – and that, put plainly, was such a quantity and quality of audacity that Goldman's middle name could well have been chutzpah! Frustrated by what he sensed was a failure of imagination and creativity, a willingness to tackle in a bold way the challenges that faced us as a community, he desperately wanted to create a culture of hope, opportunity and promise.

Buffalo activists and preservationists suddenly had themselves one very squeaky wheel who, if he had something to say, or learn, about the state of the city didn't write a letter to the editor – he went straight to the mayor, or the schools superintendent, or to the chambers of a federal court judge, often unannounced. If he saw something that needed fixing, he didn't spend time saying so, or even delegating. Instead, he rolled up his sleeves, grabbed a shovel, paint brush or broom, organized meetings, joined in protests, researched each effort as it came along – and generally put himself out there, getting the job done.

City of My Heart is a chronicle of the numerous times Goldman has been front and center among Buffalo's movers and shakers and, in that sense, is a history of many salient aspects of Buffalo's last half century.

It is also a memoir of Goldman's personal journey over five-plus decades, the public and the private overlapping as a reader watches Goldman's life and work become a part of the tapestry of the city itself.

But what sets this book apart is its cultural and sociological perspective – Goldman caring at least as much for the multiethnic makeup of Buffalo as for its past and promise, finding himself at home within the city's neighborhoods not only of many heritages and cultures, but also with the distinctive peoples of each, individuals with fierce and longtime loyalties to one another.

In this respect, "City of My Heart," is a singular narrative, told in Goldman's own, open and straightforward voice – and suffused with Buffalo names of yore, some still with us, most well known, others less so, or never having been given their due before.

My own journey through its pages brought to life long-forgotten memories, particularly of the late 1960s to the early '80s, a time when I was preoccupied with lobbying, as a *Buffalo News* columnist, for women's rights (which were still, in those decades, in exceedingly short supply).

Buffalo history loomed large in my wheelhouse as well – but as history itself, not as a great and sacred impetus toward the city's ongoing renaissance of today. Goldman, luckily, saw it as the latter and, in 1974, put together the first known tour of Buffalo landmarks and other places of interest in the Queen City.

He and I had met earlier, at a party in Allentown where we both lived with our young families, and I subsequently wrote about Goldman's tour – catapulting him to local fame (he says) and making me the first of many to document Goldman's involvement in Buffalo over the years.

Not to mince words, the extent of his contribution to the city is staggering.

Chippewa Street stands out of course: Goldman transmogrified the drab, and often dangerous, downtown stretch into a contemporary hot spot after he bought and restored the dilapidated Calumet building in the 1990s, establishing the Calumet Arts Café (known for fine food and jazz); providing the Irish Classical Theatre Company with its first home; adding The Third Room, a bar – and, later, the city's first Latin disco, La Luna.

But that was long after he, as a young PhD candidate at the University at Buffalo, wrote his doctoral dissertation on the historical development of a then-often-overlooked neighborhood – Black Rock. He soon immersed himself in other neighborhoods as well, and began his decades-long collaboration with others bent not only on protecting the Buffalo legacies of Frederick Law Olmsted but also on preserving Buffalo's priceless but long-neglected physical history.

Goldman taught at UB and, later, Empire State College, organizing a city-wide conference on Buffalo neighborhoods and seeing the publication of his first book, "High Hopes: The Rise and Decline of Buffalo, NY." An interest in desegregation of the schools led to his second book, "City on the Lake: The Challenge of Change in Buffalo."

Membership in the Jewish Community Center on Delaware Avenue, which dated from his earliest days in Buffalo, led to his staunch participation in the fight, in the 1980s, not only to keep but to refurbish the JCC's downtown building when a second JCC was built in Amherst.

Policy issues surrounding both downtown Buffalo and its waterfront – including a master plan for the city's redevelopment, the location of a new Convention Center, the controversies surrounding casino gambling and the need for improved traffic management – also consumed much of Goldman's time till the 2000s when he and others turned their attentions to opposing a prominent Canalside location for Bass Pro, the big-box retailer that city leaders didn't seem to realize would doom all hopes for a truly-revitalized waterfront, with access to all.

Goldman opened the still-popular Allen Street Hardware Café in Allentown at the same time and, in 2014, the Black Rock Kitchen and Bar. His third book, "City on the Edge: Buffalo in the 20th Century," was published in 2007; "Max Meets the Mayor," a children's offering set in Buffalo, in 2014.

"Albright: The Life and Times of John J. Albright" – Goldman's 2017 biography of the man behind Buffalo's Albright-Knox Art Gallery – and his 2019

"Tillie: A New York City Girl," a diary kept by Goldman's mother, round out his book publications to date.

Today, in his mid-70s and far from slowing down, Goldman is most involved in his Friends of the Buffalo Story, an ambitious citywide effort he founded in 2012 "to bring Buffalo history alive" to its residents.

It should be noted here that, like anyone long and frequently in the public eye, Goldman has had his dissenters over the years – individuals viewing him as an "enfant terrible," a "provocateur" or "self-promoter" – but few can deny either his penchant for getting things done, or the depth and breadth of his impact on his chosen city over the past 50-plus years.

City of My Heart is his own story of those years, including his inner thoughts, doubts, hopes and dreams. It introduces us to the members of his birth family, contrasting his Manhattan upbringing to his decades in a smaller, more manageable Buffalo – and gives us, among other fascinating chapters, the deeply personal, "Next Year in Jerusalem?: Forging a Jewish Identity in Buffalo."

It also leads us to neighborhoods throughout Buffalo – with Goldman's often- nontraditional students as guides. It expresses the meaning to Goldman of Buffalo being the birthplace not only of his three children and three grandchildren, but also of lasting friendships. It takes us into the homes of Buffalo others, letting us listen to and learn about their pasts, their presents, their dreams and desires, their families, their customs and foods

Goldman's new memoir is, in sum, an ode, a paean to the Buffalo he not only came to know but helped to grow, a city whose spirit lured him in – and to which he, in turn, has long and joyfully given back.

His energy and enthusiasm never wane here – and we are grateful for this back-and-forward-looking historian, this early soldier for Buffalo's resurgence, a man who left New York, the city of his soul, and found, in Buffalo, the city of his heart.

– Karen Brady, retired reporter and former columnist and book critic for *The Buffalo News*

Introduction

A New York State of Mind

I owe my life-long passion for cities to New York, where I was born and raised, and to my mother, Tillie, whose New York stories filled my childhood. Tillie was a marvelous storyteller. She had a great memory and an ability to recall in enormous detail the characters, settings, and events of her New York City childhood. And while she spoke often about her family and the world in which she grew up, her primary topic was the city that she adored. New York City, she said, was "My Town."

Born there in 1906, she died there 95 years later. Her life in the city spanned the century and she never lived anywhere else. She always talked about it, filling her stories with details of time and place that brought the city of her youth alive to me, my brother Tony, and my sister Barbara. Tillie was born in Harlem when it was still very white and Jewish. Many stories of her childhood contained warm and romantic recollections: long afternoons sitting on the stoop of the family's West 113th Street brownstone; hours in the kitchen with her mother, Rosie; Sabbath dinners at a long table surrounded by raucous members of her large, extended family, daytime walks to Wadleigh High School, evening walks to Ike's ice-cream parlor at 116th and Lenox, summers at the beach in Arverne, Queens, or in Tannersville in the Catskills.

Her favorite and most repeated stories were of the times she spent with her father, my grandfather, "Hymie" Schwartz. She adored her father and was thrilled whenever he asked her to join him on his weekly jaunts from their home in Harlem to his place of business, a wholesale restaurant supply company on the Bowery. She told us about his car, a blue Willys Jeep, and how they drove downtown through Central Park, stopping to look at the sheep that still filled the Sheep's Meadow. Once, she said, they stopped at the Metropolitan Museum of Art. He wanted to show her a painting by "that Jewish painter, Rembrandt." From there, they continued downtown, under the Third Ave El all the way to the teaming Bowery and the streets of the Lower East Side. Hymie had spent his childhood there, mostly on Hester Street. By 1900 or so, he was in business and soon, Tillie proudly recalled, he owned a string of tenement buildings on those immigrant-filled streets of the Lower East Side.

Tillie was a curious and energetic person. Her stories of her times with her father on the Lower East Side and her mother in Harlem were filled with colorful details of that time and place. My mother's New York City stories seeped into my soul and became my New York City stories, too. Indeed, so many years later, here in Buffalo, New York, those New York City stories have become my children and grandchildren's New York City stories as well.

My father Charlie did not tell stories. It was not until years after he died in 1966 that I learned some of the details of his early life. He was born in New York City in 1902, the youngest child of immigrant parents who'd come to America from Russian Poland a year earlier. His father was a tailor who worked in a factory in the garment industry. He worked in buildings like the one on Greene Street that housed the infamous Triangle Shirtwaist Company.

The Goldmans – father Max, mother Sophia, Charlie and his three older siblings – lived first on the Lower East Side and then in The Bronx. Charlie quit school as soon as he was legally able. In 1918, following in his father's footsteps, Charlie went to work in the Garment District, then located in and around Seventh Avenue and the mid-'thirties. My dad was smart, ambitious, and a very hard worker. By his early twenties, he owned and operated a ladies coat business called "Mode Craft Coats." Mode Craft was the center of his life and the focal point of much of our family's life too.

Our home was filled with the sounds, the smells and the feel of the coat business: fashion magazines and "swatches" (one of the favorite words from my childhood) were strewn our apartment; long and loud telephone conversations with buyers, salesmen, and the other denizens of my father's frenzied work life. The epicenter of it all was at my Dad's office and showroom in a magisterial building at 500 Seventh Avenue. On regular Saturday morning visits, we absorbed more of the color and the character of this unique industry. On side streets and restaurants – places like Dubrow's Kosher Cafeteria and Lou G. Siegel's Kosher restaurant – in offices and showrooms still filled in the 1950s with Yiddish-speaking owners and workers, the world of my father – the world of *schmatas*, the International Ladies Garment Workers Union, cigars, gin rummy and kosher food, became my world too, part of the life experiences that I enjoyed as a child coming of age in New York City.

Then there was my older sister Barbara, born in 1931, twelve years my senior. Barbara was an intense and wildly curious young woman, an artist, a "beatnik" who majored in art history at NYU. In her black tights and turtleneck sweaters, a cigarette forever cradled in her fingers, she was to me exotic and beautiful. Several times, she took me with her to NYU's Washington Square campus, once to a lecture by the great art historian HW Janson and afterwards to Figaro's, a café she loved on Bleeker Street. She adored "The Village" and together we visited her favorite haunts, including the 8th Street BookStore, Rienzi's, that fabulous café on MacDougal Street. On my 16th birthday in 1959, she took me to the Village Vanguard to see Harry Belafonte. It was with Barbara that I rode the subway to Fort Tryon Park and the Cloisters, and it was with her that I first walked across the Brooklyn Bridge.

I was particularly close to my younger brother Tony. We spent incalculable hours and days of our childhood in Central Park. There was not a nook or a cranny of the Park that we did not explore together. We rode our bikes everywhere. We played football and baseball under the long shadows cast over the Meadow by the apartment towers of Central Park West; we played basketball in the nearby playground. We climbed the rocks and, as little boys, the Mother Goose playground was our home-away-from-home. We loved the Central Park Zoo. In 1953, we won a contest to name the newborn giraffe, which was forever after known as "Frisky." Every weekday we rode the bus on Madison Avenue together up to 86th Street, transferring to the crosstown bus, then finally walking the two blocks to 88th and Central Park West where our school, Walden, was located.

But I had no better guide to the City than my mother, Tillie. Tillie came of age in New York City during the heady, liberating years between the wars. She loved the arts and she took my brother and me everywhere: to all the museums, concerts at Carnegie Hall, recitals at the YMHA on East 96th St., and, every year for my birthday, to a Broadway musical. Together we saw the original cast productions of *West Side Story*, *The Pajama Game*, *My Fair Lady*, and others. Above all, she loved Central Park. It was there, in what she called only half in jest "my estate," that she spent countless hours walking to and around the Meadow, around the Reservoir, and figure-skating on Wollman Rink. Even during the final years of her life, hardly a day passed when Tillie could not be found sitting on "my bench," near the entrance to Central Park at 61st and Fifth Avenue.

Following my graduation from Brandeis University in 1964, I returned to New York City, thinking that it was there for sure that I would find a career and make my home. I had majored in American history and, eager to continue my studies, I entered a master's program in history at NYU. I hoped that this would lead to a doctorate and eventually a teaching job somewhere in the City. I was living in a small apartment on Sixth Avenue and 13th St., on the fringes of my sister's beloved Village. From there, I was able to participate in the heady intellectual life that was all around me. I was happy and excited.

My first class was with a professor of history, a man named Bayard Still who had made New York City the primary focus of his work. I had had some extraordinary history professors at Brandeis, men (and one woman), and from them I had taken some compelling courses on topics such as the Renaissance and the Reformation, the Ancient World, Elizabethan and Victorian England, the American Revolution, and the Civil War. But a course on a city, on New York City? Who would have thought? (My mother was thrilled when I told her.) Professor Still had not yet completed his book on the topic so, in the absence of a textbook, he took us out into the streets of the city in a series of weekly walking tours. Still wanted us to visit the neighborhoods and the streets where the forces of history had actually altered the city. There was hardly a neighborhood that we did not visit. Still's ability to bring the history of New York City alive remains an influence on me to this day.

Professor Still was passionately interested in historic preservation. He, like so many other New Yorkers, was horrified and appalled by the demolition of Pennsylvania Station, which began in 1963. The massive structure was still being torn apart when we visited the demolition site a year later. It reminded him, he said, of London during the Blitz. Except this time, he said, citing Pogo, "the enemy is us."

Penn Station was falling and, if Robert Moses was to have his way, Greenwich Village would be next. For years it had been Moses' ambition to build a highway, a 10-lane superhighway, no less, across lower Manhattan. Known as the Lower Manhattan Expressway ("LOMEX"), the purpose of the highway was to connect the Holland Tunnel on the West Side with the Manhattan and Williamsburg bridges in the east. Integral to Moses' vision was the construction of a four-lane on-ramp that would, Moses said, be located in Washington Square Park. Opposition in the Village community in general and at NYU in particular was immediate and intense. Galvanized primarily by the leadership of Jane Jacobs, still a largely unknown writer for *Fortune Magazine*, those opposed to the on-ramp prevailed. Washington Square Park was saved. LOMEX, however, was still very much on the drawing board when I began my studies at NYU in the Fall of 1964.

Although I lived on West 13th Street, just outside the affected neighborhood, as a student at NYU and a devotee of New York City and its history, I cared deeply about the issue. When I learned that the soon-to-be world famous Jane Jacobs was scheduled to address a community meeting at Judson Hall (on the southern fringe of the Square), I joined hundreds of others in attendance. Her book, *The Death and Life of Great American Cities*, had been published just four years earlier. "Death and Life," as we called it, had become required reading for those of us in the neighborhood who cared about these issues.

Jacobs, despite her diminutive stature, was a woman of great charisma who could stir a crowd with her direct style of presentation. The Expressway was a cataclysmic proposal, she argued, one that would lead to the destruction of hundreds of buildings, the eviction of thousands of residents, the elimination of hundreds of small businesses and other commercial enterprises. Besides, she said, Moses' proposal made no sense. It was "stupid" and should be stopped. While the election of John Lindsay in November 1965 slowed the process, it was not until 1969 that Lindsay finally and forever killed the project. The struggle over LOMEX raised critical issues not only about urban planning and urban design, but about power and who used it. Although I would leave New York City prior to the final resolution of this conflict, the issues raised by it – what gets built and who decides – were ones that I would be dealing with later in Buffalo and for many years to come.

My interest in issues relating to city life grew as I continued my studies. NYU was emerging as a center of some of the most interesting thinking anywhere about urban issues. It was here, between 1965-1967, that I was introduced to writers and thinkers whose work would influence me for the rest of my life.

One was a city planner from MIT named Kevin Lynch, the author of *The Image of the City* (1960). Not unlike Jacobs, Lynch used human terms, writing about the senses and how people actually "feel" in the urban environment. His attention to the details of color, landmarks, "the shifting image," appealed to me as did his emphasis on the importance of "legibility" and "a sense of place." Lynch helped me to realize that urban public policy needed to be rooted in how people live and the values that they live by. It was, Lynch suggested, peoples' memories and feelings about the places they lived in – not vague, abstract and intellectualized theories about what "works", that need to be the foundation of successful urban public policy.

I also read *The Urban Villagers* (1962) by Herbert J. Gans, a professor of sociology at Columbia. He addressed the traumatic impact of urban renewal on the daily lives of the people of the West End, an old Italian neighborhood in Boston. In an effort to get a real feel for the people of the West End, Gans moved right in, living among the families and small business owners and vendors who made up what he saw to be an intricate web of neighborhood life. The West End was not, Gans reported, "the slum" that policy makers had targeted for demolition. Indeed, he cried for all to hear, the West End was a vibrant, successful and well-liked neighborhood, a place that for its 10,000 or so residents was filled with meaning and memory and therefore worthy of being saved.

Now considered to be among the most influential books of the 20th century, Jacobs' *Death and Life* was not easy to come by when it first came out in 1961. But when I, like so many of my generation first read it in the early 1960s, it hit me, as it did so many others like a thunderbolt. Its passionate and articulate critique of the urban power structure and its appeal for an approach to cities that was rooted in the way residents lived their daily life, resonated. Jacobs' principles of what constitutes good urbanism affected me to the core. She emphasized the need for diversity, the need for mixed-use, the need for small blocks, the need for concentration and finally, the need for old buildings. For me, and many others of my generation, Jacobs' ideas and the way that she presented them deeply influenced our lives.

I heard speakers too, people like Edmund Bacon whose ideas about urban planning and design subsequently appeared in his 1967 book, *Design of Cities*. Bacon's ideas, like those of Lynch, Gans and Jacobs, remain absolutely relevant today. I loved Bacon's thinking then and still do. Here are a few highlights: "Awareness of space goes far beyond cerebral activity. It engages the full range of senses and feelings, requiring involvement of the whole self to make a full response to it possible." "The architect/planner must project himself (I guess that there were not many female architects in 1967!) into the mind and the spirit of the people who are to experience his designs ..." And finally, most important then as now: "The primary purpose of architecture and city planning is to heighten the drama of living."

One of the most memorable lectures that I attended, (this one also at the remarkable community space at the Judson Memorial) was given by a man named William H. Whyte on a topic I remember vividly called "the Social Life of Small Urban Places," a project that he was working on with his young colleague, a man named Fred Kent. Whyte was in the early stages of what would by 1971 become the Street Life Project and he was here to outline and explain his ideas.

Whyte was most famously the author of *The Organization Man*, written in 1956. Like the work of similar writers, people like Vance Packard and C. Wright Mills, *The Organization Man* was a devastating critique of the modern corporate world. In his book Whyte challenged claims about the entrepreneurial vigor and daring of the world and wrote instead of the increasing bureaucratization of work in the business world. In search of more casual and spontaneous environments, by the mid '60s, Whyte's focus had become the streets of New York. He, like Lynch, Gans and Jane Jacobs, presented his ideas in the everyday language of the streets and the people who lived on them. Here, for example, are some of his perceptions on the life of the streets of the New York that he shared with us and later saw published

"The best streets are the most sociable ... Lovers are most often found on the most sociable streets." White talked about "schmoozing patterns" reporting that when men gather in groups to stand and talk, they show a distinct liking for certain kinds of places. They are, for one thing, strongly attracted by pillars and flagpoles, obeying a primeval instinct perhaps, to have something solid at their backs. They also favor edges. "Schmoozers do not stand often or long in the middle of big plazas," Whyte told those of us in his audience to watch, to observe and to learn how people behave in public places. The way people actually behave, he said, not how planners think they should behave, should guide us as we think about intervening in the public realm.

I was learning too from the work of John Lindsay, New York's mayor between 1965-1973. Lindsay was the first mayor in the country to really care about issues related to urban design and its effect on the fabric of the city. Design, Lindsay said, unlike architecture, occurs not with a building but rather at the place where the building meets the street. Namely, the side-walk. Lindsay loved the city – its streets and its parks. In 1965, he hired Thomas P. F. Hoving as New York City's Parks Commissioner. As people in cities all over the country were abandoning their parks, Hoving fought to bring them back, making them alive and fun. Lindsay and Hoving were bringing a new sensibility to the city, one in which having fun in public spaces and places was, in itself a desirable outcome of public policy. Make it fun; make it "cool" and the rest, they suggested, (and I came to believe) would follow.

It was during Lindsay's years as mayor that Paley Park, that fantastic, unprecedented "vest pocket" park on 53rd St, right around from my mother's apartment, was built. Measuring about 4000 square feet the park is an unimaginably quiet oasis in midtown. The Park's most wonderful feature is a 20-foot high waterfall that spans the entire back of the park. There is lightweight, moveable furniture, an ivy-covered wall and an overhead canopy of locust trees. Paley Park influenced generations of people and without it as a template, Bryant Park, Union and Madison Square Park, and all the others would never have been the same. When not in Central Park, it was here, to Paley Park, that my mother would come to sit quietly and rest.

Meanwhile, despite my growing interest in urban public policy, I never lost my interest in the more literary aspects of urban studies, particularly in how artists and writers depicted and represented city life in their work. I read Theodore Dreiser's *Sister Carrie*, Henry Roth's *Call it Sleep* and Betty Smith's *A Tree Grows in Brooklyn*. I was drawn too to the art work of New York City realists, painters like Reginald Marsh and John Sloan and the other members of the "Ashcan School." My sister Barbara introduced me to the work of a Greenwich Village "primitive" painter, a man named Ralph Fasanella who painted incredibly detailed, Grandma Moses-like works of daily life among the everyday people who lived in the neighborhoods of lower Manhattan. I was drawn as well to the photographers of New York, the work of Berenice Abbott, Weegee, Arnold Rothstein, Helen Levitt and the others. I loved the work of these artists and writers, with their own pulsating, yet warm and loving descriptions and images of life in the greatest city of all. And, when it came time to write my master's thesis, the topic I chose was "The artists and writers of mid-century New York: what they saw and what they said."

Upon completion of my master's, I made my first trip to Europe where I, like so many others before me, fell in love with the hill towns of Italy and the nooks and crannies of the side streets of Paris. For me, as for many others, it was the intimate scale, the powerful relationship between the different spatial elements from the fountain to the church to the market, to the square. That people could and still did live in places like this was, to me, miraculous. The scale and scope of those towns and neighborhoods were seared into my brain, becoming for me the lens through which I have forever experienced city living.

In Paris I discovered Le Marais, the oldest neighborhood in that city, where the Rue de Rivoli meets the Rue Saint-Antoine. Years before it would undergo a cascading process of gentrification that would by the 1990s transform it into one of the world's most expensive neighborhoods. Le Marais was still, when I first visited it in 1966, a working-class, largely Jewish neighborhood, a place not unlike, I thought, Gans' West End, Jane Jacobs' Village and Ralph Fasanella's lower East Side. In those days long before the Pompidou Center was built and *Les Halles* torn down, Le Marais was a dream-like cluster of tiny homes, a maze of narrow streets, alleys and cul-de-sacs lined with all kinds of stores and shops. Winding through the neighborhood, many of these little streets ended up, in a remarkable surprise for the unsuspecting pedestrian, much like those that Ed Bacon had spoken about, in the Place des Vosges. With a fountain in the middle of this perfectly symmetrical square, and sheltering arcades that surrounded it and the incredible warren of streets that fed it, the Place des Voges, like those enchanting Italian hill towns, became and have remained for me iconic urban places, images and archetypes which stayed with me as I went about my work in Buffalo.

When I came back from that trip, I wanted to stay in New York. I hoped to carve out a career there, perhaps teaching, perhaps working in urban planning. But I couldn't. Following the death of my father in early 1966, my mother's world fell apart. The warmth, vitality and creative energy that she had showered upon us as children began to vanish under a cloud of anger and bitterness. Suddenly alone after close to fifty years of marriage, she started to drink and to behave in ways that I could no longer tolerate, let alone recognize. Life with and around her, despite my love for her, became unbearable. The New York of my youth though still incredibly stimulating, was no longer that safe and secure place that had nurtured me. I had to leave. And so, in the summer of 1967 I followed my new wife Kitty, who I had met at Brandeis, to Buffalo, her home-town. But as I left, I held on tight to all that I had learned, to all that I remembered, to all that had nourished me. Yes, I was leaving the city of my soul. I had no idea, however, that I was about to enter a place that would someday become the city of my heart.

CHAPTER 1

A Brand New World

Buffalo, 1967

I arrived in Buffalo in 1967 at the perfect time of year when the weather is magnificent, soft and gentle, cooled by breezes that blow steadily off Lake Erie. Trees abound – lindens, Norway maples, flowering pears, hackberries, cherries, and hornbeams. Mornings and evenings are quiet and billowy and throughout the day, then as now, children played in the streets of their tree-filled neighborhoods. In the evenings people walked, stopping to talk with their neighbors, many of them sitting comfortably on old-fashioned, vine-covered porches. But what most differentiates the summers of today from those 50-plus years ago is that today so much of our summer activities are enjoyed in public places – in Frederick Law Olmsted's magnificent parks and parkways, on the streets and side-walks of lovingly cared for neighborhoods, at Canalside, and on the Outer Harbor.

There was nothing like these places when I arrived here in June of 1967. And while people played baseball and golf in Delaware, Cazenovia and Shoshone parks, there was a much more limited and much more sharply defined sense of the public places than there is now.

Then there was no Buffalo Olmsted Parks Conservancy, no Garden Walk, no South Buffalo Alive, no Art Alive, no Slow Roll, no Elmwood Avenue Festival of the Arts, no "Elmwood Village," no Juneteenth celebrations, no Puerto Rican and Hispanic Heritage Parade, no Burmese Water Festival, no bike paths, no running paths, no farmers' markets and, believe it or not, very few outdoor patios, no places for the public, as individuals or in groups, to sit outside, have a coffee or a drink and simply hang-out. There was, in other words, no sense that this place, Buffalo, was in any way a "special place."

Eager to recall what the city that I came to more than fifty years ago was like, I turned to the pages of the 1967 "Almanac and Fact Book" published annually by the *Buffalo Evening News*. Their findings, while certainly muscular, were grey, dour and drab. The *Almanac* showed that the population which, with 580,000 people in 1950, was dropping precipitously. In 1965, two years before I arrived, Buffalo's population was 490,000, the first time since 1915 that it fell below the half million mark. (Keep in mind, however, that despite the dramatic shrinkage, there were still at least 200,000 more people in Buffalo in the mid-1960s than there are today.)

The economy of Buffalo and Western New York was radically different then too. Industry was still at its peak, with more than 30% of the work force engaged in manufacturing (versus 9% today!). Eighteen thousand people worked at Bethlehem Steel, 17,000 at General Motors, 12,000 at Republic Steel, 5,000 at Ford. Not everybody worked on these enormous islands of industry. Indeed, a great deal of manufacturing was done on and in the streets of the city's neighborhoods. Take, for example, the intersection in the vicinity of Main and Tupper Streets. Here, in a gorgeous brick building that once housed a brewery, my friend Vincent Botticelli, a hair stylist whose shop is here, told me that in the mid-1960s, within the four block area of his shop, thousands of people once worked at places long gone: the *Courier Express* on Main and Goodell Streets, the Trico windshield wiper plant on Washington and Tupper, M. Wile men's clothing company at Washington and Goodell. There was was a time not so long ago, when corners like these in neighborhoods throughout the city provided stability and a sense of economic security to thousands of Buffalonians and their families.

Despite the 1959 opening of the St. Lawrence Seaway, which effectively killed Buffalo's function as a port of transshipment, commerce on Buffalo's waterfront was still strong at the time of my arrival. Buffalo was still one of the country's most significant flour milling centers with several thousand people working on the waterfront at places like Pillsbury, Peavey and General Mills. There were railroads too, with dozens of freight lines crisscrossing the city and thousands of men (and quite a few women) working in what was still one of the nation's leading railroad hubs. Work and the "good life" was available for tens of thousands of Buffalonians who'd left other places to come here: immigrants and their children from Europe, African-Americans from the rural South, Puerto Ricans from their island home in the Caribbean. Buffalo was filled with lots and lots of people making good money, "blue collar aristocrats," many with two cars and a cabin in the country, leading the kind of stable, middle-class life that so many desperately mourn now.

A mirror of the strength and breadth of Buffalo as an industrial powerhouse with a very solid blue-collar middle class was just how many workers belonged to just how many labor unions. There were union locals for workers in the following crafts and industries: asbestos, bakers and confectioners; barbers, bartenders, boats men, boilermakers, bookmakers and bindery. There were locals for brewery workers, for brick and clay workers; for building services employees, carpenters and joiners, textile workers, clothing workers, rubber workers, steel workers, railroad workers and unions of public employees including but not limited to teachers, police officers and firefighters.

People belonged to strong unions and, though their decline had begun, to strong ancestral neighborhoods: Black Rock and Riverside, Lovejoy, the Delaware District and the West Side, South Buffalo and the East Side, places filled with neighborhood schools, churches, parks and a steady stream of customers for the dozens of small businesses that packed the commercial and side streets of Buffalo's neighborhoods. While work was steady and neighborhoods were strong, uppermost on peoples' minds when I arrived in Buffalo in June 1967 were the "riots" on Buffalo's African American East Side.

Sometimes referred to as "riots", sometimes as "disorders", the violence that occurred on the streets of Buffalo's African American East Side over several days at the end of June 1967, sent shock waves through this city and dozens of others during that long, hot summer. Amidst cries of police brutality, small bands of African-American teen-age boys had cruised the streets, burning and looting as they went. More than 150 armed policemen were called to the scene and when forty of them marched in a phalanx down Sycamore Street, people panicked. Buses on their routes through the neighborhood were stoned and store and car windows were broken and smashed.

Arriving in the city as all of this was happening, there was little that I could do but listen to the panicked conversations of the people who I was meeting and talking to. The riots on the East Side, coming just eleven years after racial conflicts on the SS Canadiana brought an end one to the city's most cherished summer time activities, the boat-ride to Crystal Beach, were on everybody's mind, discussed by all of the people who I met during my first few weeks in Buffalo. While some people talked about what might have caused the riots, far more people were worried about how long they might last and when and if they might spread to "our" neighborhood.

By mid-summer, things seemed to have calmed down and people, those I knew at least, the white people who I had met on the West Side of the city, began to move on. Whites on the East Side however, in old white ethnic neighborhoods like the Fruit Belt, Genesee-Moselle, Delavan-Grider, Bailey-Delavan, and others did not move on. They moved out. The sweeping tide of white flight that would devastate the population of Buffalo still more during the 1970s and '80s had begun.

Other places were in turmoil, too, as the incredibly heavy hand of urban renewal swept through the city. There were bulldozers everywhere, their menacing sounds and sights dominating the landscape as they ripped through neighborhoods on the east and west sides of the city. First there was the Kensington Expressway. On my first visit to Buffalo, in the Spring of 1967, I had arrived by plane and was driven from the airport to the home of my in-laws in North Buffalo, on the side-streets of the city. The expressway isn't done yet, they told me. Soon it will be and the trip will be much quicker. They were right.

• • •

There are few people living in Buffalo today who have not learned the Humboldt Parkway story, who do not know that on the path of the six-lane Kensington Expressway there once was one of America's most gorgeous parkways, the Humboldt Parkway, designed at the end of the last century by that great American genius, Fredrick Law Olmsted. While the Buffalonians of today know about the parkway, it is less likely that they know that what was called a "parkway" was in fact a neighborhood, a landscaped promenade that connected Agassiz Circle with Humboldt Park two miles away. Lined with rows of maples and elms, with a bridle path down the middle and benches all along the sides, Humboldt was a lifestyle, a sacred place for families who for generations had called it home.

Doomed by a tsunami of inner-city highway construction that devasted neighborhoods in cities all over the country, the death knell for Humboldt Parkway was sounded in the mid-1950s. By the time of my arrival in Buffalo, that gem of a parkway, a neighborhood treasure cherished and adored by all who lived on or near it, was completely and totally obliterated. My in-laws were right. When in the fall of 1967 I picked up my brother Tony at the airport for a visit from New York, we entered the city not on Olmsted's magnificent parkway but rather on the Kensington Expressway. Not knowing what he'd missed, how much of the city's history and precious fabric had been destroyed to smooth our way into Buffalo, Tony was impressed: Now that was a quick trip, he said enviously.

Things were not much better on the old Italian West Side along Niagara Street which, I would come to know years later, had by the early 1960s been designated for demolition. For now though, what I knew of Niagara Street was limited to the inside of Muscarella's pastry shop where I was introduced to what would become the first of many Buffalo cannolis. It was not until the early 1980s when I started researching the area, that I realized that right before and indeed during my arrival in Buffalo, the whole neighborhood was coming down. It didn't matter, it seemed, that the mayor, Frank Sedita – "Little Frankie from Efner Street," – grew up on one of those streets.

Joe Ritz, a reporter for the *Courier Express*, in an article written less than a year before I got to Buffalo, described in poignant, operatic terms what was going on up and down Niagara Street in the mid-1960s. The "street," he wrote, "is still predominantly Italian-American. Gardens and fruit trees flourish in back yard plots. The interiors of the homes are well-kept and comfortably furnished." The people in the neighborhood, he reported "resent the scattering of neighbors and relatives and their relocation from familiar stores, churches and gathering places. Perhaps to understand the residents' feeling one has to be a gardener," Ritz continued. "One has to have nursed a cherry tree from a sapling, protected it from diseases, watered it, fed it, worked it so that it is capable of bearing one hundred quarts of fruit and then face the certain knowledge that it will be destroyed one afternoon by clanking bulldozer." Did anybody know? Did anybody care?

Years later I became good friends with Karima Bondi, a woman who had grown up in a home on one of those streets destroyed by urban renewal: 238 Seventh Street. Karima has the fondest memories of growing up there. The Bondis lived in their Seventh Street home as long as they could until, as Karima remembers, they could hear the bulldozers outside their front door. Only then did the family move away. It was still the fall of 1967, the year of my arrival in Buffalo, that the Bondis revisited their old neighborhood. Karima memorialized that visit many years later when she wrote the following memory piece which she calls "Summer, 1967."

> We (Mom, Dad, Me, John, Dave and Joe) are all parked in the family car (the goldish-taupe colored Pontiac Grand Prix) on Seventh Street in front of where the old house once stood. The whole block has been razed. There is a

> temporary chain link fence around the block containing the debris of so many demolished houses. My grandparents' house had been painted turquoise (at that time we were very proud of this.) Greek columns proudly flanked the lower front porch. One of these columns has "escaped" the fencing and is in the street, rolling against the curb. Dad says: "Thank God Mamma isn't here to see this." (From the collection of Karima Bondi. See photograph of Karima playing with her friends in front of their Seventh Street home)

It was worse, if possible, in downtown where, even more than in the neighborhoods, the landscape of daily life was under relentless assault, where whole blocks were crumbling on a daily basis. It had started in the '50s but continued unabated at, during and after the time of my arrival. Indeed, in the summer of 1967 one of the greatest buildings that ever graced the streets of downtown Buffalo, the Erie County Savings Bank, came crashing to the ground. 1968 was worse. Read this excerpt from a 1968 article I found in a Chamber of Commerce publication while doing research for my 2007 book, *City on the Edge*:

> "Bulldozers and cranes are cutting wide swaths through Buffalo while wreckers' balls and torches are toppling hundreds of old homes, business places and industrial buildings in an ambitious face-lifting program for the Queen City … there are hundreds of buildings involved including the following: the thirteen-story Hotel Buffalo, the eighty-two-year-old Hotel Worth, the ornate Erie County Savings Bank, the old Buffalo Times building on Main Street, the old Palace Theater nearby and the St. Paul's and St. Mark's United Church of Christ on Ellicott …"

How was it possible that I, who grew up in New York, who studied with Bayard Still, who watched the demolition of Penn Station, who stood in line to hear Jane Jacobs, could not have cared enough to know what was going on right under my nose? Where was I, during this time of radical and frightening transformation in the life of our city, a time when whole neighborhoods were assaulted, when whole blocks of the city's downtown were being demolished, when parks and parkways were being eviscerated and when fear began to insinuate and tarnish the commonweal. Where were we all? Had all of us been captured by the ethic of modernism that swept away any and all references to and reminders of our past?

A commitment to "the modern" characterized as well the cultural life of Buffalo during my first years in Buffalo. But modernism in the arts was different, dynamic and incredibly exciting. In a chapter in *City on the Edge* called "Lightning Strikes" I wrote enthusiastically about this most creative period in the artistic life of our city. It is worth quoting here:

> "The upheavals that tattered and ripped apart the fabric of the city throughout the 1960s seemed to have had little impact, particularly after 1962, the year that lightning struck Buffalo, energizing a thrilling and spectacular outburst of artistic expressions. It was in that year that this great, grey muscular giant of a city, a city known for its blue-collar stolidity, its working class neighborhoods – a "shot and a beer" town if ever there was one – burst to the forefront of the world's modernist cultural scene. It began in January 1962 when the Albright Gallery, with the addition of a sparkling new wing, became the "Albright-Knox Art Gallery." It continued in September when Buffalo's small, private commuter college, the University of Buffalo, merged with the State University of New York becoming the State University of New York at Buffalo. There was still more star power when in December 1962 the magnificent Lukas Foss was hired as the music director of the Buffalo Philharmonic Orchestra. These events created a new, shining light that served as a beacon of hope and possibility."

• • •

My first home in Buffalo was an apartment on Rand Avenue, a pleasant, tree-filled street lined with small one and two-family homes, just off Delaware Avenue across from what is still called today "The Delaware Plaza." I was curious about the place and the people who lived on Rand and who worked in the stores across Delaware, and following the nose for stories that I'd developed in New York, I began to explore the landscape of my new home, to listen and to learn from the people who I began to meet in the course of my daily life. Unwittingly, I had begun to collect the first of what would become over the course of many decades, hundreds of "Buffalo stories."

At Voskersian's restaurant, a small family diner on the corner of Amherst and Delaware, I met Jerry Voskersian, the child, he told me, of Armenian radicals, who'd spent the bulk of World War II living with his family underground in Paris. Across Delaware in the Delaware Plaza at the Amdel, a large pharmacy and general store at the location currently occupied by Bagel Jay's, I met Irv Sultz and Harvey Schiller and it was from them that I heard my first stories about Jewish Buffalo, about William Street, Humboldt Parkway, about North Buffalo and the great Bennett High School. At the Kinderloft, a small store packed with a fantastic array of children's clothing I met Maeve Mahoney, a retired school teacher who worked there part-time. Maeve lived in a place she called "The First Ward" and had taught for years at School 4 on Hamburg Street. It was from her that I first learned bits and pieces of the story of the Irish in Buffalo and heard tales of her endlessly intriguing neighborhood. Then there was Fishman's, a large five and dime, occupied today by Marshalls. Like Woolworth's, Fishman's was a precursor of the modern-day discount store, stocked to the gills with everything from buttons, nails and screws, to candy and household appliances. A lot of people worked at Fishman's and I came to know many of them. My favorite was a middle-aged woman, Angela Foglia, who spoke with a recognizably Italian accent. She was from Naples and lived in a neighborhood that, like Miss Mahoney's First Ward, I would soon come to discover on my own, a place called St. Lucy's Parish, an old Italian neighborhood on the city's East Side. An African American man worked at Fishman's too. I've forgotten his name now but over the course of many conversations I learned a little bit about how he'd come to Buffalo during World War II and went to work at Republic Steel in a part of town that he referred to as South Buffalo. He didn't live there, he told me. Blacks didn't live in South Buffalo, he said. Rather, he lived over on the East Side, on Jefferson and Ferry, near where, he said, "the riots" were.

It was at this time, too, that I discovered the Jewish Community Center, a place to exercise, to take a swim, a place, my father-in-law told me, with a *schvitz* (Yiddish for "steam bath"). The Center, with its basketball court, small weight rooms, run-down squash and handball courts and a locker room with broken tiles and rusty lockers, had the look and feel of an old neighborhood Y. It reminded me of the old card club that my father belonged to when I was a kid growing up in New York.

I felt comfortable at the JCC, a *hamish* (Yiddish for warm and friendly) place with a first generation feel. The JCC was really a "Jewish" center, filled with Jews. Unlike today, when Jews comprise barely 50% of the center's members, the Center was 99% Jewish. It was closed on Saturdays and for all of the Jewish holidays, some of which I had barely heard of and could barely pronounce.

Not only were almost all the members Jewish, but most of them were older and most from the Jewish middle class. During my first week there, I meet a jeweler who worked in the Root Building; a tailor who had a shop on Elmwood Avenue; a few auto-mechanics who came after work to clean up on their way home; and two retired public school teachers, both of whom had found work in Buffalo after arriving here from DP camps in Europe. Many of them spoke with the hard-to-lose accents of Jewish Eastern Europe. Two or three even spoke Yiddish. The staff was a fascinating collection of individuals who reflected the hard-to-generalize nature of Jewish Buffalo. Several of them – Otto and Lilli Popper, Bernard Ullrich – were Holocaust survivors and one of them, Abe Woltz, could not, despite what I thought were his best efforts, hide the numbers that were branded mid-way up his left arm.

It was at the JCC that I met Saul Berkoff, the athletic director of the Center. Saul was a warm and energetic guy, a camp counselor-type forever organizing games and activities. Saul had grown up in Buffalo on what he called "the little Jerusalem of William Street" on the city's East Side. That was all gone now, he said, "but you should have seen it when I was a kid." Orchard and Essex streets in New York, he said, "had nothing on William Street."

I followed Saul's advice and, as a result, I ventured out, discovering in the process, the wonderful Jewish and Italian world of Hertel Avenue, surrounded on all sides by middle-class residential side streets, many of them still filled with Jews, still more with a growing number of Italians. Flanked by two Italian delis – Caruso's and Sammy's – was St. Margaret's, both the church and the school, centers of Hertel Avenue's vibrant Italian community. Hertel was lined with every kind of shop imaginable, small ones like Mandelbaum's Furs, Setel Wallpaper, Six-Sixteen Shoe Store and The Sample, a fantastic neighborhood department store. Then there were the Jewish-owned food stores – Sunshine's and Kornmehl's Kosher Meat Market. There were restaurants too, a veritable Bronx-like array of Jewish food: Martin's Kosher Deli, Mastman's and the incomparable Ralph's. Ralph's was a hole in the wall, filled with characters out of a film shot in New York in the '40s: "Stumpy" standing at the front, carving the corned beef, his wife Annie, his daughter Risa and everybody's favorite waitress, the African American woman named Janie. There was no place like Ralph's, not even in New York. And the food – all traditional New York deli food and fantastic homemade soups – was to die for. Packed for breakfast and lunch, Ralph's was the favorite stomping grounds of Jews from all over the area, plus a healthy sprinkling of Italians. Ralph's was really fun and very *hamish* a place in Buffalo where Jews, Jews like me, felt at home, relaxed and comfortable.

There were a few African-Americans at the JCC and one whom I quickly befriended was a man named Willie Evans. Willie was a few years older than me and worked as a phys. ed teacher in the Buffalo public schools. We met regularly at the JCC where on several afternoons a week, in those days before exercise machines, we had some fabulous three-on-three basketball games on the Center's full court. Over time Willie shared his story with me and how he, a graduate of Emerson Vocational High School, became in 1958 an outstanding running back at the University of Buffalo. '58 was a good year for UB and after they won 8 of 9 regular season games capturing the Lambert Cup, the team was invited to play Florida State in the Tangerine Bowl in Orlando, Florida. The problem for Willie and his other African-American teammate was that blacks and whites were not allowed to play together on that field. In a demonstration of unusual solidarity that is memorable in Buffalo's long struggle for racial justice, his team mates unanimously refused to go.

Willie loved jazz and was eager to introduce me to what he promised was a jazz scene as good as anywhere in the country. One night on the town over Thanksgiving weekend in 1969 he took me to two places that I will never forget: The Little Harlem and The Pine Grill. The Little Harlem at the corner of Michigan and Broadway had been owned, Willie told me, by a woman named Ann Montgomery since she opened it as an ice-cream parlor in 1910. It's been a hotel and nightclub since, he said, a fabulous one, the jewel in the crown of Buffalo's black night-club life. "Ann will probably be there tonight." Promising to introduce me, we headed downtown.

Ann Montgomery was a striking woman, something of a cross between Josephine Baker and Lena Horne. Sometime in the nineteen-teens she married Dan Montgomery, alleged to have been one of the richest African-Americans in Buffalo. Montgomery owned hotels – a few small ones located on the east side – The Vendome, the Curtiss and the Little Harlem – which catered to blacks for whom the city's downtown hotels were off-limits. Although he died years before, "Dan Montgomery's Steak House" on Exchange Street was still open. Nothing like the glitzy steak houses of today, Montgomery's was as down-home as they come, with tables and chairs strewn casually around the large room, the walls lined with simple booths. As I remember it, Montgomery's looked very much like this description that I found on the following website:

> *http://westernnewyork.localfoodservice.com/apps/blog/view_more_detail.cfm?id=31213&catid=8449*
>
> The building stood alone on a block fairly desolate in an area that had long passed its prime. The building was three stories of all brick and painted white with dark trim, and you could see the top parapet with DAN MONTGOMERY in block print from the Thruway.
>
> Parking was never a problem. You could pull up right in front and walk the width of the sidewalk to the front steps. You entered up a set of plain concrete stairs and into the main foyer. Inside, to the left, stood a piano covered with an old blanket, and to the right was a cashier's cage. The terrazzo floor had suits of cards in-laid (maybe this was Buffalo's first casino?).
>
> Down a couple of stairs and you were in the bar room. There were leaded glass windows all carrying the initials DM in blood red. The tables and chairs were probably vintage 1920s. The tables were very similar to a rectangular table you might have in your home kitchen and the chairs were all wood with no padding or upholstery.
>
> The menu was simple. Steak (T-Bone), fried chicken or burgers in the basket, and everything came with fries and cole slaw. Friday's special was the obligatory Buffalo Fish Fry. At the time. the steak dinner cost about $6.00, cheap even in 1977 and it was worth it. No matter which way you ordered it, it came out mid rare.
>
> The server was a fairly substantial older woman. She was very soft spoken, and always greeted with a "Hiya honey" and "What're ya havin' ta drink tonight?"
>
> Go in there any time and there was never more that 2 or 3 tables with customers. Your order was taken on a scrap of paper, and that, too, was your bill. A dinner for 2 with salad a couple of drinks apiece and maybe desert was about $18.00, and the more people you had in your party the bill actually seemed to get exponentially lower the more you ordered.

Montgomery's wife Ann ran the Little Harlem and by the mid-1930s the place had become, along with the Crawford in Pittsburgh, one of best known

African-American owned hotels and nightclubs in the country. On the pre-Thanksgiving night in 1969 The Little Harlem, more than thirty years later, retained its sepia-toned, Art Deco allure. Lonnie Smith, "Dr." Lonnie Smith, a native of Lackawanna, was at the keyboard of his Hammond B-3 playing a kind of rocking honky-tonk that I'd never heard before. The place was jammed with black and white customers and sure enough, there, holding court at the bar was, as Willie Evans had promised, Ann Montgomery herself. She greeted Willie warmly, gave me a big hug and bought us each a beer. It was not till many years later when I came across the Little Harlem Collection in the Buffalo and Erie County Public Library that I realized just how significant Ms. Montgomery was in the life of mid-20th century Buffalo.

We stayed for a set and then it was off, Willie said, to the Pine Grill on Jefferson and Ferry where, he said, the great blues saxophone player Lou Donaldson was "holding court." More like a juke joint than a night-club, the Pine Grill felt like a set out of August Wilson: raucous, smoky, sweaty and filled with the sounds of the Mississippi Delta and the South Side of Chicago. Evans, it seemed, knew everybody in the place and as a result I felt comfortable and accepted.

That night before Thanksgiving that I spent with Willie Evans at the Little Harlem and the Pine Grill stayed with me for years and when, in 1990 I opened the Calumet Arts Café those two fabulous night spots were never far from my thinking. Next week, he said, "I'll take you to Governor's Inn. It's a blues bar off of Broadway owned by a guy named Peterson. You've got to hear his son, Little Lucky Peterson, play the organ." What a night … and it had all begun at the Jewish Community Center.

• • •

My growing ties to the city were strengthened by the people I met during my first year or so in Buffalo, people whose way of thinking about the city has influenced me throughout my many years here. There was Bill Hoyt, a young and dynamic history teacher at The Park School who wanted, he told me, "take history out of the classroom and into the streets." Warm and welcoming, Bill invited me to visit him at his house on Ashland Avenue, "28 Ashland," I would soon learn it was called, and it was there that I was introduced to a circle of people, friends and devotees of Bill and his wife Carol Hoyt. My small Buffalo world began suddenly to open and expand.

Bill and Carol came from the right side of the tracks, she a Buffalo Sem grad, he a Nichols alum. She'd gone to Vassar College, come back to Buffalo where she married Bill, a descendent of a long line of Hoyts. The Hoyts were friendly and very hospitable and soon their home became the center, a kind of salon/ hangout for young, socially active white liberals. I too joined the list of regulars. It was here,"28 Ashland," midst the warm and casual chaos of a house-hold of four kids, dozens of people – some eating, some drinking, some even sleeping in the attic – bonded over our shared concern for the state of the city. Undaunted by the growing number of white people leaving the city, the Hoyts – Bill more moderate, Carol ever exuberant – wanted to and felt that they could fix this city. It was this energy that propelled Carol to lead a group a group of like-minded friends and neighbors, to form a social action organization that Carol called "CAUSE": the Coalition for Action, Unity and Social Equality. While Carol and Bill were very intensely serious about these issues, neither of them ever lost their sense of fun. It was always a party with "28 Ashland" acting as party central. Carol's ability to bring a playful sensibility to the serious issues of the day were on display at the first CAUSE convention held at the Statler Hotel in the Spring of 1969. Organized by Carol and a long-time civil rights activist named Norman Goldfarb, the convention drew hundreds of people.

My recollection of the event and what information I was able to find in the archives of the *Courier-Express* call to mind not so much a business meeting as a happening, where Yippie-like theatrical effects were used to engage people. People registered, for example, at an "Aparthied Registration Center" where suburbanites were separated from city dwellers by a "commissioner of de-facto segregation." Another booth depicted conditions in a ghetto tenement, with its bare light bulb and decrepit furniture. Underlying the theatrical approach was Carol and Norman's commitment which was clearly expressed in CAUSE's mission: "to expose racism where it exists and to pursue all actions for social equality when they occur."

Meanwhile, Carol and her friend "Bunny" Castle had opened a chic and contemporary home furnishing store on Elmwood called "The Forum" (in the site now long-occupied by Aurum Jewelers) the first kind of hip and modern one of its kind. The Forum quickly became the gold standard of cool for many years to come. Indeed, it was the Forum, along with its neighbor just down the street,

Vicky Sapienza's fabulous gift shop and a café, Hello World, that lay the foundation of what would, twenty years later, become "Elmwood Village." If "28 Ashland" was more than a home, The Forum was more than a store. While the Forum did not have a pot-belly stove, the energy, creativity, imagination and good humor of Carol and Bunny did radiate a special kind of heat that made The Forum, like those old-time general stores, a hang-out for a new and interesting "smart set" of sophisticates and activists eager to bring some excitement and with it some change to their good, but very grey city. I, like so many denizens of the Delaware District, became a devoted customer. Bill Hoyt, meanwhile, in his first run for office was elected councilman from the Delaware District and from his new perch on the 13th floor of City Hall was bringing a whole new perspective and point of view to issues affecting the environment particularly, as we will see later, in Delaware Park. With Bill now in City Hall and Carol on Elmwood Avenue, the Hoyts were increasingly the focal point of all that was hip in "the new Buffalo."

Another one of the more compelling people I met during those first years in Buffalo was Lydia Wright, Dr. Lydia Wright, to be precise. Lydia Wright was a quiet, yet towering figure in Buffalo's African-American community and among the most interesting people that I've known in my more than half a century here. Dr. Wright grew up in Cincinnati, Ohio, where her mother taught in the local public schools. It was her mother's grandfather, a man named Dr. Benjamin Hickman, one of the first African-Americans to practice medicine in Cincinnati, who encouraged her to become a physician. Lydia went on to Fisk University and received her degree in pediatric medicine from Meharry Medical College in Nashville, Tennessee. After her marriage to Dr. Frank G. Evans in 1951, the couple moved to Buffalo, where, intent on maintaining a practice in the heart of the African-American East Side, they opened their office on the second floor above Dexter's Pharmacy at the corner of Ferry and Jefferson down the street from the Pine Grill. In 1954 they bought a large and stately home on Humboldt Parkway at the corner of Hamlin Road. Like everybody who lived along Humboldt Parkway, Wright and Evans came here to sit, to walk and to socialize with friends and neighbors. By 1958 the demolition of Humboldt Parkway had begun and soon, instead of the bucolic, tree-filled view from their living room window, Wright and Evans, who tried desperately to stop it, now looked out at the sea of concrete that was the Kensington Expressway. I sat with them often in their large and comfortable living room. Though they hardly heard the whizzing cars go by, they did see them and so they kept their white lace curtains drawn.

Some, like Robert T. Coles, an African-American architect I met in those years, made other choices. In 1961 Coles bought an empty lot on Humboldt Parkway. Unlike his neighbors, Coles knew how to read surveyors' maps and he saw what was coming. When he designed his house at 321 Humboldt Parkway a year later, the rear of the house, not the front, would face the six-lane highway that the Parkway had become.

Others appeared in the expanding landscape of my new life in Buffalo. There was Monte Hoffman, a young and gregarious cellist with the Buffalo Philharmonic Orchestra who introduced me to the magical world of Lukas Foss, Mitch Miller and later Michael Tilson Thomas. Peter Dow, the relentlessly inquisitive lifelong educator who, as early as 1969, talked with me about making Buffalo history the focal point of development on the city's waterfront. Irving Levick, the ambitious, first-generation entrepreneur who so clearly understood just how important the connection between arts and business is. Anthony Bannon, *The Buffalo Evening News* reporter who opened the windows of my new home to the ever-fascinating world of the arts in Buffalo. Edna Lindemann, who late in 1967 walked me through the rooms of the barely one-year-old Burchfield Center, then housed on the second floor of Buffalo State's Rockwell Hall. I met Joe Crangle, the legendary Democratic "boss," pal of both John and Robert Kennedy, and therefore, a star in my eyes. I met Mickey Osterreicher, photographer for *The Spectrum*, the student newspaper at the University of Buffalo whose images captured the frightening tensions between police and students that characterized those years. I met Lou Jean Fleron whose work at the Cornell School of Industrial and Labor Relations had begun to influence a generation of people interested in labor education, rights and social justice. I met Bruce Beyer, the anti-war activist convicted of draft evasion who led eight other protestors into the Unitarian Church on Elmwood Avenue where they – "The Buffalo Nine" – sought asylum. I met Richard Griffin the attorney who led his neighbors in Parkside to form the Parkside Community Association and in the process brought lasting racial harmony to this marvelous place. And I met Dan Higgins, the union bricklayer and South District councilman. It was through Dan that I was introduced to the weird and wonderful world of South Buffalo, the world of Franciscan fathers and Mercy nuns, of Catholic churches and Catholic schools – seven of them, if I remember correctly – packed, like the neighborhood that supported them, with large and lively families, most of them Irish, most of them Catholic.

Despite this varied and fantastic introduction to the many lives and layers of my new home town, I was still not certain what I would study when in the fall of 1970 I enrolled as a full-time PhD student in the history department at SUNY Buffalo. The primary requirement of the program was to write a doctoral dissertation, a long, detailed study of an obscure and untouched topic. Maybe, I thought, a topic drawn from the history of the city that I loved the most, New York City. Why not follow the advice of Ray Ginger, my beloved history professor at Brandeis University, who suggested a dissertation on my father's business, a history of the women's coat business? "Now's the time to do it," he said. "The founding fathers of the industry are still alive. Take one building, the one your father worked in on Seventh Avenue, and profile all the people who worked there, the owners and workers, the delivery men and the clerks, the salesmen and the models. All of them. Hang out in the building, go to the neighborhood delis and ask a lot of questions."

The lure was intense: an irresistible topic in my favorite place in the world. I was tempted and considered commuting until I finished the work. And, yet, for reasons that were not yet clear, the voices of the people who I'd been meeting during my first few years in Buffalo called to me from somewhere deep within, telling me: No, don't go. Not now. Not yet. Wait. Be patient. Stay here. You'll see. And so it was that one day late in the fall of 1970, while sitting in the stands watching a kids' baseball game in Delaware Park, I heard another voice, the voice of a woman calling out to her son who had just come up to the plate: "C'mon, Mikey. Show 'em what a Black Rock kid can do."

Acknowledgements

The recollection of the square block at Virginia, Tupper and Washington is my friend's, **Vincent Botticelli** whose hair salon is there today.

Joe Ritz's piece on urban renewal on the West Side and my references to downtown urban renewal are from Chapter 8 of*City on the Edge:* "Downtown and the Neighborhoods, 1960s."

Karima Bondi is an old friend whose stories about growing up Italian on the West Side and in South Buffalo are priceless and unforgettable.

I covered the cultural upheaval of this period in Chapter 9 of *City on the Edge:* "Lightning Strikes: Art and life during the 1960s."

Willie Evans: Following the friendship we developed at the JCC, Willie and I spent hours together over the years before his death in 2017.

Bill and Carol Hoyt: I was friends with both Bill and Carol for many years, with Bill until his untimely death in 1992, with Carol until she moved from Buffalo to Seattle in 1988. My friendship with the Hoyt family has been further cemented by my long standing relationship with their son Sam.

Allison Kimberly and Liz Kolken, once regulars at 28 Ashland, have reminded of the excitement of the Hoyt's home.

Lydia Wright was unforgettable. It was from her living room overlooking Humboldt Parkway that I first became aware of the devastating impact of the Kensington Expressway on the life of her community. Dr. Wright died in Buffalo in 2006.

Robert T. Coles was a friend of mine for many years. His death in 2020 was a blow to the architectural and design community.

CHAPTER 2

An Italian Hill Town in Buffalo?

How the neighborhood of Black Rock changed my way of thinking about life in the city

Black Rock? I'd never heard of it until that afternoon in Delaware Park. "Show 'em what a Black Rock kid can do"? What's up with that? The name struck me. "What M'am, if you don't mind my asking, is Black Rock?" She was astonished at my ignorance. Obviously I was not from here. "Everybody," she said, "knows Black Rock. It's the oldest neighborhood in Buffalo. My family's lived there for generations." Pointing to the kid at bat she said, "That's Mikey, my son. He was born and raised there too." "But why" I asked, "did you refer to him as a Black Rock boy, not a Buffalo boy?" "Well," she answered emphatically, "he's not a Buffalo boy. He's a Black Rock boy."

Intrigued by her passionate display of neighborhood loyalty and identity, I pushed further. But still, I argued, he is from Buffalo. Not really, she said, resisting insistently. I'm a Black Rock girl; his Dad's a Black Rock man and Mikey is a Black Rock boy. Barely finishing, she added quickly that his grandparents, both sides of them, were from Black Rock too. Clearly eager to talk about a place to which she was so strongly attached, she quickly revealed more. Black Rock had been a separate village for years. Same as Buffalo. It wasn't until the middle of the 19th century, long after the Erie Canal was finished, she recounted, that Black Rock became part of Buffalo. Referring to what I would soon find out was a century old rivalry, she said "that had we gotten the canal – Black Rock, I mean, do you think OJ Simpson would be playing for the Buffalo Bills? No … he'd be on the Black Rock Bills. You should go over there and check it out. Go see Jack Utzig, she said. He's a photographer on Niagara Street. He'll help you out. Tell him I sent you: Mary. Mary Degenhart."

There was something compelling about Mary Degenhart, something in our short, serendipitous conversation in Delaware Park that was provocative. Perhaps she was right. Perhaps hidden under the layers of the Black Rock story there was something, as her signs and signals suggested, special about Black Rock. All I had to do was to follow her clues. I started with Utzig.

His photography studio was on the west side of Niagara Street between Amherst and Austin and in the days after my fortuitous encounter with Mary Degenhart I made my first visit there. Utzig was warm and welcoming, thrilled and incredulous that I was interested in learning about Black Rock. "Nobody's interested in Black Rock," he said. "I can't even get the people who live here to come and look at my photos." And he had dozens of them, some that he'd taken, others that he'd collected, portraits, wedding and graduation photos and snap-shots of daily life in the neighborhood that went back to the turn of the century. Yes, it's true, he said, confirming Mary Degenhart's statement. Black Rock was a separate town. Everybody here knows that. Everybody knows about the rivalry with Buffalo over the terminus of the Erie Canal. I told him about Mary Degenhart and how she identified her son as a product not of Buffalo but of Black Rock. I had been struck by the intense sense of local pride in Mary's comments, reminding me of what I'd experienced at the Palio in Siena, one of those Italian hill towns that I held up as a model of urban perfection. There, at an annual horse race that circled the town's square, teams, each representing different neighborhoods, competed against each other. Mary reminded me of that, I told him. Well, Mr. Utzig said, with a proud grin, "she's not the only one who feels that way."

Clearly, I was on to something. I'd found a place, it increasingly seemed, which, as a result of its history as a separate town had maintained, despite its long-ago integration and absorption into the fabric of the larger city, a strong and distinct sense of itself as a separate entity, a place with the kind of strong and nurturing localism that I liked so much about those romantic hill towns in Italy. Why study the hill towns of Italy, I wondered. Why not just study Black Rock?

If you want to learn about the history of Black Rock, Utzig said in his Yoda-like monotone, you won't find it in a book. Look instead, he urged, to the landscape and the street-scape, to the bridges and the buildings, to the homes and factories, to the railroad grade-crossings and train stations. Look there, look closely and you'll see what I mean. Come back anytime, he said, and let me know what you find. As I made my way out the door, he called to me: "Go see Walter Krakowiak at the Black Rock Savings and Loan in Amherst at Dearborn. He'll tell you more."

Krakowiak, as his name suggests, was a first generation Polish-American and, like Utzig could not wait to share his enthusiasm for the neighborhood with me. He took me outside in front of the brick building that housed the offices of the Black Rock Savings and Loan Association. The whole history of this neighborhood, he said echoing his friend Jack Utzig, can be seen from right here. Did you know, he said, what was fast becoming a *de rigueur* opening statement, that Black Rock and Buffalo were once separate towns? Assuring him that yes I knew that, he pointed in the direction of the Niagara River to the right and the Thruway that passed alongside it. "You know that the Thruway was built on and over the bed of the Erie Canal, don't you?" Pointing to two large empty lots on both the north and south sides of Amherst Street he said, "that there, where those large plots of land are, that's where the Black Rock public market was, our town's market. Look to your left. See that church? That's St. Francis Xavier, the first German Catholic church in Buffalo."

Krakowiak's enthusiasm was bringing all of this back home for me. For here, right here in Black Rock, all of the elements of a cohesive community, all of the bits and pieces that I'd seen and admired in Italy and that I'd read about in the many books that I had read, were coming together. For in Black Rock I'd found what I'd been looking for: an urban community with an intense sense of local pride, fostered and strengthened by a strong array of local institutions and a story which provided the communal memory upon which the "myth" of Black Rock was built. But was it a myth? Or rather was the intense identification with the neighborhood in fact based on the actual events and developments of the past? It was to this question that I resolved to seek the answers.

I followed Jack Utzig's suggestion and with my one year old son Charlie seated safely in the rear of my car. I began what would be a lifetime of driving around the city, first in Black Rock and then the many other neighborhoods that I was on the verge of discovering. The streetscape of Black Rock, hardly changed in the almost fifty years since my initial explorations, remains as haunting and vivid today as it did then. I urge you to follow the routes that I took then. The best time to explore Black Rock is at sunset when the shadows of the setting sun project long, bright shafts of light across the Niagara River, that penetrate deep into the heart of the neighborhood. Follow this light down the east-west streets of the neighborhood: down Amherst, past the old town square, St. Francis Xavier, under the railroad overpass all the way to Assumption Church. Go left on one of the side streets in what is still known as Assumption Parish – Howell, Peter or Germain – to Austin and, shielding your eyes from the setting sun, drive west to the foot of Austin where the street meets the Niagara River. Look at the large brick buildings that still stand there – remnants of the mid-19th century – and see for yourself the powerful impact that the Austin Street lock of the Erie Canal must certainly have had on the development of this neighborhood. Turn down Niagara and go into the parking lot of Charlie Leone's enormous Gotham Antique Warehouse, (look for the large "Streng Oldsmobile" sign in the front lot). Ask for Charlie (he's almost always there) and have him show you the path of the original Erie Canal, still visible through the massive infrastructure of the NYS Thruway. Turn around and go back Austin to Dearborn and East, tiny tree-lined streets that are snapshots of a much earlier time in the life of this neighborhood. It would be hard to live in Black Rock and not be aware of the past, not to feel, as Mary Degenhart did over forty years ago, that her son Mikey was indeed "a Black Rock kid." (Over the many years that have passed since first learning about "Mikey" Degenhart I have, despite my many efforts, not been able to track him down.)

But clearly I needed to dig deeper, to penetrate beyond the ever-fascinating façade of the neighborhood to find if I could the documents and sources – the evidence – that would enable me to substantiate the assumptions that I was beginning to make about the existence in Black Rock of a unique and compelling sense of community.

Walter Krakowiak had the answers. Stored in the basement of the offices of the Black Rock Savings and Loan Association, he told me, were copies of a local newspaper that went back to the 1880s. Known as the *International Gazette*, it was that newspaper that became the foundation on which I was to build the rest of my work in Black Rock. For many months I spent days in the basement of that building on Amherst Street, poring over countless articles about all aspects of daily life in the Black Rock neighborhood.

From the pages of the *International Gazette* I was learning a new and different approach to the study of history, one that had nothing to do with the larger national and international events that I was used to studying, but one that was focused instead on the patterns, habits and routines, the likes and dislikes, of the daily lives of the people who lived out their lives in this one particular neighborhood in Buffalo.

I read the ads, the notices and the news items about events that filled the daily lives of the people of the neighborhood: picnics and church bazaars; summertime sailboat excursions to Grand Island, new stores opening and old ones closing. The paper had death notices too which offered a look far back into the pages of the neighborhood's past, small bios of men and women who'd lived in Black Rock since the middle of the last century. I was taking immense pleasure in the discovery of the intimate and intricate details of daily life that I was uncovering. Here, in the basement of the old savings and loan offices, sitting alone with this rich and exciting primary source, with nothing between me and the pages of this ancient newspaper, I was free to engage my own imagination and reach my own conclusions about the nature and the character of life in the tiny neighborhood of Black Rock.

There was more in the basement, Walter told me, urging me to read the minutes of a local business association called the Black Rock Business Mens' Association. It was from these minutes, which began in 1888 and continued into the 'twenties, that I learned about the inner workings of this small, tightly-knit local economy and the needs and wants of the dozens of small stores and businesses that comprised it. I used other sources too: the photos in Jack Utzig's studio, annual reports from the local police precincts, and pages and pages of the hand-written records of the manuscripts of the New York State census. There wasn't a person I did not interview: teachers and crossing guards at School 52, priests at Assumption and St. Xavier; store owners up and down Niagara and Amherst; neighborhood lawyers and accountants, doctors and dentists. This plus hours over lunch with Walter Krakowiak – sometimes at Santasiero's, just down Niagara Street, sometimes at The Schuper House near-by – who was ever eager to pass on to me his vast store-house of information about the Black Rock story.

There were other primary sources that I found particularly valuable and exciting. I was drawn to the City Atlases which, printed over a fifty-odd year period from the 1870s to the 1920s, revealed in bold color, details about land use on every street in the city. I struck gold, however, with the census reports, both

> federal and state, that were taken at various times throughout the late 19th and early 20th centuries. Housed then in gigantic, very heavy leather bound books stored in the basement of the old Erie County Hall, the census reports – they were all recorded and then reported by hand, hence the term "manuscript census" – are filled with fantastic information about the people who lived in Buffalo at the time the census was recorded. In the languid penmanship style of the turn-of-the-century, the census-taker entered the following details about each and every person that she (it's likely that many of the census takers, all part-time workers, were in fact, women) had interviewed: name, address, age, place of birth, citizenship status, occupation and literacy. In that basement in the old County Hall building on Franklin Street I had come into direct and immediate contact with the foundational details of "the Buffalo Story." I spent weeks there, sitting at a table in the bowels of the County Building, lost in the intimate details of late 19th century and early 20th century Black Rock. I was having a ball. Who knew that it was here, in a photo shop and in basements in Black Rock and downtown, that, after three years of digging, I would find a treasure trove of information and ideas that would form the foundation of my life-long career as a chronicler of the Buffalo story.

What I was learning in Black Rock was that the most transformative experiences and events in most peoples' lives were those that occurred as part of the process of daily life as it was lived in the neighborhood. For it was here – on the streets and sidewalks, in the stores, churches and schools – that people acquired their formative memories, the values and the beliefs they lived by and the attachments and associations that lasted a lifetime. I was learning that the intricate web of connections and relationships that were made on the streets and sidewalks of places like Black Rock, the ties that bound them to their neighborhood and to each other, were critical to the health and well-being not only of this neighborhood but of the entire city. These insights guided me as I continued to work to understand Buffalo's past and, indeed, what makes it "tick" in the present.

The people of Black Rock were proud of their history. Proud of their name, taken from the enormous outcropping of black rock that created a shelter from the fast moving waters of the Niagara River near the foot of Ferry Street. They knew their history, particularly the role of the neighborhood in the War of 1812 when, against great odds, they fought desperately to resist the British as they crossed the Niagara River, making their way down Niagara Street to the Village of Buffalo. They were proud of their many years as an independent town and proud, too, following their annexation in 1854, of the role they played in the development of Buffalo as a major industrial metropolis. When I first discovered Black Rock in the early 1970s it was still a healthy neighborhood with a strong local economy rooted in a still-strong manufacturing base. And while Black Rock, like neighborhoods in Rust Belt cities everywhere were hit hard by the economic and social trends of the millennial era, the people here, particularly those men and women who joined together under the banner of the Black Rock Historic Photo Project and in 2018 published a marvelous photographic album of neighborhood history, were still proud of their heritage and of their story. As I drove round and round the streets of Black Rock in 1971 and 1972, the sense of neighborhood pride that I'd first experienced on that pivotal afternoon in Delaware Park, was palpable. Was Black Rock, with its almost romantic connection to place and history, unique? Was it true of other neighborhoods in Buffalo too? It was with this question in mind that I, with Charlie in tow and sleeping happily in the back seat of my car, set out to answer. And as I did I quickly came to realize that Buffalo was really a collection, a collage, if you will, of distinct yet vaguely connected villages, each bearing a strong resemblance to those small, self-contained and independent Italian hill towns that had so captured my attention.

From the people in Black Rock I'd heard about a place called "The Fruit Belt." It's just off of Main Street ... at Virginia Street, Jack Utzig told me. Virginia Street is a tiny, one-way, pathway into what is immediately striking as a separate world, the world of The Fruit Belt. With its still thickly-planted trees and small, old, wooden homes set gently on the side of a slow-rising hill, the Fruit Belt, where streets were named "Grape, "Lemon," "Rose," "Cherry," "Mulberry," "Locust," and "Orange," still retained in 1972, all of the characteristics and elements of its mid-19th century origins. Though the population of the Fruit Belt had changed from being largely German-American to largely African-American, the neighborhood still bore all of the physical aspects and attributes that had characterized it for so long. The Fruit Belt with small streets arranged in a coherent grid, its forest-like collection of trees, the mid-19th century wood-frame homes that still lined it, the steeples of old German churches poking through the street-scape, bore all of the village-like characteristics that I'd discovered in Black Rock.

From here it was on to what I heard referred to as "the old First Ward." To enter it, like entering Black Rock and the Fruit Belt, was to enter what was to me a long-lost world. Again, small streets, isolated from the city's main drags, with names that conjured an American past rooted in Walt Whitman or Mark Twain – Vandalia, Indiana, Illinois, Alabama and the rest – gave The Ward a dream-like sense of mystery that I still feel today, a place where grain elevators towered over tiny, wooden houses, where the steeples of churches bearing magical names of women I found myself so eager to meet – "St. Brigid's" and "Our Lady of Perpetual Help" – loomed; where the light, at sunrise and sunset, was haunting and where, at times of day known only to the oldest residents, a long, loud train whistle pierced the quiet of the neighborhood.

I discovered other neighborhoods as well, small and isolated places with names like "Iron Island" and "Kaisertown," "Hamlin Park" and "Cold Spring," each with its own history, its own identity, its own fierce sense of pride of place.

I wanted to immerse myself in all of them, to be lost in their history, to learn their stories and then to tell them to the larger world. I vowed then that I would come back to all of these places. But first, I had more work to do in Black Rock. I'd completed my doctoral dissertation and now, wanting to push my work in and on Black Rock beyond that, to have even more fun with a subject that I'd found so engaging, I wanted, I thought, to make a film, a documentary movie about Black Rock.

I loved making home movies. Using a Kodak Super 8 that my sister gave me when I graduated from Brandeis, I'd gone all over New York, in and out of subways, up and down streets all over town, like a wanna-be Godard, trying to capture moments stolen from the daily lives of the people of New York. In my mind's eye, Black Rock was as cinematic a landscape as any in New York so why not I thought, make a film about it. It was with this in mind that I approached Mike Collins, the CEO of Channel 17 (it was not yet "WNED"). Let's make a movie, I said, set in Buffalo, about Black Rock; a documentary like the kind that the BBC was producing at that time. I'll, I said boldy, be Alistair Cooke, the renowned host. He loved the idea. Channel 17 had never done anything like that before. "Let's do it." Collins put me in immediate touch with Dan Healy, one of his producers and the station's chief cinematographer, Bob O. Lehman. These were two great guys, thrilled to be able to get their cameras "on location, in Black Rock." And what a thrill this was for me. On a large barge that Collins rented for the film, the three of us trolled up and down the Black Rock channel, shooting as we went. Then, working from a script that I had written we entered all kinds of places in the neighborhood, bars and restaurants, bowling alleys and factories, filming places and interviewing people, revisiting many of the local scenes and characters that I had encountered over the course of my Black Rock studies. After a month of filming we had a finished product, a half-hour documentary which told the story of this most intriguing neighborhood, Black Rock as I had come to know and understand it. Who and how many people watched the film (it was presented twice, once at prime time on Tuesday November 18th, 1975) I never knew. But what I did know is that the work that I had done in Black Rock, while largely invisible to the outside world, had a transformative effect not only on how I looked at and understood my work, but more significantly, how I viewed my life in Buffalo. For what was becoming gradually and increasingly clear to me was that on every day and in every way, the city to which I had so recently moved was indeed becoming my home, a place where I, like those contented passengers on that safe and secure Erie Canal boat, was also coming to know my neighbor and to know my pal.

Acknowledgements

Sadly, all my friends and acquaintances from my days in Black Rock during the 1970s have passed away (though I'm still on the look out for Mikey Degenhart!). Acknowledgements are due, however, to Professor Michael D. Frisch, my doctoral dissertation adviser at the SUNYAB history department.

CHAPTER 3

Into the 'Seventies

How people stared down decline and, with faith in themselves, rolled up their sleeves, went to work and got it done

The signs of decline, which were apparent everywhere in Buffalo during the 1970s, could not be ignored. Everything was unravelling: the industrial economy was on its last legs; long stable ethnic neighborhoods were emptying out; downtown was dying, a daily newspaper would soon cease publication, public institutions were bankrupt, and city government was crippled. Throughout Buffalo, on corner stores in the Seneca-Babcock, Bailey-Delavan, Grant-Amherst neighborhoods, were hand-written signs offering "If out of work, coffee 5 cents." There was a blizzard too, the worst in history when in January 1977 clouds and shadows and winds came roaring off the lake; blinding, relentless waves of snow followed, smothering and paralyzing the city. And yet, despite the unflaggingly gloomy and depressing statistics, there were people all over the city who never lost their faith in themselves and in their city, a belief that that they could, if they really wanted to, do what my new friend Carol Hoyt urged upon all she met: "We can," she said, "fix this place." There were men and women all over town, people whose lives and work began to intersect with mine, people, myself increasingly among them who, despite the truly depressing data that we were fed on a daily basis, believing in ourselves and in our city, rolled up our sleeves and went to work. The world that I lived and worked in was filled with people like these, people in neighborhoods and organizations throughout the city, people who desperately wanted to and knew that they could transform a city that had fallen on such desperately hard times. Their stories are well worth telling. Let's start with mine.

I was an historian, not an academic historian but an activist, entrepreneurial historian, and I wanted to use history and my understanding of it as a way to "fix" our city. What Buffalo most needed was an engaged and committed citizenry, people who cared, people who like me and my friends and colleagues, believed in their ability to "fix this place." History was the key, I felt, which by unlocking a person's interest in the past would increase the likelihood that that person would care about and become engaged in the present. I got my chance to test my "theory" when I was hired to teach a course at the UB's College of Urban Studies titled simply "On Buffalo." What I taught and how I taught it, they said (in those days of increasingly squirrely standards) was up to me. In an effort to create as broad a platform for the course as possible, to bring a range of different disciplines to the topic, I suggested a title – Learning from Buffalo" – and a subtitle: "The Past, Present and Future of the City."

What about a "textbook"? While there were a few out-of-date and out-of-print texts and hundreds of primary sources tucked away on the shelves of the Buffalo Historical Society, and in the Grosvenor Collection of the Buffalo and Erie County Public Library, there was nothing anywhere that captured and reflected in any way my interests in and approaches to studying the city. What I was looking for was a hands-on strategy to studying the city, like the one that I created for my work in the Black Rock neighborhood, a process that would engage the students directly and personally in the study of the city, an approach that would connect them, as it was doing for me, to the actual "fabric" of the city's life and history. What if, I wondered, I created a tour, a bus tour that I would lead that would take my students around and about the streets and neighborhoods of the city? What if I could, out of those many random "drive-bys" that I'd taken with Charlie strapped into the seat behind me, create a tour, one that would provide a cohesive and coherent context for learning about the city? All summer long I drove around the city, following my instincts, my nose for a story, in and around the main streets and the side-streets of neighborhoods in every part of the city, searching for large landmarks and tiny clues that might offer insight and understanding into the ways and means that Buffalo grew and evolved.

In the absence of any usable secondary sources, I created, in addition to the tour, a "work-book," a series of carefully crafted questions and exercises which, when used as a complement to the tour, would provide some semblance of the kinds of material that I would need to teach this class. The work-book was divided into sections that mirrored the stops on the tour, raising questions in each place that would, I hoped, lead the students to their own process of discovery. What meaning can we derive from the close proximity of home and work in the old First Ward? What might be the role and function of St. Theresa's Church on Seneca Street in the life of that neighborhood? What about those railroad overpasses? What do you think that the impact of those trains would have been had they crossed at grade? And what about the impact of the Scajaquada Creek Expressway and the Kensington Expressway on the life of the neighborhoods that surrounded them?

So one day, several weeks into the semester, I hired a bus and on a Saturday morning in October 1974, I and my thirty-odd students left the parking lot in front of Hayes Hall on UB's Main Street Campus and off we went. Getting off and back on at carefully planned stops all along the way, we covered the city, the skeptical and reluctant driver making hair-pin turns around tight corners into the hidden corners of the Fruit Belt, Black Rock and the First Ward. Stopping only for lunch at the Broadway Market, my tour covered the West Side driving down Niagara and onto Hudson and Allen, up Delaware Avenue past rows of magnificent mansions so recently inhabited by Buffalo's elite, and then across to the East Side where at the corner of Michigan and E. Ferry I pointed out the site of the long demolished Offermann Stadium. It is hard today, when bus tours of the city have become a fixture, to exaggerate the conceit of my bus tour. Conceived at a time when the arc of the city's history was at its lowest, a time when people could not leave the city fast enough, here I was, this kid from New York, doing what? Taking people on bus tours of Buffalo? You've got to be kidding, right?

As much as the tour itself, I liked the story and the idea behind it, so I pitched it to a friend of mine, a woman named Karen Brady whose column "Karen's Korner" in *The Buffalo News*, not unlike Sean Kirst's today, covered local human interest stories. Might she be interested, I asked her, in writing about my tour, what I was now calling "Mark Goldman's Rubberneck Bus Tour of Buffalo." Well, indeed she was and in an article that appeared in the late winter of 1974 she told the story of "the New York kid who came to Buffalo." Mark has found a home here, she wrote, and he's raising his family here too. (The article was illustrated with a photograph of me holding up my two-year-old son Charlie.) He's been studying Buffalo's history and he wants to share it with the people of his adopted city. With that in mind, she continued, he's offering weekly bus tours of Buffalo: for ten dollars, with lunch at the Broadway Market thrown in, he will lead you on a bus up and down and all around the highways and by-ways of Buffalo. Karen put my phone number at the end of the column and encouraged people to call me.

The response was overwhelming. The notion of exploring Buffalo had tapped a well of deep-seated, but seemingly long-repressed, interest in the city's history. Dozens of people called and soon, I told my businessman brother in New York, I too had "a business". The logistics were difficult and complicated but with the help of my wife Kitty's excellent organizational skills – keeping track of ticket sales, deposits, bus rentals and restaurant reservations – it worked. And so it went. Every Saturday for three months I, with microphone in hand and memorized script in my head, led no fewer than forty Buffalonians on a tour up, down, around and all over the city. Few of the passengers, and certainly not the bus drivers, had traveled any of the totally off-the-beaten-paths that I took them in and around the ancient streets of the city's neighborhoods, stopping to look at the empty and abandoned Prudential Building, the moth-balled Shea's Theater, past Frank Lloyd Wright's run-down and deserted Darwin D Martin House, "Mark Goldman's Rubberneck Bus Tour of Buffalo" penetrated the hidden high-ways and by-ways of Buffalo. The people were thrilled and I was having a ball. Word spread, the phones rang off the hook. I was making a little money from the tours (as was the Blue Bird Bus Company from whom I was renting the busses), but by the Spring of 1975 it finally became too much for me. I decided to bring my long-running hit to an end. In the meantime, however, I'd gotten a phone call from a man named John Montana, the president of Blue Bird Bus Company. He wanted to take me out for lunch. Montana, I'd heard, was the son of John Montana, the legendary local mob boss who, it was said, had once controlled private taxi and bus service in Buffalo going back to the 1920s. Montana seemed nice on the phone, saying that he had something he wanted to talk to me about. Could I meet him for lunch at the Statler Hotel? Excited, I joined him there and shortly after we sat down he told me that he liked "my operation" and that his people at Blue Bird enjoyed working with me. He said that he saw a future in Buffalo tourism; someday soon, he felt, people would realize what we've got here in Buffalo, "all that architecture and those neighborhoods," he said. He grew up in one of them, the old Italian neighborhood on Busti Avenue. He was open about his family and talked freely about his father's origins in Montedoro, Sicily and how, by the 1920s, he'd become the first Italian elected official in Buffalo. It was his father, John said, who built a large taxi and bus business that their family still owned. Anyway, he said, he wanted to talk to me about my "tour business". He was interested, he said, in "buying" my "operation." Caught completely off guard and unprepared for what was quickly turning into a business meeting, I nervously responded that in fact I had no operation. All that I had was "an idea" and I wasn't sure how, I said, I could sell that. I was tired of the "tour business" anyway and was ready to "retire". He was as befuddled as I was. Our lunch quickly broke up and as we left I thanked him for lunch and reminding him that I was done with the bus business, I told him: "You go for it. It's yours now."

I recognized that what people most liked about my tour was that I was able to offer them an historical context which helped them to understand why and how their city developed the way it did. I could sense their excitement and eagerness to share their growing understanding of their city's history. By pointing out the connection between specific places and specific events, by pointing out, for example, a parking lot in downtown Buffalo where there was once a thriving public market; or a tavern in the First Ward where the great Fenian Raid was launched, I was able to directly connect the Buffalonians of today with the people, the places and the events of the past. In the process, they, like me, were becoming more attached to the city that we all called home. They too, I sensed, were beginning to feel that they too could "fix this place."

Over the protests of many, in the spring of 1975, I had indeed "retired" and began to focus instead on other activities, some academic, some entrepreneurial, that would continue to keep me intensely and excitedly engaged in the work of learning about Buffalo. I am immensely proud of this short but most interesting chapter of my life's work. Mr. Montana was right. There was a future in Buffalo tours. But my "Mark Goldman's Rubberneck Bus Tours of Buffalo" were there first, long before those who followed in my wake and have, as a result, made bus tours of Buffalo the popular attraction that they are today. Tim Tielman, who has been leading tours on an ingeniously designed open bus, reports that over 3,000 people rode with him in 2020. And Chuck LaChiusa who founded "Explore Buffalo" in 2006 reports that he, and a full staff of volunteer guides, are operating over 80 tours, some on foot, some on boats and some in kayaks. In 2019 alone, over 20,000 went on his tours. But I was there first! The seed that I planted in the early 1970s may have been small but it certainly was fertile.

Long after I "retired," people remembered my tours and every once in a while I'd get a call and a request. "My daughter's getting married," one man said. "Dozens of people are coming from out of town to the wedding. Would you take them on one of your tours?" Once, one of my favorite Buffalonians, Dr. Lydia Wright, one of the city's all-time great leaders, called. Her family was having a reunion, she said, coming in from all parts of the county. Would I, she wondered, take twenty of them on a tour?

• • •

In the late fall of 1974, I received a call from a man who I had heard about but not yet met, the new dean of what UB called The School of Architecture and Environmental Design. Harold Cohen was my kind of guy, a smart, fast-talking Jewish New Yorker, eager to make exciting things happen. He, as much as anybody I would meet, wanted to and believed that he could, "fix this place." He'd heard about my tour, he said, and he wanted my help with recruitment. Reyner Banham, the great English architectural historian, was in town and, Cohen said, UB was hoping to hire him. Would I, he asked, take him and Banham, on a tour? Now you're talking, a real "magical mystery tour" if ever there was one: three outgoing, ebullient guys, driving around a city that was not theirs yet, and yet, through a direct process of hands-on engagement (there wasn't a nook or a cranny that we did not explore) making it theirs. Harold loved the tour and at the end of the day asked me if I would teach a course, a course he vaguely defined as "a course on Buffalo," at his "School".

Under the very exciting and dynamic leadership of Harold Cohen "The School" had become one of the most exciting "idea centers" in the city. Unlike so many other department heads, Cohen refused to move to the new suburban campus in Amherst and in the mid-1970s when I was teaching my course there, the school occupied one of Buffalo's great industrial buildings, a sleek, turn-of-the-century steel and glass factory on Main Street, the Meter Building next to Bennett High School. Under Cohen and his hand-picked faculty, "The School" was fast becoming the energetic center of a host of city-oriented projects. Cohen was a charismatic, fast-talking "Brooklyn boy" whose Jackie Mason-like lilt and intonation had never been heard in Buffalo's WASP-dominated architectural environment. He was an exuberant and unabashed booster of Buffalo's potential. He wanted to save the H. H. Richardson Buildings on the grounds of the

State psychiatric hospital, to fix the schools, rethink the Peace Bridge to Canada, create a Conservancy for Olmsted's parks. He was very popular on the local lecture circuit, and people responded very positively to his energetic and hope-filled message of renewing the city, as for example the members of the Twentieth Century Club where in early 1976 he delivered a speech on "Fixing Buffalo: Using Brain Power, Our Best and Most Reliable Resource."

I soon became fast friends with Professor Banham and his wife Mary, and during the summer of 1977, I helped them teach a three week course that focused on the three surviving buildings of the Larkin Soap Company. Banham had fallen in love with these buildings, recognizing instantly the role that these buildings played in the development of modern architecture. He wanted them to be the first in what he hoped would be an ongoing effort to measure, document, photograph and make field drawings of all of the structures from what he called "Buffalo's Golden Age of Industrial Architecture." We worked throughout the summer and at an event in the building in November 1977, we sponsored "Larkin Day" at which the students who'd participated in the summer workshop presented their work. Forty years before anybody had ever heard the term "Larkinville," Harold Cohen and Reyner Banham and those of us who worked with them were proclaiming the importance of these buildings not only to Buffalo's past but to its future as well.

At that time, the main Larkin building was owned and occupied by Graphic Controls, a large, multi-national specialty industrial printing company owned and operated by Max and Will Clarkson. The Clarkson brothers had come to Buffalo from Toronto in the late 1960s and adapted quickly to their new surroundings. As a resident of Allentown, older brother Max was one of the founders in 1971 of the Allentown Community Center, a cultural incubator, as we'll see, of enormous importance in the life of the city. Will, meantime, a life-long devotee of architecture, had met Dean Cohen and in the summer of 1977 was working with us on our efforts to document the Graphic Controls Building, aka, "The Larkin Building" on Exchange Street.

In September 1977 we were all invited to the official opening of the School's new quarters in Hayes Hall. It was, like pretty much everything Dean Cohen touched, exciting, elegant and ever stimulating. To commemorate the event, Harold had invited one of my favorite thinkers on urban issues, Edmund Bacon from NYU. Bacon was to deliver a lecture on a topic near and dear to Dean

Cohen: "Values and Ethics in the Design and Planning Professions." What a way to start the school year!

Meanwhile, Will Clarkson and Harold Cohen become friends and together they created a support organization for Dean Cohen's school called "The Friends of the School of Architecture." While raising money for "The School" was part of their mission, their larger intention was an ambitious one, an attempt to engage the community in a sustained and city wide effort to do nothing less than "improve the built environment of the city of Buffalo." Under their leadership, the Friends created lecture series and symposia and organized a docent program that sent volunteer apostles of Buffalo's architecture into local schools. More than forty years later, "The Friends" of what is now known as the School of Architecture and Planning, remains a significant part of its work.

Banham wanted a book on Buffalo architecture. Sometime in 1978-79, he turned to Will Clarkson who, forming an entity called the Buffalo Architectural Guidebook Corporation, began to organize the project. Clarkson was putting together a team of writers, an august crowd: Frank Kowsky, soon to become the nation's leading expert on Olmsted and Vaux; John Randall, the passionate advocate of the work of Louis Sullivan, Austin Fox, dedicated expert on Buffalo architecture, Jack Quinan whose pathbreaking work on Frank Lloyd Wright would be critical in the preservation of the Martin House, Terry Lasher, a first-rate librarian and archivist, and the great Banham himself.

Not satisfied with that line-up, Clarkson, in an effort to beef it up still more, called on "Yours Truly." Obviously flattered, I at first demurred. I was not, I told Will, an architectural historian and I had no particular expertise in that field of study. Yes, that's true, Clarkson countered. But you know Buffalo's history. We need you to provide an historical context, he insisted, a narrative that would enable the reader to see and understand the individual buildings from an historical perspective. Clarkson was beginning to talk my language. What if, I suggested, the book be divided not by architectural styles, not even by dates and periods. What if, I said in what I sensed to be a different and more interesting approach to Buffalo's architecture, we divide the book into seven different sections, each covering a different neighborhood. I could, I suggested, write the neighborhood narratives, setting the stage for the architectural historians who would take it from there. He agreed and so it was. Clarkson raised the money and made the deal with MIT Press, which in 1981 published the book *Buffalo*

Architecture: A Guide. It was then and remains today, the first and most important and credible effort to bring to the attention of the world the incredible legacy of Buffalo's architecture. I am extremely proud of the role that I played in this most significant effort.

I had a ball working on it too, collaborating with such interesting, smart and really enjoyable people. Working sometimes together in Hayes Hall and sometimes alone, our small group of writers constituted a lively and deeply engaged coterie of friends and colleagues. I became particularly close to Pat Bazelon, an extraordinary photographer, an Englishwoman who had moved to Buffalo with her husband, a professor at the Law school. Pat was hired to be the project photographer. Together she and I drove all around the city, lugging her massive, large-format camera in and out of my car, setting it up at busy intersections, at the still-bustling entrance to Bethlehem Steel, at long-empty East Side factories and in the shabby, abandoned but still-glorious lobby of the Prudential Building. Our work together became the backbone of the book and launched a career for Pat as a world class architectural photographer. *Buffalo Architecture: A Guide* was released in time for Christmas 1981 and was immediately successful. Tim Tielman, who was working as a manager in the Walden book store in the Main Place Mall, remembers that the book was "flying off the shelves. We couldn't keep enough of them in stock." Word was spreading, knowledge of our heritage was building and with it, slowly, but surely, a faith in the future.

• • •

Meanwhile, I was teaching two different kinds of courses, both on Buffalo. One, a history course that focused on its past; the other a "contemporary issues" course that focused on its present. This was a perfect combination for me which with one foot planted firmly in the past, the other in the present, allowed and encouraged me to explore the two areas of urban studies that I enjoyed most. In the absence of "texts" and/or other secondary, I developed my own learning materials. With my head buried sometimes in the archives and sometimes in the pages of Buffalo's two daily newspapers (remember the *Courier Express*, RIP?), I proceeded.

The mid-1970s were an exciting time in the world of local politics, particularly following the passage of the federal Community Development Act of 1974. One of the most ardent advocates of this act was a man recently elected to the Buffalo Common Council from the University District named William D. Price. Bill Price was a singular leader, cut out of the same cloth, I still believe more than forty years later, as Bobby Kennedy, a gutsy fighter, a man with a vision as to how to stabilize the escalating crisis in race relations that he believed was brewing here. In addition, he had an abiding faith in Buffalo and the ability of the people who lived here to renew it. I was following his work in the press, particularly his efforts in the Fillmore-Leroy neighborhood. In partnership with Walter Kerns, the priest at Blessed Trinity Church on Leroy Avenue, Price had created a community organization which became a city-wide model of community engagement. Known as FLARE – Fillmore Leroy Area Residents – the primary purpose of the organization was to do what never had been done: to bring racial balance and stability to a rapidly changing neighborhood. I first met Bill at Walter Kerns' office at the church in the early Spring of 1975 and it was there that he talked to me about his high hopes and expectations for community engagement and citizen participation. Sometime later he came to talk to my urban studies class in Foster Hall. To my great surprise he brought with him a friend and a colleague, a man he introduced to me as Joe Ryan.

Bill Price and Joe Ryan had a lot in common. They were both Irish-Americans not, like so many others, from The First Ward and South Buffalo, but from North Buffalo, from St. Mark Parish. Both were veterans of the US Marine Corps, both having served in Vietnam. Both were extraordinarily charismatic, tall, handsome, idealistic, hardworking, forward thinking young men who had come of age in the 1960s, believing deeply in the promises of their generation. They were very restless, very smart and, by the way, very funny. I became good, lifelong friends with both of them. They wanted to talk to the class about what they both felt was "the radical potential" of the Community Development Act of 1974.

Theirs was a fascinating, exciting, extraordinary presentation in which these two "Young Turks," as passionate as they were articulate, outlined the terms of the Act. Federal monies, they said, would no longer be awarded in "categories" but rather in "blocks." There was a world of difference, between these two approaches, Price and Ryan argued. Whereas categorical grants must be used for a specific, designated purpose, block grants can be used for any purpose decided upon by the entity, in this case the city, that receives it.

Price and Ryan talked about how they wanted to create a system that would allow Federal funds in the form of block grants to pass as directly as possible into the neighborhoods themselves. The men were excited by this promise, eager, as Price said, to "jump at the chance to try out our notions about how a city is rebuilt and preserved." In order to overcome the opposition of the existing leadership in the city, they knew that they would have to a power base of their own, rooted as much as possible in the streets and neighborhoods throughout the entire city. Price's and Ryan's inspirational vision and their full embrace of citizen participation had a permanent impact on me, a point of view and an approach to the making of public policy that continues to influence me almost fifty years later. Together, it was clear, there was nothing that these two could not do. (Much of my initial contacts with Price and Ryan were reported in my earlier book, *City On The Lake*, Buffalo, 1990.)

It was at the College of Urban Studies that I first met members of Buffalo's Puerto Rican community, people like the students Casimiro "Caz" Rodriguez, Jose Pizarro and Alberto Cappas. Some, like "Caz," were raised in Buffalo. Others, like Cappas and Perez, had come from New York to attend the State University here.

Rodriguez's family, like so many of the Puerto Ricans who settled in Buffalo, had come here in the early 1950s, working first on the fruit farms in the area and then moving to Buffalo to work in the steel mills. Jose Pizarro and Alberto Cappas had come to Buffalo in the late 1960s, among the several dozen "Nuyoricans" who had come from New York to study at UB. Bringing with them the energetic and impatient swagger of New York, they quickly began to organize their fellow Puerto Rican students. In 1968 they formed a group called PODER: Puerto Rican Organization for Dignity, Elevation and Responsibility. By the time I met them in 1973, the two young men were respected members of the growing number of campus activists. I first became aware of Pizarro and Cappas in the Fall of 1974 when a poster hanging in Norton Union caught my eye. El Gran Combo, a fantastic Puerto Rican salsa group that I had heard in New York, was coming to the Statler Hotel for a concert. Tickets, the poster said, were on sale in the PODER office. It was there, in a large room on the second floor of Norton that they shared with the Black Student Union, that I met Jose and Alberto.

While I had no Puerto Rican friends growing up in New York, Puerto Ricans were a part of our daily lives, filling the side streets of the upper West Side neighborhood of my high school and the baseball diamonds that we played on in Central Park. In fact, my high school, Walden, had a "sister school" in San Juan and it was there that I and a few other members of my junior class went on a field trip in 1959. The sights and sounds of Puerto Rico and the Puerto Ricans that I'd come across growing up in New York were familiar to me and I was thrilled to find at least some of it here in Buffalo, at least in the office of PODER in Norton. Intent on bringing leading Puerto Rican writers and artists to Buffalo too, Perez and Cappas, several years before the Nuyorican Poets Café opened on the "LOISIDA" (street acronym for a Puerto Rican from New York City's "Lower East Side") in New York in 1980, had brought some of the leading Puerto Rican poets (Miguel Algarin, Miguel Pinero and Pedro Pietri) – to the UB campus. Ever eager to fill the often empty slots of my urban studies class while at the same time exposing my students to interesting outsiders, I invited Jose and Alberto to come talk to my class about the work that they were doing on behalf of the Puerto Rican students at UB. They brought some props with them: a portable record player and a El Gran Combo record. "We're gonna salsa," they said. "All of us. Let's get up and dance."

We started to hang out and now Jose took me to Virginia Street. He wanted me to meet somebody, "somebody special," a friend of his named Francisco "Frankie" Perez. Now that was a story. Frank was one of the most charismatic people that I've met in my more than fifty years in Buffalo. Warm and friendly, supersmart and a great guy to be around, he was a natural and extremely effective leader. I first met him in the winter of 1974 at the home of Jose Pizarro on Tenth Street on the increasingly Puerto Rican West Side. I watched Frankie closely in those years and, in 1975, my idea for a documentary film on him and his work on the Lower West Side was accepted by WBEN-TV. Working together with a reporter named Allen Costantini, we co-wrote and produced a half-hour film. It was a great story, filled with the color and characters of Frankie Perez's neighborhood. Allen and I were thrilled with the work that we did on this project and were very disappointed when we got so little response or feedback from the viewing public. I revisited the story again in 1990 in *City on the Lake* and again it fell flat. I still believe that the story of Frankie Perez and the work that he and others did on the lower West Side of Buffalo in the mid-1970s is one of the all-time great Buffalo stories. Maybe now, forty-odd years after the fact, the time is ripe to tell it again. I hope you agree.

Frankie Perez was born in the small town of Moca, in the northwestern part of the island. He had come to Buffalo in 1953 when his father, a fruit picker, sent for him, his mother and his brothers and sisters. By then his father was working at Bethlehem Steel and living on Niagara Street on the lower West Side. It was here, in this rapidly changing neighborhood of exiting Italians and entering Puerto Ricans, that Frankie grew up. He went to old School 73 on Seventh Street, torn down, like Karima Bondi's house down the street, as part of the Shoreline urban renewal project, then onto Grover Cleveland High School, followed by two years at the University of Puerto Rico. But it was here, on the West Side, at what he called "the University of Virginia Street," that he got his real education.

Frankie Perez's lower West Side was nothing like the grim, drab, posed and purposefully depressing photographs that local photographer Milton Rogovin made for his book *Triptych* that appeared at this time. Unlike the miserable looking people in Rogovin's agitprop work, Frankie and his co-conspirators were hopeful and energetic, vibrant, filled with music, hope and joy. It was inspiring to see what was happening on the streets of the lower West Side and to feel their people's hope for the future.

By the early 1970s, Puerto Ricans had planted firm and increasingly deep roots on the lower West Side. Group after grassroots group, politics heavily on their minds – the Puerto Rican-Chicano Coordinating Committee, Alianza, the Spanish Speaking Political Caucus, the Buffalo Hispanic Association and Pucho Olivencia's Puerto Rican American Community Organization – were, together and separately wrestling with the challenges of being Puerto Rican in Buffalo. Virginia Street was the focal point of the community, the place where everything came together. By the early 1970s, the Virginia Street Festival with its parade, its ragtag tumble of booths, homegrown salsa and *son* bands, its profusion of Mexican and Puerto Rican delicacies and its real air of "Dancin' in the Streets," had become an institution. Virginia and Niagara were now lined with bodegas and, as shabby as they may have looked to outsiders, these tiny stores, with their supply of plantains, mangos, aguacate, Café Bustelo, and bright green and pungent olive oil, were important centers of community life, building blocks of strength and self-confidence.

By the time that I met him in late 1974, Frankie was the leading power broker on the West Side. As chairman of the three leading grassroots organizations in the neighborhood – the Puerto Rican Chicano Coordinating Committee, the

Lower West Side Resources and Development Corporation, and the Virginia Street Festival – Frankie was the go-to guy, "the Fiorello LaGuardia," he called himself, "of Virginia Street." He would need all the influence and power that he could muster for he was about to fight a battle to save his community, the fight against the West Side Arterial.

Although little known in the annals of Buffalo's long history of city planning disasters, there are few more shameful episodes than the efforts in the early 1970s to build a highway, a grade level one at that, across the city connecting the Kensington Expressway on the east with the New York State Thruway on the west. While I have described this appalling project in detail in *City on the Lake* and *City on the Edge*, it is worth recalling here that, as recently as the early 1970s, there were still planners and politicians in the area who did not see nor understand the incredible devastation that such a project would have caused. Frankie and his followers on the lower West Side, people who'd struggled to finally find a place for themselves in this neighborhood, sure did and now, with Frankie Perez at their command they fought back. After a two year struggle they won when, on January 12, 1976, a resolution introduced by Buffalo's new assemblyman William B. Hoyt, finally and forever killed this ghastly plan. Later that evening, Frankie Perez threw a party at PRCC headquarters on Virginia Street. Dancing to the music of El Gran Combo, Celia Cruz and Tito Puente, dozens of us celebrated. Now, finally, Frankie said in a toast to the ecstatic crowd, "We are free to build our community." I stayed close to Frankie over the years and when, twenty years later in 1995 I opened La Luna, our Latin dance-club on Chippewa Street, Frankie Perez was our guest of honor.

• • •

Not only the neighborhoods but the parks, too, particularly Delaware Park, were crumbling. Growing up in New York, I had lived my entire youth on the fringes of Central Park. It was there, on the Great Lawn in the shadow of the Belvedere Castle, that my gang of friends met on weekends to play football, basketball and baseball. It was in Central Park, too, around the Reservoir, that I and my family walked almost each and every Sunday. The park was an extension of our living room really, an integral daily part of my growing up in New York. Within days of coming to Buffalo in 1967, I discovered Delaware Park. It was in Delaware

Park remember, that I first heard about Black Rock. And it was here too that I first became involved in the public affairs of the city.

It started with long distance running and, like so much of the rest of my life in Buffalo, with a personal relationship, my friendship with another transplant, a man named Jesse Kregal. Jesse moved from Portland, Oregon to Buffalo in 1970 to become the principal timpanist with the Buffalo Philharmonic Orchestra. He fell in love with Buffalo instantly and over the course of his many years here (Jesse died in 2016), he would stop at nothing to "fix it." I met him at the Jewish Center, sometime in 1970-71. (At that time there was still only one JCC.) In those days before machines, when working out meant playing sports, the JCC had a full-court basketball court and it was here that I met Jesse, running round and round it. (There were 26 laps to a mile and he was a long-distance runner.) I was too and Jesse, ever friendly, energetic and enthusiastic, encouraged me to join him. Soon we were joined by Alan Gross and now we were three. Alan was born and raised in Buffalo. He'd grown up, he said, around Delaware Park and in the early summer of 1972 he suggested that we run there, on the Ring Road which circled what he called "The Meadow."

By that time, The Meadow and the Ring Road that circled it had long been in the sights of highway planners. There'd been a public golf course on The Meadow here since the mid-1920s and MUNY (municipal sports baseball games) had been played here for years. By the 1950s, however, Delaware Park, with its location smack dab in the middle of the busy commuting route between downtown and North Buffalo, had become vulnerable, easy prey for automobile-happy planners and politicians. It was from my father-in-law, Milton Friedman, who lived in a house on near-by Middlesex Road, that I first learned about the tragedy of the Scajaquada Creek Expressway and how its construction through the heart of Delaware Park began what became a decade-long assault on the park. "Miltie's" memories led me to want to learn more about this particularly compelling story and soon I was poring over documents in the files of the New York State Department of Transportation in the Donovan Building on Washington St. It wasn't long before I began to uncover the details of this tragic tale. The files were filled with the kinds of grizzly details that I could not resist. The attack on the park started, I learned, during the first car-happy era of the 1920s when planners, calling it a "barrier to traffic," suggested that Delaware Avenue be doubled in width as it passed through the Park. Referring to this part of the Park as "little used lands," this report suggested that a wider "roadway" would relieve traffic. Thus the "S-curves" near the lake and cemetery. Then, of course, there was the Scajaquada Creek Expressway which I was amazed to learn, was built with hardly the slightest opposition, not even from the affluent residents of the area. As if the Scajaquada were not enough, in 1958 NYSDOT proposed something called the "Delaware Park Shortway" which, had it been built, would have taken a large chunk of parkland on the northside of the Meadow, transforming Amherst Street into a divided highway parallel to the Scajaquada. (I have written about these events in much greater detail in *City on the Edge* (2007).)

The Ring Road, meanwhile, had become something of an access route for the Scajaquada and by the time of that summer afternoon in 1972 that Jesse Kregal, Alan Gross and I ventured there to run around it, it was a traffic nightmare. Cars circled in both directions, the speed limit was 30mph and, worst of all, there was a ramp at the bottom of the road, where the restrooms are located, which enabled motorists to enter directly onto the expressway. The Ring Road then had become a shortcut for motorists speeding around it, hoping to save some time by cutting through the park and onto the highway.

It was hard in those days to find people who cared. Indeed, the park, like so many of the city's extraordinary assets, was being increasingly abandoned by a middle class hell-bent on leaving the city. Delaware Park was a mess: the lake was a sinkhole of pollution, closed to the public due to sewage overflow; the hill behind the Rose Garden had not yet been discovered and reimagined as "Shakespeare Hill" by Saul Elkin; the golf course and the Meadow were untended. The same was true of the other six parks known today as "Olmsted Parks." Ignored by politicians who saw little political advantage in fighting for them, the parks were terribly neglected. Unlike New York City, where Thomas Hoving as parks commissioner provided dynamic and creative leadership, there was no public official in Buffalo who saw or understood the importance of public parks in the life of the city. Until that is, in 1970 when William B. Hoyt, running on a platform that included his passionate insistence that the lake in Delaware Park be "cleaned-up" was elected Delaware District councilman. Hoyt cared about the Meadow too and when we approached him about our concerns about it, he was immediately supportive. Indeed, citing conditions at both the lake and the Meadow, Hoyt persuaded Mayor Stanley Makowski in December 1972 to allocate $25,000 for the creation of a master plan for Delaware Park. Hoyt insisted upon citizen input, and in the Spring of 1972 he called for the creation of a citizens' committee called the Delaware Park Steering Committee. Under the smart and passionate leadership of Bette Blum and Joan Kahn who one year earlier had founded The Buffalo Green Fund, the DPSC quickly became an effective forum for citizen participation that stood the normative model of top-down planning on its head.

A coalition was developing around the efforts to reclaim the parks from automobiles, and the runners were a critical part of it. By the early 1970s, long-distance running, (perhaps in response to a new found sense of environmentalism, not to mention the gas crunch of 1973) was taking off in Buffalo as it was in cities throughout the country. There were several running clubs in Buffalo – the Belle Watlings (named for the infamous owner of the brothel in *Gone With The Wind*), Checkers, named for a popular Hertel Avenue bar and the one I belonged to, The Buffalo Philharmonic Athletic Club, founded by the ever-inventive and energetic Jesse Kregal.

Basically "run off" the Ring Road by cars, in the Spring of 1973 we moved to the Niagara Parkway, across the Peace Bridge on the Canadian shore. The parkway is a magnificent, beautifully landscaped, gently rolling, two lane road set down on the edge of the Niagara River like a carpet. Beginning its fast- moving journey just over the bridge in Fort Erie, it ends in a crashing finale (clearly this appealed to the timpanist in Kregal!) at the foot of Niagara Falls. We were running there weekly now and, inevitably, on those long, slow and gorgeous runs, we (our group included Alan Gross of the Buffalo Philharmonic, Norm Schwendler of The Belles and Joe Jordan from Checkers) conceived the idea of a marathon, an international marathon, one that would start in Buffalo, cross the Peace Bridge to Canada and end, 26 miles later, at Niagara Falls. We called it "The Skylon International Marathon." The Skylon was more than a running race. It was, rather, a celebration of place and of community, an event that represented and embodied in many ways our increasing oneness with the city. The Skylon, I still feel, symbolized our full devotion to the city, for at a time when so many people were running away from Buffalo we, exuberant runners all, were running through it, embracing it as we ran. The course took the runners down the Olmsted-designed parkways of Chapin and Bidwell, around Soldiers Place and Colonial Circle, down once stately Richmond Avenue, around Symphony Circle past Kleinhans Music Hall, down Porter Avenue to the Peace Bridge. The Skylon, conceived, organized, staffed and operated by citizen volunteers, was a communal event, one that made those of us who created it and who ran in it proud of ourselves and of our city. The first Skylon International Marathon was in 1974, the last, ten years later in 1984.

We now turned our attention to the Ring Road where, despite the fact that it required dodging motorists who were getting onto the Scajaquada Expressway, we chose to do most of our training. Following the Skylon, the number of runners in the park grew, and while significant improvements had been made – by 1977 the entrance to the Scajaquada Expressway had been closed, traffic around the Ring Road was one-way and the speed limit had been reduced to 15 miles per hour – our vision of The Meadow as a place for passive recreation required that far more traffic-calming measures were necessary. This was particularly true when in early 1978 we learned (discovered, really) about the Zoo's plans and intentions for the Meadow.

Our discovery was serendipitous, happening when one of the members of our club, an anthropologist familiar with measuring and surveying, discovered the tell-tale signs of orange markings on the Ring Road across from the Zoo's entrance, and orange stakes planted in various parts of the Meadow itself. While we fought it, the Zoo insisted on closing its entrance on Parkside Avenue where it was accessible by public transportation, and moved it instead to the Ring Road. The stakes in the ground and the markings in the road suggested why: the Zoo, we learned in the Fall of 1978, was planning to build a five acre, five hundred car parking lot across from the Zoo's new entrance in The Meadow in Delaware Park.

As hard as this may be to believe today, there was a time, not so long ago, when one of the great creations of one of America's greatest creators was a prime target for the kind of catastrophic despoliation that was being considered by the Buffalo Zoo. But true it was, and the Zoo's plan was all that we, a small group of well-trained, intense, long-distance runners needed to hear. In the fall of 1978, we sprung into action. Our goal was to stop the Zoo from implementing its masterplan and then, once that goal was accomplished, to replace it with a series of measures that would "take back the park" and return it to the hands (and the feet!) of the people who Olmsted had intended it for.

With the support and encouragement of Tim Swift, the new Delaware District Councilman (his predecessor Bill Hoyt had been elected to the New York State Assembly) and the Delaware Park Steering Committee we organized, we gathered signatures of hundreds of park users and enthusiasts including the members of the Golden Tee, one of the oldest African-American golfing associations in the country and from the many high school and MUNY league baseball teams that played in The Meadow. We worked closely with Ruth and David Lampe at the Parkside Community Association, lobbying Mayor James D. Griffin and the Common Council, focusing particularly on the Zoo board. I desperately wanted to make an impact; to show what people who cared about their parks in other cities had accomplished; to show what we could do in Buffalo. I had followed developments like these in New York City and had become familiar with the Central Park Conservancy, formed in the early 1970s to do just what we were trying to do in Delaware Park. I'd been aware for some time of Fred Kent, one of the early advocates for traffic-calming in New York, a man who, working for Mayor John Lindsay, organized the first Earth Day celebration in 1970. In early 1975, Kent founded an organization which I have avidly followed since, the Project for Public Spaces. Fred was a passionate, persuasive, if quiet speaker. I'd heard him in New York and now, to help us fight the Zoo, I wanted him in Buffalo to help us convince the Zoo board to drop their parking lot plan. In March, 1979, at a crowded meeting held within the compact surroundings of the Parkside Lodge, Fred talked about parks, about public space and how people used them; about his experiences in Prospect and Central Parks and about how, in cities all over the world, people and planners were trying to tame the automobile and to reclaim public spaces for pedestrians.

Our group of true believers was joined two months later by one of Buffalo's greatest public officials, County Legislator-turned-Assemblywoman Joan Bozer. Working through her recently formed group The Buffalo Friends of Olmsted Parks, she convened a one-day conference held at the Historical Society. The purpose of the conference was to "discuss a national Olmsted historic park system" and the keynote speaker was New York's Senator Daniel P. Moynihan. Pointing to the Central Park Conservancy as a model for Buffalo, Moynihan was adamant in his insistence that an organization be created in Buffalo which, independent from politics, would preserve and protect the city's seven Olmsted parks. The impact of these two meetings, one specially focused on The Meadow, the other on the entire Olmsted system, began to shift public opinion in our favor. In the summer of 1979, Finley Greene, President of Zoological Society stated that, "due to opposition from neighbors and others," the Zoo foreswore any further efforts to create a parking lot in the park. Then, on October 12,

1979, we cheered when Greene officially announced that "The Zoo will delete from its plans any intention of constructing a parking lot in the Delaware Park Meadow." (See the minutes of the DPSC in the Archives of the BOPC. I am particularly gratified by the specific references in those minutes to the role that "Mark Goldman" played in these efforts.)

Our successful efforts in this campaign was a critical turning point in the recognition by the people of Buffalo of the truly historic value of Delaware Park in particular and the Buffalo parks in general. Fredrick Law Olmsted, whose name and work was then known only to a few scholars and park activists here, is now recognized throughout the city and his work regarded as among our city's greatest assets. The efforts that we put forth in the mid and late 1970s laid the groundwork for what came later when, in 1995, twenty years after the Friends of Olmsted was created, the Buffalo Olmsted Conservancy was formed. It was Joan Bozer, we all knew, who deserved much of the credit. But there were others, too, no less important than the runners who, with their feet on the ground and their eyes on the prize, had worked so hard to make this happen. "Fix this place" indeed!

• • •

The work that we were doing to protect and to preserve Delaware Park during the 1970s and 1980s was reflected in the work that other like-minded people, a growing group of preservationists, were doing to preserve and protect the historical landscape of downtown Buffalo. I had my personal introduction to Buffalo's nascent preservation scene when, following the attention to my bus tours and my increasing efforts to advance the cause of local history, a man named Olaf "Bill" Shelgren, asked me to join the Board of the Landmarks Society of the Niagara Frontier. Shelgren, a second generation Buffalo architect and a passionate preservationist, was one of the founders of the Landmark Society in 1961 when the oldest building in the city – the Coit House (c. 1820) was being threatened with demolition. (1961 was an important year in the history of the preservation movement in Buffalo, the same year that Olive Williams on Irving Place, Max Clarkson, Bill Magavern in Allentown formed the Allentown Association.)

While the Coit House was saved, other far more interesting and important buildings, architectural wonders like the Central Library with its cozy corners, window seats, inviting form and function perfect for a library and the Erie

County Savings Bank, notwithstanding the existence of the Landmark Society, were mercilessly demolished. Consisting of members of the city's old guard – there were no blue-collar types and no minorities among the membership – the group appeared, at least to me at least, to be more of a genteel social club than the kind of hard-fighting preservationists that Buffalo desperately needed. Meeting for drinks in either Shelgren's home on Crescent Avenue or in Austin Fox's wonderful Victorian on Lexington Avenue, I was not convinced that the group had the necessary gumption to take the fight to the developers and the politicians who during the '70s were doing their best to destroy much of the historic fabric of downtown Buffalo. Indeed, in the early '70s, right in front of their eyes, much of lower Main Street, lined with mid-19th century commercial buildings, many of them cast-iron, was being torn down, making way for a sky-high office building that the Marine Midland Bank was building. Simultaneously, Joseph Ellicott's extraordinary and unique 1804 radial street plan was under siege. While one whole side of Niagara Square was being cruelly amputated (to make room for the construction of perhaps the worst building ever built here – the City Court Building), Ellicott's transcendent radial street pattern was mindlessly compromised when in 1973 the convention center was built, plopped down in the middle of downtown like, to use a term that Tim Tielman coined to describe another convention center almost forty years later, "a death star." Where was the Landmark Society while this was going on? Where was anybody?

By this time I'd become friends with David Stieglitz, a young architect interested then in what he still calls today, creating "a city with a brain." He had a small office on the 12th floor of the Prudential Building, Louis Sullivan's fantastic building which is today ranked internationally as one of the world's great buildings. By 1973, the building had fallen on desperately difficult times. It was almost completely empty and only wild, crazy and creative people like Stieglitz, his colleague Jay Burney and an architectural historian named John Randall inhabited it. Randall was a starry-eyed Louis Sullivan freak who, it seemed, went around the country trying to save his hero's seemingly often threatened masterpieces. Before arriving in Buffalo to save the Prudential, he'd camped out in St. Louis where he'd organized a citizens' campaign that successfully saved Sullivan's Wainwright Building. By 1974 the Prudential was on the road to destruction. Neglected by its absentee landlord who had forfeited on its mortgage and defaulted on its taxes, the building's tenants were leaving in droves, and this remarkable building was left to the likes of Stieglitz,

Burney and Randall. It was here, in Stieglitz's office, part sleeping quarters, part office, part sculpture and painting studio, that I met John Randall.

By 1974, Randall was living in the Prudential Building, squatting really. While it was never clear how – was he a tenant, was he a squatter? – there he was, in an old abandoned office on the 12th floor – which he was carefully filling with the long neglected decorative elements of the building: salvaged door knobs and fixtures, window frames etc. He was a one-man restoration and salvage crew: chipping away at drywall and removing the drop ceilings that had for so long covered the building's fabulous decorative elements. Then, a fire struck the building and the mortgagors, a bank in Oklahoma, announced that it was time to tear it down. And in a moment I'll never forget, yours truly saying that "I'm not going to let them tear down that building, Moynihan pledged his support to its preservation."

Randall desperately needed help and it was with that in mind that in September 1977, I brought him and Stieglitz to a board meeting of The Landmark Society one of whose members was Erie County legislator Joan Bozer. At the time of the meeting with Randall, Bozer was up to her eyes in her effort to save the recently decommissioned US Post office at Ellicott and South Division. The site in 1971 of an infamous anti-Vietnam war demonstration (the anti-draft resisters, known as "The Buffalo Five," were subsequently tried in Federal District Judge John T. Curtin's courtroom), by 1977 the post office was empty and in the absence of any viable reuse plan, the US Postal service announced its intention to demolish it. Appalled by this prospect and sensing support within the community, Assemblywoman Bozer effectively mobilized the voters behind her plan to convert the building into a downtown campus for the Erie County Community College, now Erie Community College. Following her victory, it was her efforts and a steadily growing group of people willing to define themselves as "preservationists," that led to the transformation of the Post Office into the downtown campus of the Erie County Community College, one of the most successful and exciting adaptive reuse projects in the city's history.

Bozer had already established contact with Senator Moynihan. She convinced him that as part of his upcoming visit to Buffalo, on behalf of the Olmsted parks, he would speak as well on behalf of the Prudential. Preservationists were still a small group of people, more of a family and not yet a "movement," and so there was much overlap of people and projects, many of us members of both the Landmark and the Delaware Park Steering Committee. Collaboration and communication was easy, and we were thus able to get the most for our money. On that same day in June, 1979 when Moynihan spoke so persuasively about the need for an "Olmsted Conservancy," he visited as well the Post Office and the Prudential Building where, in the company of Joan Bozer, David Stieglitz, Jay Burney, John Randall, and, in a moment that I'll never forget, yours truly, he pledged his support for the building's preservation.

Moynihan's day long trip to Buffalo in 1979 had a lasting impact on the city's nascent preservation movement. His strong support for both the conversion of the Post Office as well as insistence that the Prudential Building be saved, turned the tide politically and financially for both of these projects. Finally, in what I felt was the most compelling statement of the trip, Senator Moynihan urged the creation of a broad, comprehensive and assertive approach to historic preservation that would preserve the whole of Buffalo's built environment.

Moynihan would get what he wished for when, three years later, in 1981, Sue McCartney and a handful of her supporters founded the Preservation Coalition. McCartney's Preservation Coalition members had their work cut out for them. So much of the fabric of the traditional city had been lost that many of us wondered if there was enough left to create the foundation of the kind of city that we so desperately wanted. The demolition of individual buildings and whole neighborhoods that had occurred during the '50s and '60s had been devastating and traumatic; their loss was magnified by what was built to replace them. But Sue, joined in the mid-1980s by her husband Tim Tielman, were bold and fearless fighters for the cause and I, like many of my co-conspirators, did what we could to support them in their most important work.

No one more than Joan Bozer has been Buffalo's undisputed champion of historic preservation. Starting with her herculean efforts to transform the Post Office, continuing with her pivotal role in the creation of the Buffalo Olmsted Conservancy and her passionate and ongoing efforts to bring renewable energy to Western New York, Joan's role has been transcendent. When I asked her years later why she had become so involved in these issues, she told me the story of her first visit to Buffalo, one she made to visit her fiancé John's family here in 1951. John had picked her up at the airport, she recalled and drove her home to visit his parents who lived on Meadowview Place, just off of Agassiz Circle. Their route, she distinctly recalled, was down and over the Humboldt Parkway. Driving slowly down these tree lined parkway, filled with kids on bikes, couples walking and even a cluster of people on horseback, she was thrilled. "It's an Olmsted parkway," her fiancé John told her. "You know. The same fella who built Central Park." That evening from the Bozer home overlooking Agassiz Circle, she called her parents. When they asked her how she liked Buffalo she replied, tears filling her eyes: "It's the most beautiful city I've ever seen."

• • •

By the late 1970s and early 1980s, there was finally, and perhaps belatedly, a growing awareness of and sensitivity to questions relating to "the built environment," not queries about architecture or urban planning per se but rather the softer, more qualitative issues about "place" and how people feel in and respond to their urban environment. In November 1983 a few people, calling themselves "The Spirit of Buffalo Study Group," organized a conference in Buffalo called "Imagining Buffalo: Reflections on our City". Its purpose, the organizers said, was to create a "gathering for story-telling about how we feel about our city." In its Fall 1984 issue, a fascinating but short-lived journal called *The Buffalo Arts Review* devoted an entire issue to the conference. In his key-note address, James Hillman, the renowned Jungian scholar from Dallas, Texas, set the tone: "We are speaking of the city as if it were a living being, a body with a soul, a dreamer. A place with a shadow." Moving way beyond the usual discussion of plans and drawings, Hillman said that "we inhabit a psychological city before we enter the actual city."

Urban renewal may have destroyed the streets and the buildings of the city, but it did not dampen the creative and artistic spirit of the city which, for those of us who experienced it, offered so much joy in the present and so much hope for the future. 1970s Buffalo was filled with some of the most exciting artistic and intellectual developments in the city' s history, a litany of firsts that remains inspiring today. Despite the decline, the bad news, the city's horrific reputation in the outside world, it was clear to those of us who lived here during the challenging decade of the 1970s, that something special was in the air and something wonderful was happening. Writing in a publication that celebrated Hallwalls (a unique and now nationally known Buffalo arts organization that celebrated its twentieth anniversary in 1995) here's how I described that atmosphere of Buffalo during the seventies:

> *"What is New York the capital of?"* The New York Times *recently asked dozens of doyens, critics, literati, paparazzi, politicians and anybody who'd answer. It's an easy question, with a hundred and one different answers, all of them accurate. But what about Buffalo? Was there anything that Buffalo is the capital of? Well, yes, I answered my own question. For twenty years I wrote, it has been the capital of Hallwalls; the capital too of the Just Buffalo Literary Center, the Creative Associates, Media Studies, the CEPA Gallery, the UB English Department, Saul Elkins' Delaware Park Shakespeare Festival, the Buffalo Philharmonic Orchestra, of Artpark and the Talking Leaves Book Store. These fantastical developments were born in Buffalo during the dark night of the mid-1970s, a time of melt-down and despair, a free-fall, a time that marked the visible beginning of the end, when the bottom was falling out from under us. You couldn't avoid it anymore as those ugly, nasty, devastating, long-term, insidious, subterranean developments which had been eating away at the city for years finally took over. But yet, it was here and then, amid the growing wreckage of the city, that this great renewal occurred. Like Athena? Like a Phoenix? Where did the energy and imagination come from? When were these seeds planted and by whom? We didn't know and we didn't really ask. We did know however that the sudden, most unlikely flowering of things so new, so fresh and so dynamic gave us reason to hope and even believe that Buffalo had indeed become the capital of something wonderful."*

• • •

And then there was the Blizzard of 1977. For me, as for so many Buffalonians, the Blizzard of 1977 was a transformative event, an experience that solidified in ways that I was not even consciously aware of at the time, my growing ties to and affection for the city of Buffalo. Everybody who was living in Buffalo in January 1977 remembers where they were and what they were doing on that morning when a vicious, awesome, swirling torrent of wind and snow struck the Buffalo metropolitan area. The weather had been overpowering for months. We had a foot of snow in October and temperatures in November broke a record set in 1880. Two feet of snow fell on Thanksgiving Day. Though there had been storms throughout December, Christmas Day was mild and pleasant, sunny with temperatures peaking in the mid-thirties. Then, suddenly, the weather changed. It happens this way often in Buffalo: the wind roars off of Lake Erie, the powerful gales forcing their way up Court Street, whipping around Niagara Square into the heart of downtown, roaring up Delaware Avenue. Traffic lights hang helplessly across the city's streets, dancing like kites while pedestrians cling desperately to street lamps. Then the sky starts to darken and the temperature starts to drop. Things got dramatic the day after Christmas 1976. It was 36 degrees at noon. By early evening it had dropped to 10. The snow and cold continued through New Year's and, with temperatures peaking at 14, it was impossible to plow the streets. Along with a much heralded "snow blitz," and endless pleas to motorists to get their cars off the streets, the city crawled to a halt. On January 18th, it was 6 degrees below zero. On the 19th and 20th temperatures rose to the low teens but fell to single digits overnight. It hovered there – lows near zero, highs near 20 – through the weekend of the 22nd and 23rd. Meanwhile, the snow was mounting: 34 inches had already accumulated and snow plowing proceeded at a snail's pace, hampered by scores of abandoned cars strewn all over the streets. The forecast on the morning of January 26th was a bit more encouraging but, by the end of the week, officials at the National Weather Service at the Buffalo airport had become concerned about reports coming out of Ohio. The weather had worsened throughout the Midwest and a storm was moving rapidly across the 250 mile plus expanse of Lake Erie. By 7am on Friday January 28th, a vicious storm had struck Cleveland, Toledo and Erie, PA. On Friday, January 28th, between 11 a.m. and 1 p.m., the storm finally arrived in Buffalo. According to *The Buffalo Evening News*, the area "lay prostrate, flattened by the most destructive and most disruptive storm in history." With winds up to 60 miles per hour, thick and heavy falling snow and temperatures close to zero, the storm was now classified as a "severe blizzard." Thirteen thousand people were stranded downtown, scores elsewhere in places both central and remote, as the entire metropolitan area came to a frightening and frigid standstill.

The storm continued over the weekend. The sky finally did clear for a few hours on Sunday afternoon, but by four o'clock whirling black clouds again covered the city. On Monday and Tuesday of the next week the snow and wind increased again and on Thursday still more snow fell. On Friday, one week after the blizzard first struck, squalls and heavy drifting continued with near-zero visibility, producing conditions similar to the week before. Finally, at dusk on Saturday, the sun slipped down behind Lake Erie and the sky cleared. The night was bitter cold, five to ten degrees below zero, but the wind had stopped and the clouds had disappeared and now the rich, deep blue winter sky was filled with stars. The next day, everyone knew, would be a beauty.

People awoke on Sunday morning and looked out at the sparkling, glittering, powdery, white streets. The snow was piled high everywhere and sidewalks and driveways were buried under thick, white blankets of snow. Dressed in layers of our warmest clothing, I, like the rest of the people of Buffalo ventured out to explore our snow-bound city. Pushing out against the masses of piled-up snow, I forced open the door and stood outside, silently looking and listening. I was struck by the shimmering beauty of the snow-filled street-scape and by the overwhelming quiet of it all. With all but emergency vehicles banned from the streets, the whole city was plunged into a deep, eerie and awesome silence.

For some it was a time of fantasy and imagination: the quiet, white city, the city in the clouds, the city without streets and sidewalks, without cars, without work, the city on vacation. There were snow mountains everywhere and, making it more fantastical still, dozens of people with food coloring and water colors, pouring out the contents of their jars on the mounds of snow.

Spring was unusually beautiful that year and the summer of 1977 was one of the most pleasant in memory. While people gradually stopped talking about the blizzard, they did not forget it. These were hard times for Buffalo, years when the economic and demographic foundations of the city were undermined. Like the blizzard, the battering of Buffalo's economy and the loss of so much of its population, were occurrences over which the people who lived here had no control. In my mind there was a poignant connection between these phenomena and as we, for I now considered myself one among them, the people of Buffalo struggled through them, the ties that bound us to our community were strengthened.

Michael Morgulis spent a good part of the Blizzard of '77 holed up in his basement studio in the Great Arrow Building. By the early 1970s, Michael, who was born and raised in the Cold Spring section of the city and got his start in the retail business working in his father's fruit and vegetable stand at the corner of Jefferson and Ferry, was living on Cottage Street in Allentown in what he refers to as the "Cottage Street Collective." It was here that he started a small printing company whose name – "New Buffalo Graphics" – offered a hint of what was to come. Michael was intimately involved in Buffalo's dynamic arts scene of the 1970s, a well-known and liked member of the city's avant-garde. He'd come of age hearing the empty and meaningless slogans and sayings that touted his city, things like "Boost Buffalo: It's Good For you" and "We're Buffalo Talking Proud." Tinkering at his desk deep into one long, cold night towards the end of January 1977, he came up with something else, something that he believed in his bones captured the essence and reality of his city for his generation. Michael, like Debra Ott, understood that Buffalo was "just Buffalo," simply Buffalo, a "city," he said, "of no illusions." "Buffalo, City of No Illusions." Michael, it seems, was suggesting a different kind of city, a city of the psyche, a city in which we take seriously and listen to our notions and fantasies, our dreams and our words. The lack of illusions did not prevent, indeed it may well have fostered, the incredible outpouring of energy that filled the streets of the city during the 1970s when groups of people, I proudly and happily among them, armed with a faith in ourselves and in our community, proceeded "to fix the city" that we loved.

On a personal basis nothing strengthened my deepening emotional ties to Buffalo more than the birth during this period of my first two children, Charlie in 1972 and Lydia in 1976. For it was their birth above all else that solidified my increasing ties and connections to Buffalo. Instantly, upon their birth, Buffalo became their city, their home town; not mine, but theirs. They were connected to Buffalo by and at birth. That resonated deeply with me, leading me to engage more, to care more deeply about the city around me and as a result to take my commitment to the city much more seriously.

While the most powerful event, the birth of Charlie and Lydia were not all that gave me hope in and for Buffalo during this time of my life. Indeed, everywhere I looked, midst the overwhelming devastation of the landscape of the city, the ominous and relentless facts and figures that spelled doom, I saw in the faces of the people who walked in the streets and lived neighborhoods throughout the city, small, but telling signs of vibrancy, creativity, intelligence and commitment, a faith that led so many of us to say: "Yes, we can fix this place."

Acknowledgements

Karen Brady: An Allentown neighbor, a columnist for *The Buffalo News*, Karen has been a friend for most of my fifty-plus years in Buffalo. I was thrilled when she agreed to write a forward to this book.

Harold Cohen: Buffalo became Harold's home in 1974 when Harold took up the post of Dean of the University at Buffalo's School of Architectural Planning

& Design. Within years he transformed "the School" into a vibrant center of super-smart thinking about architecture and urban planning. While most of this information comes from vivid memories of my contact with Dean Cohen, I have been helped here by the detailed information available in the Harold Cohen papers at the Archives of SUNY Buffalo.

P. Reyner Banham: Banham was a world-renowned architectural historian whom Dean Cohen recruited to teach at the "School" from 1976-1980. He, like Cohen, had a big personality and together they created an ongoing sense of drama and excitement on the Main Street campus. Through Banham I became friends with his wife Mary who was the editor of the book we wrote on Buffalo Architecture. Banham was convinced that the roots of European modernism lay in the industrial architecture of Buffalo, particularly the grain elevators. That was the main argument that he advanced in his 1989 book, *A Concrete Atlantis*.

Will Clarkson: A pillar of the city's early preservation movement. Born in England, Will moved to Buffalo in 1950 to assume control of Graphic Controls, an off-shoot of his family's business. With his older brother Max deeply engaged in the Allentown Historic District, Will, fascinated by modern architecture, became active at Harold Cohen's "School" in the mid-1970s. It was Will's energy and commitment that in 1981 that led to the publication of *Buffalo Architecture: a Guide*. When and if there's a history written of "Larkinville", Will deserves a loud-shout out as it was he who he turned over his buildings to Reyner Banham for what would become the blueprint for the revitalization that later occurred there.

Pat Bazelon: Pat Bazelon, an English-born photographer, moved to Buffalo in 1977. Soon, we were both retained by Will Clarkson to work on *Buffalo Architecture: a Guide*. We became life-long friends. Before Pat moved to Brooklyn in 1988 to become chief photographer at the Brooklyn Museum, she had a fantastic show of her grain elevator photos in a memorable 1987 exhibit at the Burchfield-Penney. Pat died far too early in 1998. In 2020 the Anderson Gallery hosted a retrospective of her photos of Buffalo's steel mills called "The Color of

Steel." I am proud that it was I who accompanied her on her many photographic field trips around the city.

Jason Aronoff, another of Buffalo's preservationist founding fathers, provided most helpful background information on the early preservation movement.

Arlene Price and **Eileen Ryan**: Both Bill (1999) and Joe (2016) died way too early. I have maintained contact with their wives, Arlene Price and Eileen Ryan, who have helped refresh my memory about these two fantastic Buffalonians.

Jose Pizarro and **Alberto Cappas** were two "Nuyoricans" who, like me, came to UB and then stayed, exerting an enormous influence on the West Side.

Casimir "Caz" Rodriguez: Currently head of the Hispanic Heritage Council, has been active in the affairs of his community since I first met him at UB in the 'seventies.

Francisco "Frankie" Perez: The "Mayor of Virginia Street" during the 1970s when he, as much as anyone, lay the groundwork for the future development of Buffalo's Hispanic West Side.

Jesse Kregal: Came to Buffalo to join the BPO as principal cellist, a position he held into the new century. Jesse conceived and was a founder of the Skylon International Marathon between Buffalo and Niagara Falls, Ont. It was the first marathon to start in one country and finish in another. Mr. Kregal was also the founding director of the Scajaquada Pathway, a multi use trail parallel to Scajaquada Creek that provides an inland connection from Erie County Riverwalk to Delaware Park Lake. In his honor, the pathway was renamed the Jesse Kregal Pathway.

The **Donnelly Brothers**, **Mike**, **Tom** and **Bill** were an intimate part of our community of runners. While all three brothers ran in the races, Tom organized the races, Bill as a free-lancer, wrote about running as a sport and as a life-style in regular articles in the North Buffalo Rocket and other publications.

Saul Elkin: Born and raised in New York City, Saul came to Buffalo in 1969 to teach theater at UB. Inspired by Joe Papp of the NY Shakespeare Festival, Saul did what no one thought possible: he launched a free Shakespeare Festival on what has become "Shakespeare Hill" overlooking Hoyt Lake. A jewel in Buffalo's summer cultural crown, Saul's Shakespeare festival which he began in 1976, is the oldest, free-Shakespeare festival in the country.

Bette Blum and **Joanie Kahn**: Founders of Re-Tree Buffalo and, since the early 1970s, among the earliest advocates for the Olmsted Park system. Joanie, along with Joan Bozer, has been relentless in her efforts to create a twenty-first century park system on the Outer Harbor.

Martha Neri, archivist at the Buffalo Olmsted Conservancy made available the wealth of material at the Buffalo Olmsted Conservancy so that I could read the minutes from the Delaware Park Steering Committee.

Fred Kent: For more on Fred Kent see "acknowledgments" for Chapter 7.

Joan Bozer: Joan is the doyenne of Buffalo's preservationist movement. Beginning in the 1970s when, as an Erie County legislator she championed the reuse of the old Buffalo Post Office, continuing into the 'eighties as a New York State Assemblyman she led the efforts that resulted in the formation of the Olmsted Conservancy, Joan has been the most influential and effective advocate for preservation and park planning in our area. It was her efforts that have led as well to the opening, in the Spring of 2021 of the solar powered carousel at Canalside

"Bill" Shelgren, a well-known architect (he died in 2010) and Austin Fox, the legendary Nichols English teacher and an early advocate for the importance of local architecture, (he died in 1996) were among the Founding Fathers of our preservation movement and very encouraging of my efforts to join them.

David Stieglitz: There have been no more interesting nor innovative architects in Buffalo over the past half-century than David. Whether it be environmental concerns (his work at Times Beach) or educational issues (he and his wife Bunny were the architects who created the concept of and then built the "Zoo School"), David has had his hand in so much that has been innovative in the life of our community.

Jay Burney: A preservationist when I first met him in the mid-1970s, Jay has remained one of Buffalo's most committed environmentalists. He is among the founders of the Times Beach Nature Preserve and of Buffalo's Outer Harbor Coalition.

John Randall: John was the most passionate preservationist you'd ever meet. Born in Chicago he grew up in a landscape dominated by the work of Sullivan and Wright. Upon hearing that Sullivan's Wainwright Building in St. Louis was threatened with demolition, he moved there and headed a movement that was responsible for saving it. He did the same when he came to Buffalo in 1973, moving into and then doing all that he could do to save Sullivan's Guaranty Building. To save the building, Mr. Randall offered to become the building manager for free. He set up a museum of artifacts with original Sullivan ornaments and Frank Lloyd Wright furniture so people would come in to see the building, and he and Joan Bozer eventually persuaded US Sen. Daniel Patrick Moynihan (D-NY) to take a tour. With Moynihan's help, the building was restored. Without John that never would have happened.

For **Hallwalls** see Ronald Ehmke and Elizabeth Licata, ed., *Consider the Alternative: 20 years of contemporary art at Hallwalls* (Buffalo, 1996)

Michael Morgulis: Michael and I have been friends for over forty years, from the time he created the marvelous "Buffalo: City of No Illusions" logo in 1977. In 1990 he designed the iconic logo for the Calumet Arts Café, his "Six characters at the Calumet" as well as the cover for my second book on Buffalo, *City on the Lake*. In 2020 he obliged me once again by designing the fabulous cover of this book.

Debora Ott: Born and raised in NYC Debora, a poetry student at UB, organized her first poetry reading at the Allentown Community Center in 1974. That year she founded Just Buffalo Literary Center which is, almost half a century later, one of the leading centers of poetry and the literary arts in the nation.

Vicky Sapienza: Vicky grew up on the Italian West Side. She could cook and run a business better than most and her shop/café, *Hello World* on Elmwood and Bryant was the center of all that was sophisticated in Buffalo during the 1970s through the early '90s.

Susan McCartney: Susan grew up off of Hertel Avenue where she first came to appreciate the value of dense, walking neighborhoods. In 1981 she founded the Preservation Coalition and along with Tim Tielman has been the city's most powerful and prescient preservationist in town. We have remained colleagues and friends for all these years.

Trudy Stern: Poet, Bohemian entrepreneur, a founder of the Greenfield Street Café and the original Lexington Avenue Coop, Trude, along with her husband Michael, have been for years at the center of all things artistic and offbeat.

Nancy Tobin: As a long-time writer and arts critic for *The Courier Express* and *The Buffalo News*, Nancy has a unique overview understanding of cultural life of our community that spans more than fifty years.

CHAPTER 4

Into the 'Eighties

How a teacher and his students discovered their city ... together

At about this time, I started teaching at Empire State College, a marvelous college within the SUNY system. There was much about "Empire" that was special and unique. For one, most all of the students were older, "non-traditional" students. They were men and women who matriculated with a wide range of life experiences the college recognized as "life learnings." For another, learning at Empire was collaborative and rooted in close personal connections with the students. It was not based on a professor's syllabus reflecting his/her interests alone. Instead, a student and "mentor" (not professors!) developed a "learning contract" designed by both in which we worked together on topics reflecting the student's interests. My goal as a mentor was to create a model for the study of Buffalo history based on the kind of work that I'd done in Black Rock. The model was to collect the bits and pieces of peoples' stories and from them to create a larger narrative about the city's history. By encouraging students to look at the fragments of their families' histories, the small pieces that comprise the whole mosaic of their lives in Buffalo, I wanted to lead them down a path of greater understanding of themselves and of the city that they lived in.

By working individually with each of my students, most all of whom brought a wealth of prior knowledge and experience, I was able to develop relationships that allowed me to learn as much from them as they did from me. One of my first students was George Arthur. George was the councilman from the Ellicott District, on Buffalo's East Side. As a life-long resident and as a serious student of its history, there was little that he did not know about his district. We held our meetings anywhere – sometimes in our offices at Franklin and North, sometimes "in the field." Soon after we started working together, George suggested that we meet at Gigi's, then Buffalo's premier soul-food restaurant. We'd get something to eat and then he'd take me for a drive around the Ellicott District. By weaving together in a free-flowing narrative the life and times of his family and the neighborhood that he lived in, George's "story" and the "story" his neighborhood became, like some mesmerizing film, indelibly planted in my brain.

There was hardly a place that we did not go: the Michigan Street Baptist Church, the Colored Musicians Club, the railroad yards where so many African-American men worked, including George's father and grandfather, both waiters for the Pullman Company. As we drove by Vine Alley, the heart of Buffalo's early 20th century Black Belt, the original location of the Vine Street AME Church and the all-Black Vine Street Public School, George told me about Henry Moxley, the African-American who in the mid-1860s challenged segregation in the Buffalo public schools. George also told me about music and about the storefront jazz clubs on East Ferry Street and Jefferson Avenue: the Revillot and the Pine Grill. George talked about working in his mother's BBQ stand on William Street. He reminisced about the people that he met delivering newspapers all over the Ellicott District: Dan and Ann Montgomery, the owners of the Little Harlem; Sherman Walker, the funeral director and political power broker; and the Miles Brothers, Marshall, Mitchell and Percy, who ran the city's numbers' racket from their table at the Little Harlem. He told me about his great uncle, George C. Sarsnett, who became Buffalo's first African-American police officer in 1918. And he talked about the house that he grew up in, a double at 65 Pratt Street with the Arthurs downstairs and Mr. and Mrs. Samuel Arluck, the parents of Harold Arlen, the popular music composer, upstairs. George talked fondly about his street and his neighborhood, and how Black and Jews shared the same turf on friendly, even intimate terms.

One day many years later, I came across a 1963-64 edition of *The Travelers' Green Book*, recently made famous by the Oscar winning movie. Promising "assured protection for the Negro Traveler," the *Green Book* promised its African-American readership "vacations without aggravation." To read the Buffalo listings is to be reminded of just how deep was the chasm of racial separation of the city in the mid-1960s. All of the listings were in and around William and Michigan streets, the heart of what is now called The African-American Heritage Corridor. There were hotels like Costello's, the Claridge, Dan Montgomery's, the YMCA and the Williams. Restaurants included Gerald's, the Hickory Tavern, the Horseshoe and Mother Dear's Bar-b-que. There were "safe" taverns and music clubs including the Holiday, the Bon Ton and the Pine Grill. I wish I'd found the *Green Book* when I arrived in Buffalo in the summer of 1967. Maybe I would not have gone to Europe that summer after all.

Though painfully aware of the devastating impact that the prevailing ethos of white supremacy had on his community, George was very proud that African-Americans in Buffalo, in response to a rigidly enforced color line, had developed a strong and largely self-contained community of their own. The economic, social and cultural needs of the people who lived there were met largely by individuals and institutions within the community itself. George valued the strength that this kind of self-contained community offered its residents and, like so many of his generation all over the city, mourned its loss. George's views, when added to what I had learned in my study of Black Rock, increased in my mind the "power of place," of the importance of localism and compelling need that we all seem to have to be rooted in and connected to "place."

George Arthur completed his degree at Empire State College, majoring in political science. Already a member of Buffalo's Common Council, George eventually became the council president. Upon his retirement from politics, George became the passionate leader of a community-based effort that led in 1995 to the creation of Buffalo's African-American Heritage Corridor. He remained, until his death in December 2020, Buffalo's indispensable expert, the ultimate "go-to-guy" on all questions related to the history of Buffalo's African-American community.

Another student from those early days at Empire State was Joe Tanzella. Tanzella, like George Arthur, grew up in the Ellicott District, in and around the Swan and Seneca Street neighborhood in the all Italian St. Lucy's Parish. (This was the home turf of the "Na-bo-li-tans," Joe was quick to remind me. Not the Sicilians living on the West Side!). By the time I met him, the Insalacas, like most of the original parishioners at St. Lucy's had long ago moved to South Buffalo. He was, he said, deeply attached to his old neighborhood, the chairman of the annual St. Lucy's banquet, the guardian of his family's treasure trove of old photos and, he boasted, the "GodFather" of what he called the "St. Lucy's Society," a group of "goombahdies" who met once a week for lunch at DiTondo's. "C'mon," he said, "we'll go together."

DiTondo's on Seneca Street, which was founded in 1904 by Sebastiano DiTondo, and was operated by the same family until it closed in 2018. Filled with dozens of former neighborhood residents, this fabulous, "right-out-of-The Godfather" restaurant, was the perfect place for us to meet.

Joe Tanzella was in the process of preparing a celebratory history of his neighborhood called, "St. Lucy's Parish: Our Old Italian Neighborhood." The booklet was as juicy as the gigantic, mouth-watering plate of chicken "parm" that we shared at DiTondo's. Drawn from his childhood in the forties and fifties, Joe's list included a wide range of places and businesses, including bakers, butchers, tailors, drug stores, funeral homes and restaurants. They had names like Mangano, Ervolino, Delmonte, Antonioni, Guarnieri Hardware, Ruggieri, Delbello and Vastola. He had begun to create a list as well of what he called "ricordi" of neighborhood life: St. Lucy's playground on Chicago Street; the sound of church bells ringing through the neighborhood; the smells of bread, onions, and boxes of wine grapes; drying "conserva" (tomato paste) in the sun; dice games and penny pitching before Sunday mass on the corner of Eagle and Hickory; and all night wakes with men in the kitchen smoking and drinking.

My goal as mentor was to create a credible course of study based on Joe's deep interest in his neighborhood's history. With that in mind we decided that he would create a neighborhood "album." Joe started with his memories, his large collection of photographs, and other memorabilia. Then, over the course of several weeks of research, he added information from the same kinds of primary sources – newspapers, census reports, etc. – that I had used in my work in Black Rock. The result was the creation of a piece of work that not only added to our body of knowledge of Buffalo history, but did so in a way that had deep personal meaning for Joe. His study of his roots in Buffalo history had served for him the same purpose that it had for me: history was becoming the glue that bound us to each other and to our home town.

Another neighborhood that I discovered as a result of my teaching at Empire State was Riverside. I'd first been introduced to Riverside while working on my dissertation on Black Rock. It was, I knew, a kind of suburban extension of that older neighborhood. By the early 1920s, Riverside had begun to fill up with the children of the German and Polish residents of Black Rock who were attracted to the many good paying factory jobs and the best views of the Niagara River of any neighborhood in Buffalo. By the 1950s however, the completion of the New York State Thruway ended forever the ease of access to the Niagara that had made life in Riverside so pleasant and attractive. The river, with its fishing and boating clubs, its tiny fishing huts, hot dog stands and several postage-stamp size beaches, was the neighborhood's most significant and, after Riverside Park, most popular public space.

It was not until I met Mary Waltz in 1981, another one of my students at Empire, that I learned this story and about how hurt and angry the people of Riverside were when they lost direct access to the Niagara River. Mary had lived her life on Crowley Avenue and as a child, like all of the children from Riverside, had spent the bulk of her summers hanging out on the shore of the Niagara River. She and her neighbors fought hard against the Thruway's separation of the shore line. When they lost and the Thruway was completed in 1958, they held a mock funeral for their suddenly lost neighborhood waterfront.

Mary was encouraged by my approach to local history. She, like Arthur, Tanzella and the others, wanted to pursue her interest in and knowledge of this story as part of her studies at Empire. So off we went, with Mary riding shot-gun, on a personalized tour of the neighborhood, led by another eager and avid student. She wanted me to meet a friend of hers, a woman named Irene Gardner. Irene, like Mary, lived in a house with a large front porch with what had once, like the Canadian shore just across the Niagara River, been an undivided, uninterrupted view of the Niagara River. Not now, she said, not since 1958. It wasn't until the early 1970s, Ms. Gardner told us, that she and a handful of neighbors, (all women, Mary Waltz who was one of Gardner's co-conspirators, chimed in adamantly) began to actually do something about the situation. What if, they wondered, a bridge could be built, a pedestrian bridge over the Thruway that connected Riverside Park on one side with the Niagara River on the other? The women gathered over one thousand signatures and relentlessly lobbied their local officials. Finally, Ms. Gardner and her group of neighborhood activists got for their neighborhood what they had been denied by the Thruway. The Irene K. Gardner Pedestrian Bridge was dedicated in March 1980, once again connecting Riverside Park to the Niagara River.

Mary had another idea in mind for our work together at Empire State. She wanted to study the history of Riverside High School and the extent to which the school reflected the history of the neighborhood. Using a combination of materials that included high school yearbooks, a local newspaper called *The Riverside Review*, interviews with former graduates as well as other documentary evidence culled from local resources, Mary was able to write a paper, not unlike

Joe Tanzella's St. Lucy's "album" that reflected her deep interest in and connection to the history of the neighborhood in which she grew up. She, too, was strengthening the ties that bound her to her neighborhood and her city.

And then there was Thomas John, a Seneca Indian and a descendent of the great early 19th century Seneca leader, Cornplanter. John was born and raised on the Cornplanter Tract in Allegheny County, about an hour south of Buffalo. He moved to Buffalo in 1966, as the federal government evicted the last of the Senecas from the Cornplanter Tract in order to build the Kinzua Dam on the Allegheny River.(While the Dam did protect Pittsburgh from flooding it had a devastating impact on the Senecas on the Cornplanter Tract.) Uprooted, Thomas moved to Buffalo where he studied to become a licensed electrician. He later became an officer in his union, IBEW local #41. By the early 1970s, he'd married and together they raised their children on a street called Fenton just north of the Buffalo Creek in South Buffalo. Thomas once told me proudly that his home was located in the heart of what once was the Buffalo Creek Reservation.

Thomas was a voracious reader with a particular interest in Buffalo history and the place of the Senecas in the early history of the city. He was particularly interested in his roots because he was raised and remained a follower of the teachings of Cornplanter's brother-in-law, the great 19th century Seneca religious leader, Handsome Lake. Blending some of the messianic aspects of Christianity with traditional Seneca practice, Handsome Lake preached a return to the traditional Haudenasee religion of the long-house. Thomas was a disciple, a regular visitor throughout his years in Buffalo to the Tonawanda Reservation where the Code of Handsome Lake is still practiced today.

Thomas was familiar as well with the basic outlines of his peoples' history. He had read and indeed brought to our first meeting, a long out-of-print history of early Buffalo written by Robert Bingham called *The Cradle of the Queen City*. Thomas was fascinated by a reference in Bingham's book to his street – Fenton Street – where, Bingham wrote, on a terrace overlooking the Buffalo Creek, "returning hunters brought their game, women pounded corn for their daily food and children played." (Bingham, p. 11.) Thomas was haunted by the serendipity of this, that he, a displaced resident of the Cornplanter Tract, was now living in the heart of what in the early years of the 19th century had been a settlement belonging to his Seneca ancestors.

While Thomas had already done a great deal of reading and was very familiar with the general outline of the history of his people in Western New York, he wanted to do more. Indeed, he told me, his long-held hope was to write a history of the Buffalo Creek Reservation from its initial settlement in the 1770s to its demise less than eighty years later. Though I knew nothing about this topic, I was very eager to learn and so, over the course of the next year and a half, Thomas John, with me as his helpful assistant – his "mentor" – plunged into this fascinating history.

Despite the demands of his full-time work and leadership in the IBEW, Thomas spent many of his available hours in the archives of the Buffalo and Erie County Library. He studied the history of the Senecas and their Buffalo Creek Reservation including the impact of Sullivan's Raid during the American Revolution, the larcenous treaties, the arrival on Seneca lands of the "black coats," (Red Jacket's term for Christian missionaries) the tortured yet fascinating history of Red Jacket, and the War of 1812. Thomas, however, did not get to finish his magnum opus as in 1983, he died suddenly of a heart attack. About a year later, his wife called me to say that she had all of her husband's notes and wondered if I would like them. Perhaps, she said, I could finish the work that her husband had started. In recognition of the importance of the material that he uncovered and the work that he did, I would like to highlight some of the initial notes and drafts of what Thomas John had hoped to be his "History of the Buffalo Creek Reservation, 1794-1850."

One of the books that Thomas had been reading was Anthony F.C. Wallace's 1969 work, *The Death and Rebirth of the Senecas.* He was struck by Wallace's term, "slums in the wilderness" to describe the reservations that the Senecas were being put on in the 1790s: "… places in the wilderness where non traditional Indian culture could long survive and where only the least useful aspects of white culture could penetrate." In his notes, Thomas highlighted Wallace's words that resonated most with him: "The Senecas had lost much to the ravages of war, hunger, pestilence and disease. But more damaging to the spirit was the loss of confidence in their own way of life, a lessening of respect for themselves." Thomas cited a quote Wallace attributed to a "sympathetic" missionary at Buffalo Creek: "Suicides are frequent among the Senecas. I apprehend this despondency is the principal cause of their intemperance. Their circumstances are peculiarly calculated to depress spirits, especially those contiguous to white settlements."

Following his own heartbreaking experiences on the Cornplanter Tract, Thomas was drawn to Wallace's critique of white settlement patterns. Referring to "the exploitation of the area," John pointed out that actual settlement was accomplished not by random, unintended actions of pioneer settlers, but rather by the collaboration of the government and land companies. Wallace reported the first settlers of the land were not pioneers but rather real estate speculators. As a result, by the time that "the common pioneer" arrived in the 18 teens and 'twenties the land had already been "explored, bought from the Indians, garrisoned, pacified, surveyed, mapped and picked over by the land companies, public officials and private speculators seeking the most probable localities for quick profit." Thomas was struck by the notion that this process created a common underclass in which many of the white settlers were "as demoralized as the natives on their reservations," because they, too, were trapped in "slums in the wilderness."

It was the treaties though, the countless broken treaties – Fort Stanwix, Big Tree, Canandaigua, Buffalo Creek – that so littered the landscape of Buffalo and Western New York, that most interested Thomas. Though never angry, Thomas was sad and frustrated. He wondered when and if his people would ever be adequately compensated. Thomas did not live to see the "treaties" between New York State and the tribal remnants of his people that led at the turn of the last century to the creation of legalized casino gambling on what was traditional Seneca land. I doubt that he would have considered the casinos which now plague our community to be the compensation he hoped his people would receive.

• • •

Empire State maintained close connections in the community. We were aware of the changes that were occurring in the local economy, particularly the need among a growing number of displaced industrial workers to find new ways to create a life for themselves in our increasingly deindustrialized world. With this in mind, the college administration reached out to Westinghouse Electric. In 1947, Curtiss-Wright, the Buffalo based airplane manufacturing company, sold its plant near the airport to Westinghouse Electric, a manufacturer of electric engines. The company with 7200 employees in 1970, continued to grow, but rather than expand in Buffalo, it began to move its production out of town. Production at the Buffalo plant dropped precipitously. In 1987, with fewer than eight hundred employees still in Buffalo, Westinghouse announced that it was going to shut down. Westinghouse pledged to initiate "the most humane plant close-down to ever take place" and began to work with Empire State College to help them. Working with the company, a small team of the college's mentors created a program whereby laid-off Westinghouse workers would, with their tuition paid for by the company, enter into college degree programs at Empire State. "De-industrialization" was no longer merely an academic term disconnected from the reality of peoples' lives but rather for me and the others at Empire State, a direct, in-your-face look at a global phenomenon that was happening in our own back-yards. Our students from Westinghouse wanted desperately to get an education, to be able, as one of my students said to me, to "finally get to use my brain."

• • •

Meanwhile I was using my position at Empire State College to seek a larger audience for issues around and about Buffalo history. It was with the support of the college that in October 1981 I organized a day-long conference called "Buffalo: A City and its Neighborhoods." Here's how I described it: "Buffalo is a city of diverse neighborhoods, each of which possessed unique characteristics and traditions .... As Buffalo celebrates its one hundred and fiftieth birthday, there is some talk about the revival of these neighborhoods. Given that, it is appropriate that we dedicate a day to the serious study of the place and the function of the neighborhood in the past, present and future of Buffalo."

The large and magnificent sanctuary at St. Paul's Cathedral where the conference was held was filled to capacity as I walked to the raised lectern in front of the eager crowd to deliver the opening lecture which I called: "A Historical Approach to an Understanding of Buffalo's Neighborhoods." No power points, no YouTubes, not even a slide-show. I just addressed some straight-forward questions: What have been the historical forces responsible for the growth and development of the city's neighborhoods? How have economic, political, and ethnic patterns shaped our neighborhoods? How can an understanding of the historical development of our neighborhoods help us to understand and develop public policy for the neighborhoods of today?

Following my opening lecture, the conference divided into a series of concurrent panels led by people who I had asked to make presentations: Angelica Keil, an expert on Buffalo's Polonia, spoke on "Women and the family in Eastern

European Immigrant neighborhoods"; Father David Gallivan, soon to become a monsignor and one of the great spiritual leaders in the city, presented on "The Parish Church: Cultural and Political focal points"; David Stieglitz, my favorite architectural visionary, spoke on "The City's Neighborhoods in the present and the future"; Alberto Cappas, increasingly well-known Puerto Rican poet, spoke on "the Lower West Side: the problems and promises of a heterogenous community"; James Pitts, councilman for the Ellicott District spoke on "Race Relations on the City's East Side", while Lawrence Quinn, Commissioner of Community Development spoke on "Programs and policies for Neighborhood Revitalization."

The conference concluded that evening with a wonderful, celebratory cocktail party. I was exhausted and elated that the work that I had been doing for almost ten years was beginning to catch on. I wanted to bring the issues that I cared about to a larger audience, to share my enthusiasm for the history of my adopted city with as many people as possible. The neighborhood conference that I'd organized for Empire State College inspired me to do so and now I pitched two stories, one to *The Buffalo Evening News*, the other to T*he Courier Express*: one on the history of Black Rock, another, called "East Side Story," about African-American history in Buffalo. These two articles, both on the front page of each of the papers' Sunday magazines were, I believe, the first effort to bring to the attention of a large audience themes and topics dealing with the history of Buffalo. The articles examined the impact of history on the contemporary city. How and why did Black Rock become such a strong, self-reliant neighborhood? Could the patterns of neighborhood development that had created Black Rock be replicated in other parts of the city? What were the historical patterns that led to the creation on the East Side of a strong, if segregated, African-American neighborhood? What had been the impact of urban renewal on the area? And what, if anything, could be done about white flight?

In 1984, I became involved with *The Buffalo Arts Review* (BAR), a quarterly publication dedicated to arts and cultural affairs. Published by The Irving Collective (one of the founders, George Howell, lived at 22 Irving in Allentown), this loosely-knit band of writers included some of the most interesting writers in the city. In the winter of 1984, in response to Mayor James Griffin's disgusting attack on the owners of City Lights, Buffalo's leading gay bar, who were trying to move into Theater Place, I offered to write a piece for the *Review* on the importance of gays in the artistic life of the city. Mayor Griffin's position, I argued revealed "not only narrow-minded homophobia but an ignorance of the process by which so many sections of so many American cities have been revitalized ... "From Portland, Oregon to Portland, Maine," I wrote, "gays have been our true urban pioneers who at their own risk, dared to go where the straights feared to tread." I pointed out that while Buffalo's straight population was "dwindling rapidly," the city's gay population was growing. This was a "significant demographic phenomenon and as long as it persists, Buffalo can expect to enjoy continued urban revitalization ..."

Taking advantage of a "write-anything-you want" editorial policy, I followed that piece with a blistering, somewhat hysterical (or at least it so seems today) critique of "Buffalo Buildings" in the Spring, 1984 edition of the *Buffalo Arts Review*. Using terms like "architectural narcissism" and phrases like "form follows fantasy," I cited the "excessive concern with the vagaries of changing architectural styles" and the need for architecture "with a social conscience." My writing was filled with heart-felt yet sophomoric adjectives: The M&T Buildings was "bland and faceless". I referred to the "grotesque giganticism" of what was then called the Marine Midland Tower, nothing less, I screamed, than a "massive, overwhelming and oppressive structure, the Bauhaus gone berserk." The convention center was, I said, "irredeemably inappropriate for the dense urban street-scape, destroying forever the truly human scale that characterized the area." Boy was I pissed. I hated the massing of the ugly new buildings along the lower Terrace – the WKBW building and the Hilton hotel which with its "enormous moat-like parking lot, I torched as an architectural insult to the people of Buffalo." What we needed in Buffalo, I wrote in conclusion, was "an architecture of ideas, architecture with a social conscience, architecture whose form, by building on the past, by reflecting its surroundings, by supporting and strengthening the human environment, continually enriches the built environment. We have a right to demand nothing less." Clearly, my stake in the fate of Buffalo had become increasingly personal.

Acknowledgments

All my students at ESC: A rare and wonderful bunch, adults, men and women who, as returning students with vast life-experiences, brought their own individual uniqueness to their studies at the college. We learned so much, together.

Bob MacCameron: My work at Empire State College was graced by my friendship with Bob MacCameron. I met Bob when we were both graduate students in the history department at UB. Over the years we developed an extraordinary relationship. It was Bob who introduced me to Empire State and as office mates there from 1977-1990 our close relationship became even closer. I was bereft when he died of a terrible illness in 2005 and I miss him still.

DiTondo's Restaurant: Located on Swan Street since 1904, DiTondo's was one of my go-to places until it closed in 2019. Owned by the same family since it opened, DiTondo's offered incredible old-school food in an old-school atmosphere. DiTondo's was quintessentially Buffalo. We've all got our fingers crossed that it will soon re-open.

Mark Maio: Mark was a specialist in biomedical photography when he came to work with us at Empire State. The work that we did together, photographing the last of the grain scoopers on the Buffalo waterfront has become the foundation of an internationally recognized career as an art photographer. In 2007 a (12) print portfolio of his *Against the Grain* that he did with me at Empire State was purchased by the George Eastman House International Museum of Photography and Film for their permanent collection.

CHAPTER 5

Judge John T. Curtin

Struggling with the challenges of a changing city, he helped restore my faith in Buffalo

My work in Buffalo history had taken on an increasingly personal meaning: the study of the city's past was tying me ever tighter to the city's present. Working in Black Rock, I had devised a process of first-hand learning about by-gone Buffalo that had allowed me to become more intimately involved with the process of history. In libraries and basements, I had explored rarely-seen documents; in the streets and homes of the neighborhood, I had had countless conversations with the people who lived there. Those personal connections that I was making to Buffalo's past – its "story" – were strengthened still further by my bus tours. I was becoming intimately familiar with the intimate details of the fabric of the city: its street corners; sunsets and sunrises; homes; churches; and factories. I liked the ironic conceit of the tours, the notion that it was me, the "New York kid," who'd come to Buffalo to introduce the people of this city to their history. People loved the tours – I could have, as John Montana, the bus company owner who would have "bought" my tours years before knew, kept them going forever – and I loved leading them. I was becoming deeply attached to my adopted city.

Meanwhile, my work at the UB's College of Urban Studies, the School of Architecture and Environmental Design, and at Empire State College had allowed me to meet some of the most interesting people of my many years in Buffalo. My students and colleagues with a shared excitement about Buffalo's history and the issues and affairs of the contemporary city were a steady source of inspiration.

While happy in my work, the creative arts scene, and my personal life (in addition to Charlie and Lydia, my second son Jonathan was also born in Buffalo during this time), the 1970s and '80s were not happy times for Buffalo. The steel and auto plants in the region were unravelling, department stores, restaurants, shops and service organizations were going out of business on a near-daily basis. Even venerable institutions like the *Courier-Express*, the Buffalo Philharmonic, the Albright-Knox Art Gallery, the Buffalo Science Museum and the Buffalo Historical Society teetered on the brink of bankruptcy.

Even the *New York Times* got down on Buffalo. On February 9, 1975, on the cover of the most widely read Sunday magazine in the world, was a photo montage of the faces of Buffalo's unemployed men and women. The story was called "Down and Out in America." On the front page was a quotation from one of the people interviewed for the piece: "I didn't realize it was this bad." Accompanied by a gallery of sad-faced and somber Buffalonians, the article, out of the pages of Walker Evans and James Agee, painted a picture of devastation and hopelessness.

And then there was the "Blizzard of '77," which, notwithstanding its romantic whiteness, delivered a gut-wrenching blow to the image and the self-esteem of the city. The "we can fix-it" mentality that had characterized so much of the 1970s seemingly was being replaced with a deepening sense of despair. Maybe the nay-sayers had been right: maybe it was too late to fix Buffalo. I, too, was affected by the changing mood. As I began in the early 1980s to write a narrative of the city's history, the energetic and optimistic state of mind that I had maintained through the '70s had disappeared. The name of the book – "High Hopes" – had a subtitle that said it all: "The Rise and Decline of Buffalo, New York."

The first half of the book was a generalized narrative of the well-trod themes in the city's history, topics like the Erie Canal and the emergence of an economy rooted in commerce, the coming of immigrants, and the late 19th century transition to an economy rooted in industry. In retrospect, the book seems compromised by a moralizing and judgmental tone. I took personally what I saw happening in Buffalo. In a manner unbecoming to a detached historian, I blamed it all on what I considered to be short-sighted leadership. Shouldn't "they" have anticipated and even have prevented the litany of catastrophic events that had battered the city: the decline of industry; the St. Lawrence Seaway; the loss of local ownership; the restriction of immigrants; and the decline of the population in the city? And what about our marvelous streetscape, destroyed by urban renewal and our unique landscape trashed by highway construction? Should "they" not have known better? Why, damn it, I asked in anger and dismay, didn't "they"?

Looking back on it so many years later, I wish that I had assumed a more measured, even-tempered tone. Wanting to believe in the city's future, I sought out local historical figures who passionately engaged with the challenges of their time. I found them a-plenty. There was Red Jacket, the noble Seneca leader who, in resisting the seductive allure of Buffalo's white settlers and in standing up for the traditional values of his people, offered a heroic figure for members of minority groups in the contemporary city, who were wrestling with identity issues of their own. I admired Mordecai Noah, another Jew from New York like me. But Noah's ambition was not just to find a home in Buffalo, but to found a Jewish state called "Ararat" on Grand Island.

I was drawn to the charisma of John Timon, who became the first bishop of the Roman Catholic Diocese of Buffalo in 1848. Bishop Timon was a proud Irishman – he boasted that though born in the States, he was conceived in Ireland. When confronted by the vicious anti-Catholicism of the WASP gentry, he fostered a whole new world of churches, schools, hospitals, and orphanages, which the city's Catholic immigrants could call their own. And, in one of my all-time favorite demonstrations of Buffalo bravado, Timon, when faced with a decision as to where best to locate St. Joseph's, his diocesan cathedral, he chose not the safety and the isolation of the Irish neighborhood in the First Ward, but rather the heart of Protestant Buffalo right across the street from St. Paul's Episcopal Church. He ensured that two imposing church steeples, one Protestant, one Catholic, would forever highlight the skyline of Buffalo.

There were more: African-Americans like William Wells Brown and Mary Talbert, who, like Timon, were heroic in the face of bitter prejudice. Brown was a runaway slave from Missouri who settled in Buffalo in the late 1840s. Brown soon became a leader in the city's abolition movement and an active agent in Buffalo's underground railroad. In the year 1842 alone, just during months when the Niagara River was free from ice, Brown was said to have led over seventy fugitive slaves over the "River Jordan" to freedom in Canada.

Mary Talbert, who lived fifty years later, was a Buffalo public school teacher, an advocate at the turn of the century for justice for the city's growing African-American population. Appalled by the representation of African-American life embodied in two exhibitions on the Midway at the 1901 Pan American Exposition in Buffalo (one was called "Darkest Africa," the other the "Old Plantation"), Talbert demanded that they be dismantled. Replace them, she argued, with a new and different exhibition, one that documented the achievements of African-Americans in industry, science, culture, and education since the Emancipation Proclamation. Though her petition was denied, Talbert was energized by the experience and began to organize a greater event. Four years later, W.E.B. DuBois, John Hope, Monroe Trotter and other African-American leaders responded to Mary Talbert's invitation to meet at her home on Michigan Avenue. There, together, they lay the groundwork for the formation of the Niagara Movement, which by 1909 became the National Association for the Advancement of Colored People.

• • •

The annals of the city's history were filled, I discovered, with heroic figures. These were men and women who saw things as they could be, who, with confidence in themselves and faith in their fellow citizens, had been able to overcome the challenges of their era and make a real difference in their communities. Gradually, I felt myself emerging from the funk that I'd found myself in, rediscovering my own energy and my sense that we could, in fact, "fix this place." My faith was restored and replenished still more when during the late 1970s and early 1980s I began to learn about Judge John T. Curtin and the Buffalo school desegregation lawsuit.

The Buffalo school desegregation case has all the elements of legal drama, a great story filled with great characters. Although its roots were planted firmly in the history of the country, the case itself did not start until 1972 when a coalition of individuals and civil rights groups filed suit in the court of United States District Judge John T. Curtin. The suit, known as "Arthur v. Nyquist" (that's right… George Arthur, my student at Empire State College, was the lead plaintiff, Nyquist was the New York State Commissioner of Education), charged that, in violation of the US Constitution's 14th amendment's equal protection clause, the public schools of Buffalo had been deliberately segregated along racial lines. The charges were momentous, the outcome potentially devastating. Judge Curtin, fully aware of the explosive implications of the suit, was in no rush to try it. Indeed, it was not until the fall of 1974 that the trial actually began. By then, the temper nationally and locally around what was generally referred to as "forced busing" had become increasingly volatile. Many Buffalonians followed the details of the trial as it unfolded in the fall of 1974 with talk about it filling the air-waves and living rooms throughout the city. What would Judge Curtin decide? Would he, like Judge Garrity in Boston, impose busing? And if he did, how would the people of Buffalo react? Would we, like the people of South Boston, throw rocks at African-American students? Tear up our country's flag? Would some people up and run, leaving the city and its public schools behind?

Curtin took his time deciding. Indeed, it was not until April 30, 1976 when the nerves of the community were frayed, that Judge Curtin was ready.

"It is the finding of this court," Curtin ruled in a decision that dominated the local press for days, "that the plaintiffs' Fourteenth Amendment rights to equal protection under the law have been violated by intentionally causing and maintaining a segregated school system.... The problems presented by the case are difficult and will require rigorous effort to overcome." Concluding firmly, Curtin said: "But overcome them the defendants must."

Following Curtin's ruling in 1976, the case moved into "the remedy phase" and, over the course of the next ten years, the Board of Education, gently but steadily prodded by Judge Curtin and led brilliantly by School Superintendent Eugene Reville and his deputy Joseph T. Murray, implemented a series of sweeping changes whose goal was to create and then sustain a school district that was racially balanced. Unlike Judge Garrity, his imperious colleague on the Federal bench in Boston, Curtin had an abiding faith in "the opinions of the community" and he believed deeply in "common sense, practical views of the parents and the teachers and all the other people who are involved in this very complicated process."

This was, Judge Curtin knew, a critical time in the life of the city. School desegregation would not be easy. But in language that was as aspirational as much as it was inspirational, Curtin tried to calm the people of Buffalo. Curtin encouraged his fellow Buffalonians to meet the challenges of change, to desegregate their schools and in the process work with them to create a new and different sense of community. Exhorting the people of Buffalo to rise to this historic occasion, Judge Curtin quoted Tennyson's "Ulysses": "Come my friends, 'tis not too late to seek a new world."

By the mid-1980s, it began to look as if they had. Buffalo's public schools had achieved a level of racial integration and educational excellence that was the envy of cities throughout the United States. People came from everywhere to see for themselves how Buffalo seemed to have accomplished what no other city had been able to.

Among them was a reporter from the *New York Times* who in May 1985 came to Buffalo to cover the story. The report was lavish: Buffalo was "a national model of integration … confidence has been restored in Buffalo's public schools.'" The report stated that "integration has worked because parents and teachers received a major role in designing the city's 22 magnet schools; because millions of dollars in extra Federal funds were available to make the magnet schools special, and because a Federal judge brandished a court order that kept things moving."

Calling the effort a "velvet steamroller," the paper credited Buffalo school officials with having "crafted a system of magnet schools so appealing that of the 30,000 students who were bused four years ago, only 15 percent had to be ordered onto buses by the Federal judge. Nearly one of every three Buffalo schools is a magnet school." And, *The Times*, said, it was working: "Residents of the city's neighborhoods were accepting the changes, putting their kids on buses that were taking them all the way across town to magnet schools." *The Times* article quoted Judge John T. Curtin: "Yes," he said, "we've had a number of setbacks and it hasn't all been perfect." But, he added, "I'm distressed by people who make statements nationally that integration doesn't work. It does work. It's plain wrong to say it won't. It's working in Buffalo." In addition, he pointed out, "I'm convinced that our school system is much better than 10 years ago or 20 years ago …. Of course I'm pleased. We're all pleased. But the school system is like most things in life; it calls for attention all the time. People want instant results. For heaven's sakes, it takes a while." A good sign, he said, was that he'd not been yelled at by parents in a long time. They used to come to his home, he said, write him notes and call him on a phone in the middle of the night on a number he never took out of the phone book. "I've been sleeping much better these days," he noted.

So too, it seemed, were the people of Buffalo. For here in a city whose history was so defined and so divided by ethnic and racial divisions, the impossible seemed to have happened. It was an incredible story and I wanted to know more. So in the late 1980s I began a process of research and writing that in 1990 resulted in the publication of my second book, *City on the Lake*.

For well over a year beginning in 1985, holed up in tiny cubicles – first in Judge Curtin's chambers, and then in Superintendent Reville's office – I pored over hundreds of pages of documents, reports and newspaper articles. I interviewed dozens of the participants – parents, teachers, school administrators, particularly Gene Reville and Joe Murray, and, much to my distinct and unforgettable pleasure, I spent hours in the presence of Judge Curtin himself. Covering the story was a thrilling experience because I had the opportunity to spend time with some of the most important, even heroic, people in the recent history of the city.

Curtin, Murray and Reville were part of a group of liberal Catholics that I had come to know, people who worked feverishly to counter the tide of racial enmity that, since the riots of 1967, was surfacing throughout the city. There were people like attorneys Richard Griffin from St. Rose of Lima in North Buffalo and Vincent Doyle from St. Mark in Parkside, who as founding members of the Parkside Community Association, did so much to bring racial harmony to that changing neighborhood. In 1972, Griffin became the lead counsel for the plaintiffs in the school case. There were others: Monsignor Walter O. Kern, the priest at Blessed Trinity on Leroy Street, who was working with Councilman Bill Price to ease the white flight then affecting the Fillmore-Leroy area; Father Bill Stanton who, like Curtin, had been raised in St. Teresa's but now was serving as the priest at St. Ambrose on Okell Street in South Buffalo. There, working with two teachers at the school, Father Joe Bissonette and Father John Weimer, Stanton formed an interracial CYO branch at the church. Doyle, Griffin, Bissonette, and Weimer were classmates at Canisius High School, continuing on together to Canisius College. For them, at least, the Catholic pipeline from neighborhood parochial school, to Canisius High School and College, was a liberal one, where the localism of the neighborhood was leavened with the more open-minded Jesuit education of Canisius. Linked by their faith and their foundation in Buffalo's immigrant Catholic neighborhoods, these men were ready to join Judge Curtin in his ambitious efforts to create a new kind of community for a new kind of Buffalo.

There were dozens of others, too, particularly community leaders in both the white and the African-American communities who, recruited by Curtin, Reville and Murray played a transcendent role in this monumental effort. Community activists in South Buffalo and Riverside like Carol Holtz, Joe Pirakas in South Buffalo African-American educators like Marva Daniels, Florence Baugh, Mozella Richardson, Evelyn Cooper and so many more. At community meetings and in their offices I met and talked to dozens of people – parents, teachers, school administrators and all the others involved in the monumental changes that were occurring in our city. Given the energy and commitment of so many (yes, there were certain die-hard obstructionists, most notorious among them Mayor James D. Griffin) I was drawn not to them but to the citizen soldiers of Buffalo who I believed were fighting a front-line battle for the soul of the city. It was a joy for me to get to know these men and women and to hear their stories, one of the great highpoints of my fifty-plus years in Buffalo.

No one appealed to me more than Judge Curtin who, while I was writing *City on Lake* during the late 1980s, became kind of a fixture in our household. I talked about him a lot and kept a photo of him taped to our refrigerator. My star-struck references to his "blue eyes" and "Paul Newman-like" good looks was a source of constant amusement to Charlie and Lydia, who teased me that "Dad has crush on Judge Curtin."

I first met Judge Curtin in Delaware Park where, though a member of the Belle Watlings, a rival running club to our Buffalo Philharmonic Athletic Club, he was among the most affable runners in the park. He was an avid runner, a good competitor and a regular participant in Buffalo's active racing scene. In 1988, at close to 70, he was third in his age group in Buffalo's Runner of the Year competition. For years he ran indoors at the track at the old downtown YMCA but since he started running marathons (he, like many of us, ran in the first Skylon in 1974), he ran only outdoors. Sometimes he ran on The Ring Road at The Meadow; at other times from his office, at lunchtime. Taking off with a bunch of his running buddies from the Buffalo Athletic Club 'round the corner from his chambers on Court Street, they took the five mile run down to the Erie Basin Marina, through LaSalle Park; up the Riverwalk and then back downtown to the club. Sometimes, on nice days when there wasn't much wind coming out of the south, Curtin ran what he called his "grain elevator run," through the streets of the old First Ward, over the Ohio Street Bridge, around the hulking, lofting strangely graceful grain elevators long before this area was known as "Silo City." An hour later, Curtin walked back to his office, his sweat-drenched running clothes stuffed into the crushed gym bag that dangled in his hand. Always smiling, always friendly he sat down at his desk and went back to work. How could I not have had "a crush on Judge Curtin?"

And the others too. The outgoing, politically astute Gene Reville, the South Buffalo boy from Holy Family parish with a universal world view. Joe Murray, the Irish Catholic kid from Riverside, from All Saints Parish, the son of a cop who, like Reville, understood the fears of the people of the city and yet knew, at the same time, how to inspire them to achieve greater things. Murray was a gentle visionary who knew instinctively that good public education was built on the foundation of a strong civic culture. He worked tirelessly to achieve both. Above all, though, there was Judge Curtin: wise, humane, super-smart and deeply sensitive. In all my years in Buffalo there has been nobody who I have admired more than Judge Curtin. From the time that I met him in Delaware Park, through the years that I followed him as he monitored the Buffalo school desegregation case, there has not been a person who I have been more thankful to have known than him.

Despite, or because of, their upbringing in the strong working-class, Catholic neighborhoods of South Buffalo and Riverside, these three men dedicated their lives to the creation of a diverse and pluralistic sense of the city, a place where people of different races, ethnic backgrounds and levels of wealth live, work and function together. I believed deeply in their hopes for Buffalo and, at the end of the 1980s, I felt those hopes were on the verge of being realized.

Perhaps we really were, as Curtin had hoped, on the brink of a new age, one in which the historic neighborhood patterns and affiliations that had characterized our city for so long were being transformed into a bolder vision of ourselves as a far more unified and pluralistic place. Could it be that finally, Buffalo was really becoming "the City of Good Neighbors?"

But that was then when hopes were still high. I believed in Curtin, Reville and Murray as I believed in Red Jacket, Bishop Timon, Mary Talbert and the others. I believed in the promises of a pluralistic city, one where neighborhood customs and traditions were strong and respected, a city where pride in place did not mean racial exclusion. I believed deeply in that vision and in the ability of hard-working, idealistic people to realize it. It was that belief and that faith that led me in the late 1980s to Chippewa Street and the Calumet Building.

Acknowledgements

It was the incredible importance of the school desegregation case that led me to write ***City on the Lake*** (1990) a detailed study of that case, the findings and the remedy, set within the context of the 1970s and 1980s in Buffalo. Some of this material is drawn from that. The final written record of this case gives some testimony to its complexity and to the fervor with which it was contested. Pretrial motions and discovery procedures consumed many months; the actual trial lasted ten days in the Fall of 1974, with a transcript running 1,695 pages; parties submitted many pre-trial and post-trial briefs. Over 180 exhibits were admitted into evidence.

Over the course of researching the school desegregation case in 1987-1989 I left few stones unturned. I spoke with dozens of people in the schools, in government and in the community, a list too long to print here. Below, however, are the people whose friendship and support meant so much to me at this time and whose role in this most significant chapter of our city's history was critical.

Richard F. Griffin: Born and raised in the Parkside neighborhood, Griffin, along with long-time Buffalo public school teacher Jack Anthony, formed the Parkside Community Association in the early 1960s in an effort to sustain and stabilize Parkside as a racially mixed neighborhood. Griffin became one of the city's preeminent civil rights attorneys who, working with his colleagues Marilyn Hochfield and David Jay, represented the plaintiffs in Buffalo's landmark school desegregation case.

Eugene Reville, Joseph T. Murray are among, along with **Federal District Judge John T. Curtin,** the most important figures in Buffalo during those critical years of the last quarter of the last century. I admired all three of these men intensely and was thrilled that I was not only able to know them but to interact with each of them on a friendly basis. Reville's success in Buffalo led him to be recruited by the Clintons to come to Little Rock to help them create a metropolitan wide school district. In 1990 he was killed tragically in a car accident. Joe Murray continued his work in Buffalo. I consider myself blessed to have remained a friend and supporter until his death in 2020. There are no more words for Judge Curtin, a transcendent figure in the history of our city. Curtin died in 2017 at the age of 96. His legacy is incalculable.

CHAPTER 6

The Calumet Arts Café

The arts as a tonic for an ailing downtown

By the end of the 1980s, I was itching for change. I wanted to do something different – something really exciting, something entrepreneurial, something bold and risky, something that would make a splash. After years teaching history, I wanted to get into the mix, to use my talents and to get my hands dirty. I had been following my brother Tony's work in SoHo (i.e., South of Houston Street) in New York City and in South Beach, Miami where, almost single-handedly, he was bringing new life to old, abandoned sites. Tony worked at the place where architecture, design and the arts came together. His approach to historic preservation combined sensitivity for underappreciated architecture with an astute business sense. I wanted to do something similar for Buffalo, and I wanted to do it for myself.

I had a vision, if not a plan. I'd known for years of the power of the arts and artists to transform long-decayed places. I'd watched what was happening in New York's West Village in the '60s and '70s, where squatting artists transformed an officially designated "commercial slum" into what would soon become known as "SoHo." I understood the role of artists as effective change agents in the public realm, and I had a vision for how that could happen in Buffalo too. Besides, I loved the arts, particularly the off-beat, small-scale stuff, the kind that took place in tiny, tucked away locations. In New York City, I was fond of The Nuyorican Poets Café on the Bowery, the Knitting Factory, a hole-in-the-wall art gallery, performance space and café on Houston Street, and, on a somewhat grander scale, my brother Tony's eponymous Greene Street Café. I could see in Buffalo too, the impact that small arts groups, like Hallwalls, CEPA and Just Buffalo were having on the spirit of the city. I'd followed closely the evolution of Artpark in Lewiston, and began to wonder what might happen if all of the elements of that dynamic institution could somehow be replicated in downtown Buffalo. What if

I could create a venue that was part classroom, part performance space, part café where, under one roof, a range of artistic and cultural activities could take place. I wanted to "follow the artists." As the song says, "I could do that!" All that was missing was the right building. With that in mind I called Tony. "Find a building, a really great one, on a corner," he said. "Then, let's talk."

• • •

The focus of my interests in Buffalo had been the city's neighborhoods, so I was far less familiar with the streets of downtown. I was well aware of the decline that had been eating away at the city's core since the early 1960s. In 1983, in *High Hopes*, I wrote in scathing detail about the years of ill-conceived urban renewal projects that left downtown Buffalo in worse shape after than it had been before. Writing about downtown in *City on the Edge* (2007), I noted that even as late as 1990, there was in downtown "a palpable sense of uncertainty about the future." In an article he wrote about downtown in 1994, *Buffalo News* arts critic Richard Huntington was glum: "The whole area," he wrote, "is devoid of people. It is one big stretched out mood piece, a stage set for dancing bears and organ grinders."

It was onto this "stage set" that I walked in the summer of 1988 in search of a location. It didn't take long. Driving down Chippewa Street past Holzman's Pharmacy, Todd's Shoes, The Style Shack, Arnak's Art Gallery and the great, gabled building called "Fisherman's Wharf," I saw, on the southeast corner at Franklin & Chippewa, a glorious, three-story building. With its burnt sienna terra cotta tiles, its undulating windows, its energetic face, the building – called the "The Calumet" – had the look of an Art Nouveau masterpiece, unlike anything else that I'd seen in Buffalo. It was indeed "a great building." I didn't care that the windows were filthy, and that the building was nearly empty. In the one plate-glass window, with a faded, neon sign reading "LaRussa's Men's Shop," was a large piece of cardboard with the two magical words that I was looking for: "For Sale." The instructions were below: "Call Charlie at 855-XXXX if interested."

Call Charlie … Call Charlie … Who could this Charlie be, I wondered? Call Charlie … So, from the phone booth across the street, I did just that: I called "Charlie." A man with a heavy Sicilian accent (I could always tell the difference between a Sicilian and other Italian accents!) picked up: "This is Charlie. Charlie LaRussa." "Wait right there," he said energetically, when I told him I was interested in his building. "I'll be right over. I want you to see the building. You gonna love it."

Charlie was great, very friendly, very Sicilian, dressed nattily in black, his thick, silver hair combed back neatly over his head. He wanted to get out of Buffalo, he said. He had family "in Vegas." Besides, he could act there, getting bit parts as a character actor in night-club revues. He'd already played in *Guys and Dolls*, he told me. "I played Nathan. Nathan Detroit." He proceeded to show me around. There were three storefronts on the ground floor: his old store, LaRussa's Men's Shop, was an open 2,000 square foot room with high ceilings covered in magnificently intact, chiseled tin tiles. In the next store-front was, well, he said, "You don't want to know what that is," his raised eye-brows communicating silently his disdain for the place. "It's a joo-le-rhee store," he said. "They sell stolen joo-le-rhee. But hey, they pay $500 bucks a month. Ya ain't gonna get that much from anybody else on Chippewa Street, that's for sure." Next to that, in a space currently occupied by an outpost of the restaurant Bacchus, was a large deli and convenience store, a Holly Farms, like LaRussa's store on the corner, big, no less than 2,000 square feet. Run by three generations of the D'Aloisio family, Holly Farms was a fantastic store. Though gritty, run-down with a mechanical system that didn't work as well as it should, it was an old-school kind of store, filled with bubble-gum, chips, magazines, racing forms, beer and pop. Most important, Nick and his brother Mark made the best and the biggest sub sandwiches anywhere.

Charlie took me upstairs. There was only one way up, a small wooden staircase, original, I sensed, to the building. It led to a vast space that had been subdivided years ago into separate offices, most of which still had their original doors of oak and glass with the name of each occupant lettered in gold: Herman Goldstein, DDS, read one. Levick's Jewelry Appraisals, read another. The building was supported by rows of steel beams which made it easy to divide the large spaces on each of the three floors into a warren of smaller ones. It was these large steel beams that made possible the high, approximately fourteen-foot ceilings on each of the three floors. While the second floor was thus subdivided, the third floor was not. Indeed, a whole half of the third floor was one large open space supported not by a vertical beam but rather by a horizontal steel beam embedded into the ceiling. "You know what was up here," Charlie asked. "You won't believe it. You're Jewish, right? The Buffalo headquarters of the Ku Klux Klan," he said with a smile. "Now you have to buy the place. Let's go somewhere and talk. Let's go to Holzman's on the corner. I'll buy you a caw-fee."

We crossed Chippewa at the corner down the street. Chippewa had the look and the feel of the Bowery: men hanging around the street corners, standing in the doorway or sitting on the stoop of the House O'Quinn. Directly across the street from the Calumet was a badly run-down single-room occupancy hotel – The New Chippewa Hotel – where upward of fifty men in various stages of despair lived, much of the time on the street in front of the hotel. While shabby, run-down and bedraggled, there were a mix of stores that would be the envy of the street today. Todd's, an independently owned men's shoe store that had been there for years; Forget-Me-Not Flowers, another fixture from decades past; The Style Shack, selling clothes worthy of John Shaft; two strip clubs – (The Cozy and Radice's); The Bradford Grill; and The Arnak Art Gallery, featuring Native American art. Holzman's was at the south east corner, (in the store front occupied since the mid-1990s by Spot Coffee). The place was out of the history books, combining in that one big space a pharmacy, a lunchroom, and its specialty, a full line of stage make-up. A remnant of Buffalo's glory days as a pre-Broadway theater hub, Holzman's offered all kinds of "theatrical makeup for both professionals and amateurs." The lunch counter was long and serpentine with close to twenty stools. With a menu that featured ice-cream sodas, milk shakes, malts and a list of hamburgers with names like "The Chippewa," "The Delaware" and "The Franklin," Holzman's was a very popular downtown lunch spot. We found two stools at one end of the counter and there, looking out at Delaware Avenue, Charlie and I, over a piece of pie and a cup of "caw-fee," talked.

We're both chatty people. We liked each other and spent a fair amount of time talking. Charlie, like so many Sicilians in Buffalo, was from Valledolmo. He'd been in Buffalo since the early 1950s, working first as a laborer in Buffalo's infamous labor union, Local 210, before he opened his men's clothing store on Chippewa Street in the late 1970s. Charlie's first love, though was acting. He had small parts in local amateur theater companies but it was in Las Vegas, where his brothers lived, that he got his first taste of real theater getting small parts in nightclub shows. He wanted to go there permanently, but he needed to sell his building first.

"So," he asked, "whaddaya think?" I loved the building. It was easy to look beyond the dirt and grime that covered the gorgeous terra-cotta exterior and see a clean, brightly lit façade lighting up the dark Chippewa Street night. Easy to imagine the large plate-glass windows, newly washed, the faces of dozens pressed up against it, peering in, hoping to get a glimpse of Milt Jackson playing the vibes or McCoy Tyner playing the piano. Easy to see, too, beyond the drop-ceilings and dry-wall partitions and visualize one large open space, dimly lit, with a stage against one wall, a bar against the other, a room filled with patrons who'd come in out of the cold of the Chippewa Street night and had stepped into, into, into … what? … The Calumet Arts Café?

"What do I think? Waddaya mean what do you think? "I like it," I said. "I love it." "Well," Charlie said, "This is a big deal for me. I'm trying to move to Vegas. I'm trying to start a new career. I gotta get $200,000 for the building … cash." Yikes … that was a big number, a bigger one certainly than I was used to. I hesitated: "I gotta talk to my brother. I gotta talk to Tony." Charlie was surprised: "Tony? You got an Italian brother? I thought you were Jewish." It was fun and a pleasure to deal with Charlie LaRussa but … two hundred grand? … *managia* … that was a lot of dough in 1988. "Charlie, I'm gonna talk to Tony and I'll get back to you in a few days." "That's fine," he said. "You're a good man. I can tell. Take your time. You might as well. You're the first person who's called in months. Nobody else wants the place." We walked out, shook hands and parted ways.

While Chippewa was clearly no "miracle mile," with its variety of small stores and businesses, at least during the day, it was a pretty busy commercial street with a fair amount of foot traffic. There was certainly more activity on Chippewa than there was on Main Street where the vast and empty space had led reporter Huntington to call downtown a mood piece. Given my focus on the city's neighborhoods, I had paid no attention to Chippewa Street. I knew that there were bars and that in the Calumet there was a storefront that housed The Friends of Night People. I had no idea that it was, as *The Buffalo News* had described it, the "epicenter of dereliction," "the boulevard of broken dreams," "home to and hang-out of winos, prostitutes, drug-dealers and other "notorious low-lifes." So eager was I to make this deal, so excited by the prospect of turning the glorious, yet semi-abandoned Calumet Building into something fabulous, I was not willing to either see or hear anything about what most people in Buffalo considered the dread realities of the street. Indeed, it was not until many years later that I stumbled onto a *Buffalo News* article that described my neighbor, Fisherman's Wharf, circa 1969. The restaurant, the article said was "perhaps the seediest of

Chippewa's seedy joints during the strip's heyday as Buffalo's de facto red light district. At a State Liquor Authority hearing, Buffalo Police said the place was frequented by disorderly women, dope peddlers, and people looking to employ disorderly women and dope peddlers. Three cops said they were approached by women soliciting them for immoral purposes and offering marijuana for sale inside the tavern. It was the city's center of vice; during the 1970s, one judge estimated that up to 40 prostitutes worked the street each night. The going rate was $20; the bargain rate $15." Would I have called Charlie had I known all this about Chippewa Street?

While I knew nothing about Chippewa Street's bad reputation, I did know something about the Calumet Building, which had been featured in the our 1982 book, *Buffalo Architecture: A Guide*. The photograph that Pat Bazelon took of the building said it all: a starkly empty building with jerry-rigged doors and windows and in one window a sign that read simply: "Available." (How much was it worth then, I wondered.)

The Calumet Building met all of my brother's criteria. It was architecturally unique, covered in sparkling and exuberantly colored cream and burnt sienna glazed terra cotta with sinuous "calamus reeds" woven into the building's façade. And, as per Tony, it sat proudly on the corner, an absolute stand-out, not-to-be-missed building in the center of downtown Buffalo.

I called Tony. "Make him an offer," he said. "'Don't argue the price. Give him his price and argue the terms." "Yeah, but Tony, $200 grand is still $200 grand." "Listen to me … don't negotiate the price," he repeated. "Negotiate the terms. He wants to sell the building, right? And move to Vegas? How many offers has he had? Not one, you told me. So … here's the deal … tell him you'll give him $20 grand now and that he has to hold a mortgage on the balance …. Wait, wait, wait," he hesitated. "Tell him it's got to be a 7% interest only mortgage with a 20-year balloon. (I wondered, still a total ingenue in the world of real estate, what "balloons" could have to do with all of this, but anyway.) This way, Tony said, you will own the building for almost nothing and have a very small monthly carrying cost of $1,050 per month. "You'll have twenty years to come up with the balance. Do it that way," Tony said, "and save your cash to rehab the downstairs."

I was nervous, never having done anything like this before, so I delayed calling back Charlie. Until the end of the week. We met again, this time at the Bradford Grill, a remnant of 1950s Buffalo. The Bradford had great burgers cooked on a grill behind the bar. Charlie, in his head already out of Buffalo, talked excitedly about a revival at the Sands Hotel of the musical *The Most Happy Fella* that he was going to Vegas to try out for. "Well, what did he say? What did your Italian brother Tony say?" "Charlie, I don't know, this is all very new to me. So don't blame me. Blame Tony. Maybe he is Italian after all." "So … Tony said your price is fair and he wants me to pay it. But," I said stumbling, "he said that he wants you to hold a mortgage. I'll never get a mortgage for the building, Tony told me, and the only way I could buy it is if you, Charlie, hold the paper."

Tony was right. Charlie wanted to make this deal. "For how long?" he asked. I breathed deeply and spit it out: "Twenty years, 7% interest only. Twenty thousand now. $180,000 in a balloon payment in twenty years." Charlie didn't seem to care about the terms, but focused instead on the $20,000 down payment. "You mean you're gonna give me $20,000 in cash? Now?" "I guess," I answered sheepishly. "I like it," Charlie said quickly. "I think we can work this out. I'll call you tomorrow." But wait, he said: "Do you know the musical "*The Most Happy Fella*"? Actually I did, the fabulous Frank Loesser show about the Italian immigrant who falls in love with a mail order bride. "I love that show," I said. "You gonna play Tony? Tony Esposito?" "I'm gonna try, that's for sure." Charlie got up, shook my hand and said with a broad smile that he'd call me in the morning.

Next morning I got the call: "The building's yours kid. I'll get the papers drawn up. I wanna close fast." (While we did lose track of each other, I learned that Charlie did in fact move to Las Vegas and did get some small movie parts. He was particularly proud of his role as a casino gambler in Steven Soderberg's *Ocean's Eleven*. He might still be there today!) I called my mother in New York. "Lotsa luck, son," she said. Better be careful what you wish for."

Now what? Good question. Armed with my twenty-year interest only note from Charlie and its $1,050 monthly payment, I, despite my ignorance about real estate and business, believed in myself and I was confident that I could, in the desolate storefronts on the "street of broken dreams," make something really great happen.

I knew what I wanted, but had no idea how to get it. I knew nothing about construction and certainly nothing about the rules and regulations surrounding it. I wanted to do everything on my own, to get my own hands and clothes dirty in the reclamation of the Calumet Building. I wanted to look the part, too, to wear the paint-splattered clothes, the hard hat, the steel-toed boots, the many-pocketed carpenter's tool belt that contractors wore. In my mind, the work that I was doing at the Calumet paralleled and reflected the work that I'd been doing studying Buffalo's history. I wanted to embrace the work, to make it intensely personal, intimate, and very real. Excited and impulsive, with no plans and no architect, with no permits, and under $100,000 to my name, I went to work.

Shortly after I closed on the building in the fall of 1988, I set out to repair the badly damaged sidewalk in front of the Calumet. Now wearing my newly acquired steel-tipped shoes from Hook's, a handy-man's belt, carrying a bucket of concrete, a trowel and a wheel-barrow that I rented from Chi-Chi's on Grant Street, I set out to do the work. It was theater as much as anything else. I wanted the people of Buffalo to see me, on my hands and knees, actually, with my own two hands, healing the broken pavement of Chippewa Street. Writing about the city's past at night, restoring the present during the day, I felt that I was involved in transformational work. I wanted people to see what I was doing, to take notice and applaud my efforts, and I was saddened when they didn't. Perhaps they were threatened by my efforts, my willingness to put myself on the line in such an exposed and vulnerable way. Or maybe they really didn't care. It was their loss, though, I thought, as I watched pedestrians by the dozens simply walk by, their heads down, indifferent to what I sensed was my existential engagement with the very fiber of the city.

Luckily, one person finally noticed. One day, a young African-American man poked his nose through the door that I kept open on Chippewa as I worked. Perry Young had just gotten off a Greyhound after a five day trip from his home in Alligator, Mississippi, to Buffalo where he had an aunt (an "Awhn't," he called her.) Perry announced that he was looking for work. "There's nutthin' in construction that I can't do," he told me. Perry was a wonderful young man, energetic, smart, very hard working, and true to his word--there was very little in construction that he couldn't do. So, together, we went about the work of taking down the partitions from LaRussa's Men's Shop, knocking down the drop ceiling that hid those beautiful tiles, and pulling up linoleum tiles, which covered a gorgeous hardwood floor. Interrupting our work at noon for one of Nick's fantastic sub sandwiches, we were making progress and having a ball doing it. (Sadly, Perry didn't stay around for long. He was a "rambling man" and within a month or so he was on his way.)

Others started coming through the open door at the Calumet. Curious as to what was going on, a cast of characters soon became part of my growing network of friends and colleagues in downtown Buffalo. Among the most memorable was a tall, attractive woman who on one day in December 1988 came wandering through the open door. She took off her long overcoat and set down a large box of paints. With an unforgettably energetic smile, she said, "Hi. I am Joanna Angie." Like Perry, she had recently gotten off the bus. "I'm an artist, a muralist," she announced. With large, brown eyes casting an envious look at the enormous fire-tiled walls and the partly exposed tin-ceiling, she said, "I sure would love to paint all that." I immediately said "Yes."

Joanna spent the next several weeks working like Michelangelo on the Sistine Chapel ceiling. Standing on a rented rolling scaffold, Joanna painted and then stained the hundreds of tin tiles that comprised the ceiling of what was becoming the Calumet Arts Café. From the ceiling, we moved to the walls. Stripping them of several layers of drywall, we revealed floor-to-ceiling walls of one square foot ceramic "fire-tiles," the kind that were used in turn-of-the century buildings as fireproofing. Joanna adored the large, blank walls. Handling the wheeled scaffold like an accomplished skate-boarder, she moved up and down the walls, turning them into breathtaking giant, abstract canvases.

One day, Joanna wanted to see what was upstairs. The wide open spaces on the second and third floors were made seemingly larger and lighter by huge ribbons of windows. "These have got to be artists' studios. It's written all over this building," Joanna declared. She now began to tell me that she had come to Buffalo with the hope of creating a community here of artists who could all working the same space. She already had a name for it – Buffalo Arts Studio. "Let's put it here," she suggested.

I wanted people to see what we were doing, to have a cup of coffee from the gigantic pot that I set up in the front window, to ask questions, to get engaged in the project I had almost randomly begun to create on Chippewa Street. And they did.

In the Spring of 1989, three people, two men and a woman, each in their mid-thirties, came walking down the street. In a way that made me think of the Marx Brothers, they poked in their heads in rapid succession through the open doorway. "We heard you're making an arts space here," said one of the men. "A performance space. Can we look?" "My name's Vincent O'Neill. This here's my wife Josephine and," with a slight smile and a glint in his eye, he added, "that there's my brother Chris. Just in from Dublin and we're looking for a theater. We call ourselves 'The Irish Classical Theater Company.'" The O'Neills were irresistible, each bursting with talent, each filled with life, each possessing personal charm and charisma. We clicked immediately and vowed that somehow we would find a place for them to perform within the Calumet Building.

There were others too: Debora Ott, the founder and director of the Just Buffalo Literary Center, stopped by. She'd been to LaRussa's once, she said, when Clifton Joseph, a well-known Jamaican "Dub" poet was in town looking for a "hat like Shaft wore." She, too, heard that we were working on an arts space. She talked to me about Just Buffalo, wondering if there might not be some room for them. Michael Morgulis came, too. He was my friend who created our city's everlasting brand: "Buffalo: City of No Illusions." Might there be room, he wondered, for a silk-screen print shop upstairs?

Another day, there was a tall, slouched-over man wearing a long overcoat, a cigarette dangling from his lips, a character out of Robert Frank's *Pull My Daisy*. He was David Kane, a keyboardist and composer for his band – *Them Jazzbeards*.

David didn't talk much, but it was clear as he walked slowly all around the room that he liked the way it was shaping out. "It'd be pretty cool to play in here someday. Stay in touch," he said, waving as he ambled out and back onto Chippewa Street.

Other people stopped by, curious about the gossip on the street. Several other musicians came by, wondering whether it was true that there would be a new jazz club in downtown Buffalo.

People believed what they wanted to and I, unclear in my own mind about what exactly I was doing, soaked it all up. I was beginning to feel that something really good was happening here in this long derelict space. What it was, though, I wasn't sure. Was it the O'Neills' theater? Was it Joanna Angie's artists' studio? Was it a music club? Was it a restaurant? A bar? Somehow, maybe, all of the above? Meanwhile, I worked and, listening to my brother, I waited. "Let the walls speak to you," Tony said, "Don't worry. It will come."

One day in the early months of 1989, a motorcycle pulled up in front of our open door. The cyclist was a skinny, grizzled guy like me in his late forties, wearing a tight-fitting leather jacket out of *The Wild Ones*. As he helped himself to a cup of coffee, I, ever eager to greet anybody who came in, went over and introduced myself. His name was Jamie Moses. He had heard about something cool happening on Chippewa and he wanted to check it out. Jamie had recently moved to Buffalo to be closer to his mom, a jazz singer from New York named Peggy Farrell who was beginning to make a name for herself here in Buffalo. Jamie had grown up in Greenwich Village, so we spoke about the places he'd been and the people he'd met there. He'd even had his photograph taken by the great photographer for *The Village Voice*, Fred McDarrah. He liked Buffalo, and had begun a musical career of his own as the singer and piano player for his rock group called "The Jamie Moses Band." What he wanted to do most of all, though, was to start a newspaper in Buffalo, one modeled on *The Village Voice*. He was appalled by *The Buffalo News*, its overindulgent coverage of the Buffalo Bills measured against its lackluster coverage of the arts. In the short period of time that he'd been in Buffalo, Jamie had become impressed by the high quality of the artists who lived here and the vitality of the arts scene in general. He wanted, he said, to create a publication that would document the efforts of the artists in Western New York, and to enable them to communicate with one another.

I was impressed by his background and by the obvious sincerity of his commitment to the arts. "We're kind of on the same page," I told him. What he hoped to do in print, I was planning to do in the Calumet Building – make a place where artists of all kinds would be able to present their work. He had met the O'Neills and knew David Kane. While he had not yet met Joanna Angie, he loved the idea of her Buffalo Arts Studio. "Let's stay in touch," he said. "We need each other." About a year later, in June of 1990, the first issue of Jamie Moses' ARTVOICE hit the streets. For the next twenty-odd years Jamie, often writing under the pen name of The Khanasamah of The Muse, and ARTVOICE offered the people of Buffalo a fresh, vibrant and important perspective on art and life in our community.

Yet another visitor showed up, a man who introduced himself as Ralph Viola, a "building inspector." Mr. Viola was a big guy who looked the part, as if he'd been hanging around construction sites for most of his life. Kind, friendly but clearly a no-nonsense type of guy, Viola wondered "what the hell's going on here?" Believing deeply in the value of the work that I was doing and defensive when faced with any questioning of it, I replied that I was only cleaning out the place. "What are you doing with it?," he wanted to know. "Well I don't really know yet." Nervous and uncertain, I told him that I was thinking about some kind of a "mixed-use arts space, a music room, a performance space." I told him what my brother said, that I should wait and "let the walls speak" to me. He chuckled and replied, "that's all well and good. But while you're waiting, you will need a permit." Actually it was two – a demolition permit and then a building permit. "Who's your architect," he wanted to know. "Don't know yet … haven't got one." "You got a half hour?," Viola asked in mocked exasperation. "Come with me. I'll buy you a cup of coffee at Holzman's."

I put down my cool contractor's leather belt and, somewhat nervously, feeling as if I were being taken into custody, I walked down to the corner with my companion, City of Buffalo Building Inspector Ralph Viola. "Listen, you just can't do what you're doing," he said. "I know you're trying to do the right thing but there's a right way to do the right thing and you, my friend, are not doing it." Sitting at two corner stools at one end of Holzman's counter, Viola pulled out a yellow legal notepad and outlined the process, offering me a crash course on what I would need to do to bring new life to that old space in the Calumet Building. He'd help me but, he warned, it was going to take a lot of time and effort. "Get yourself an architect … a good one, one who knows the codes … get a drawing and then come back and see me." Viola could tell that I was upset, nervous, afraid that my little "do-it-yourself" project was getting hijacked by a cold and callous bureaucrat. Sensing my anxiety, he reassured me. "Don't worry, you can have your arts café. But," he said firmly, "it's got to be a legal arts café! I'll help you to get there."

And now, with Ralph Viola as my guide and the help of architects Steve Carmina and Phil Silvestri, I was on the right track. It would not be easy. Everything started and, often ended, in City Hall. While we had included City Hall in our MIT guide book and I was aware of its uniqueness as a great civic building, I knew little about the actual denizens of the place.

Despite the somewhat macabre interior – the dirty, dark halls, the elevators operated by any number of bedraggled, half-shaven ancient men in ratty, Buffalo Bills sweatshirts, the often endless lines – there was something about the run-down mustiness that appealed to me. I particularly liked the people who filled the offices. Most all of them were African-Americans and second generation Italians, Poles and Irish, people who still lived or who had just recently left the old ethnic neighborhoods that were in proximity to City Hall. I came to know and to like the secretaries and the inspectors, as well as people like me who were working their way around the intriguing maze of this giant building. I enjoyed sharing with them my enthusiasm for their varied ethnic backgrounds, wishing them the best on St. Patrick's Day, St. Joseph's Day, on Dyngus Day, Kwanzaa and all the rest.

And so began a year-long period during which there was hardly anything about reviving an old building that I did not learn. I'd never done anything like rehabbing the Calumet. Now, for the first time in my life, I learned about groups of Buffalonians who I would never have come into contact with, had it not been for the work that I was doing at the Calumet: architects, contractors, plumbers, electricians, drywall installers, plasterers, roofers, painters, tile and floor guys. The list was fascinating, endless, and expensive! I had already discovered Chi-Chi's but, in those days before Home Depot opened in Buffalo, I needed and found others, places like Lenco and Frontier Lumber, Shanor Electric and Licata Plumbing and Sherwin Williams and Schuele's paints and, *primus inter pares*, Allen Street Hardware, that century old mecca.

Working on the Calumet Building quickly became a family affair. My son, Charlie, who by now had come back from college, contributed brains and brawn. His friends – Pat Gallo, Ange and Russ Canna, among them, came along too and together, day after day, stopping only for those big subs at Holly Farms, we worked to transform the interior of the old clothing store. (Several years later, after college, Lydia came to work there too, as a bartender. Jonathan, meanwhile, went off to college at Indiana University.)

There was nothing that Joanna Angie would not do to help, even when Inspector Viola told us that we would have to either take down or cover the building's original tin-tile ceiling that she had so lovingly painted and restored. "You need a two-hour, fire-rated ceiling. You can either sprinkler the place or cover that ceiling with drywall." Ever strapped for money, I, in a decision that I still regret today, opted for dry-wall.

Our work began to pay off. With the focal point of my efforts on the Calumet Building, in early 1990, I joined forces with Tim Tielman's and Sue McCartney's Preservation Coalition of Erie County to have the building officially recognized as a protected landmark. I'd been a preservationist since I first heard Jane Jacobs in New York; now, close to thirty years later in Buffalo, I valued and sought the prestige that historic designation conferred. Despite the restrictions that designation imposed, I was happy to have my property join the ranks of Buffalo's most noteworthy buildings. We celebrated the designation and, weeks before we actually opened in September 1990, we hosted a lecture on Frank Lloyd Wright sponsored by the Preservation Coalition.

Meanwhile, I was trying to figure out just what the heck an "arts café" really was. I began to put my thoughts into words: In early 1989 I wrote a memo to myself in which I outlined my goals and objectives for what I was increasingly referring to, to myself at least, as the Calumet Arts Café. "I want," I wrote, "to create and MAINTAIN (my caps!!!) in the heart of downtown Buffalo a meeting place, a place of entertainment and fun, a place where all kinds of people can come to enjoy good food, good drink and good entertainment. I want to create a place in downtown Buffalo where people of different and varied backgrounds can enjoy themselves together, can overcome barriers and can come away with an experience that transcends simply eating and listening to music. I want to create an environment that nurtures cosmopolitanism and multiculturalism, a space, in the heart of downtown that will lead the people of Buffalo to think about how, together, we can create "the good city." Looking back at this document, printed on my dot matrix on my Apple II word processor, I am proud of what I wrote more than thirty years ago.

"An arts café sounds great," Tony said. "I like it. A lot. But what," he wanted to know, "about a cash register?" "You can't have an 'arts café' unless you have people spending money. You gotta sell them something. You gotta serve food and drinks. You gotta have a restaurant and a bar!" Now that's something I really knew nothing about. I was an historian, a teacher. What did I know about "a restaurant and a bar?" Learning about construction was hard enough. Now this? "Well," he said, "you better learn." He rattled off some tips, talking mostly about managing expenses. Low costs, that's the key. Food should never cost you more than 30% of what you sell it for; booze no more than 20% and your payroll no more than another 30%. That leaves you 20% for everything else. "Tiny margins, my brother. You better be careful," he warned.

Well, I dug in. Confident that I could do this and ever-willing to try, I plunged into learning about restaurants and bars. There was no "Idiots' Guide," no Internet, no easily accessible way for me to learn what I soon came to appreciate was a complex business. I asked around, talking to people I knew in the business: Stavros Malliaris at Ambrosia, Joel Lippes at The Rue, Don Warfe at

Just Pasta, Dave Shatzel at Cole's. With bits of information gleaned from them and from my ongoing talks with Tony, I was able to pull together just enough knowledge to lead me to believe that I could open the Calumet not only as an arts café, but as a full-scale restaurant as well.

A varied menu of cultural arts and entertainment was a critical component of my vision. For ideas and inspiration, I drew not only from my own experiences in New York but also on the eclectic Buffalo scene. Despite the dreariness of parts of downtown Buffalo, there was a beating heart of cultural activity nearby. Much of this was due to the work of Harold Cohen who in 1978, at the request of Mayor James Griffin, created a master plan for what he called "Buffalo's Entertainment District."

For most of the century, Main Street between Tupper and Chippewa was a bustling strip lined with theaters, restaurants and music clubs. By the time Cohen arrived in Buffalo in 1974, almost nothing of that remained. The Market Arcade was boarded up and empty; the magnificent Shea's Theater was destined for demolition. Main Street, torn up by the never-ending project to build an above-ground rapid transit line, was a shambles. Cohen had a lofty vision for a revised "theater district," one that was rooted in the concept of downtown as a twenty-four hour destination, a place where great architecture, hosting a lively arts scene, would bring the area back. To many, it seemed preposterous.

And yet, by the end of the 1980s, much of Cohen's vision had begun to fall into place. In 1981, local stakeholders formed the Theater District Association and in September of that year announced the first celebration of what is still known, almost forty years later as "Curtain Up".

The above-ground portion of the rapid transit system was complete and Buffalo Place, the business improvement district charged with managing it, had been created. Shea's had been meticulously rehabilitated and the adjacent Theater Place, which combined offices, apartments and The Tralfamadore Café and night club, was fully occupied. The Market Arcade theater complex had been built and steps were being taken by the city to reimagine the rest of the building.

So, by the fall of 1990, as I prepared to open what would soon be "The Calumet Arts Café," the blocks of Main Street between Tupper and Chippewa were in the process of becoming a regional cultural arts and entertainment destination. As a result, the Curtain Up 1990 line-up was plentiful and impressive. The Theater of Youth was offering *The Belle of Amherst* in its theater just up from Chippewa, at 282 Franklin. The Studio Arena was presenting Feydeau's *A Flea in Her Ear*, UB's Pfeiffer Theater, two Albee plays, *American Dream* and *Zoo Story*; The Kavinoky had *Death of a Salesman*, directed by Chris O'Neill and starring Stu Roth, and the Paul Robeson Theater presented *Driving Miss Daisy*, directed by LaVerne Clay. At 700 Main Street, an emerging arts space shared with the CEPA Gallery and Arts Development Service Hallwalls presented its annual "Ways of Being Gay Festival". The Buffalo Entertainment Theater, also round the corner from the Calumet on Franklin, was presenting a play about August Strindberg called "The Night of the Tribades" while at the Theater Loft on Elmwood Avenue, Lorna Hill was starring in Ujima theater's production of "For Colored Girls …." My favorite spot, The Cabaret, a tiny, totally funky room run by Erica Wahl housed in what is now "D'Arcy McGee's," mounted a magical presentation of a play compiled by Wahl called "Conversations with Dali," with original music composed by David Kane and performed by "Them Jazzbeards". It was at The Cabaret in October 1990, that many of us who were beginning to stake a claim to Chippewa Street as our own, came to hear Ani DiFranco debut her first album.

There was lots of live music everywhere, much of it at Nietzsche's, a music club on Allen Street opened by Joe Rubino in 1988. Rubino promoted music every night of the week: Mondays and Tuesdays Michael Meldrum ran the best open-mic nights in town. Wednesdays were reserved for a fantastic rock 'n roll band called The Thirds; Fridays, for Stan and The Ravens. Saturdays for Billy McEwen's Buffalo Blues Band. At least once a month, the Outer Circle Orchestra, featuring a flexible ensemble of percussionists and other instrumentalists (like incredible guitarist and sax player John Allen), performed to large crowds at Nietzsche's. Plays and poetry readings too were regular features on Nietzsche's ambitious entertainment menu. You could hear punk rock at the Continental, just down from Chippewa on Franklin. (I'd been to the dungeon-like Continental once, during the presidential election of 1984 when the club produced a rollicking show called "Rock against Reagan.") There was plenty of jazz too, at Anchor Bar where Jimmy Gomes Trio held forth every weekend; at the Central Park Grill and at the Colored Musicians Club and at the Cloister on Delaware, (where Al Tinney and Peggy Farrell, Jamie Moses' Mom, performed.) On Main there was Andy Vitello's Blue Note featuring R&B and Jazz, presenting such greats as Jimmy McGriff and Dr. Lonnie Smith. At the Tap Room in the old Lafayette Hotel, you could hear some of the best blues anywhere, a steady line-up of local bands and such major blues stars as Clarence "Gatemouth"Brown, Buddy Guy and Robert Jr. Lockwood. And, of course, the jewel in the crown, The Tralfamadore, one of the great jazz clubs west of the Hudson, presented the world's leading jazz artists on an almost weekly basis. And, you could dance too: to Stan and The Ravens at Rosy Rum and Rations on Elmwood, to Shakin' Smith at the Schuper House on Niagara and to Terry Sullivan's rock 'n roll band at The Brick Bar on Allen.

Given the vitality of the cultural calendar of downtown Buffalo, where could my Calumet Arts Café fit in? What role in this vibrant downtown scene could it play? I sensed, but could not clearly articulate, that something was missing. The Calumet building offered me the opportunity to prove myself, to demonstrate that I could build on a broad-based program of cultural arts programming, creating in this most extraordinary building a new, different and better model of "urban renewal." I was, in the words of Lin Manuel Miranda's Hamilton, "not throwing away my shot."

With the building's status as a city landmark secured, I began to focus on programming, to create as diverse and varied a lineup of events and activities as possible. So the Calumet offered live jazz on Fridays and Saturday evenings, regularly alternating the lineup in an effort to create a stage for as many local jazz musicians as possible. We mixed it up as much as we could: A double bill featuring Irish singer Gerry Beirne and local musician Ani DiFranco; and any number of programs and events that celebrated ethnic holidays and traditions: a Columbus Day dinner highlighted by historian Marvin Lunenfeld and his provocative lecture, "Was Columbus Jewish?" There were Hanukkah and Purim programs; Three Kings events; Chinese and Japanese musicians and dancers, Cuban nights and African days; poetry readings and benefits and, one of my favorites, a spectacular Halloween party featuring the miraculous costumery and the magical sets of Franklin LaVoie.

On Sundays we offered a "Classical Music Brunch," sometimes featuring musicians like BPO violinist Diana Sachs whose sensuous performance of the Kreutzer Sonata I remember to this day. Yvar Mikhashoff, the extraordinary contemporary artist from UB's music department performed here too, once offering a not-to-be believed performance of tango and ragtime piano pieces. Sometimes I invited Tom Crann and Stratton Rawson, the learned announcers from WNED-FM, who presented the kind of music "informances" that I had heard as a child at Leonard Bernstein's Young Peoples Concerts. Crans' first program, on Valentine's Day, 1991, was called "Dvorak in Love."

I was proud as well of our program of Saturday tours which were, I wrote in a press release and a brochure (remember, there was no "social media" available!) nothing less than "part of the Calumet's interest in increasing the awareness and knowledge of issues critical to the well-being of our community." The tours were many and varied and offered me the opportunity to showcase the work of people in the community who I most admired. There was Joe Murray's tour of Buffalo's schools; Tim Tielman's tour focusing on important planning and land use issues; Jack Randall's tour of the Prudential Building; David Anderson's tour of his eponymous gallery, Stan Lipsey's tour of *The Buffalo News* newsroom, Judge Curtin's tour of his chambers; Mike Billoni's behind-the-scenes tour of what was then Pilot Field. And then, that old stand-by, always good for sellout crowd, "Mark Goldman's famous Rubber Neck Tour of Buffalo."

• • •

There were four storefronts in the Calumet Building. The first two we'd transformed into the Calumet Arts Café. The fourth was occupied, the long-standing home of Nick's Holly Farms. But the third was empty, a vast, two thousand square foot space that we'd use for storage: "Just put it in the third room." It was getting expensive operating the Calumet and the cost of our ambitious programming was rarely covered by our sales. We needed cash flow, a steady source of income that could help cover our mounting programming costs. My brother, in his loving Yoda-like way, now dropped a hint. "Open a bar there," he said, "in that empty third room. You're gonna need the cash flow." Well, I knew less about bars than I did about restaurants. Bars were simply not part of my experience growing up in New York and socializing in a bar was something that I rarely did. But Charlie, on the other hand, did as he and his Elmwood Avenue buddies had been regular, if underage, habitues of that street's many watering holes. (They were particularly fond of Tuesday "Ladies Nights" at Coles.) "I'll do this, Dad. Let me open a bar. I can do this. We'll make it very cool, I promise." While there was a busy bar scene a few miles away on Elmwood Avenue, other than a handful of down and dirty Bowery-type saloons on and around Chippewa Street, there were no places downtown where the "hip," "artsy" crowd could hang out and have a beer, a kind of neighborhood drop-in place like The White Horse in the

West Village or that I seen in SoHo. Charlie was insistent and enthusiastic. "I can do this, Dad. We'll call it The Third Room."

From the minute Charlie opened the Third Room in the winter of 1992 people flocked to the place. Featuring a DJ who spinned hip-hop and reggae, (music not heard in any other bar in Buffalo at that time), an authentic French Art Deco poster of a Parisian barmaid named "Genevieve" on the wall ("Ask for Genevieve when you come in," one of our ads in *Artvoice* ran. "She's sure to show you a good time"), very dim lights and a Lautrec-like outside mural painted by Jeffrey Paul Lane, The Third Room quickly became an iconic destination. And Tony was right ... we did need the cash, and the high-margin, low-overhead Third Room provided it.

Then there was the Irish Classical Theater Company, less a company when I first encountered Vincent, Josephine and Chris O'Neill than three vagabond Irish actors who'd come to Buffalo in the mid-'80s in search of a place to perform. By 1990 and 1991, they had begun to appear in theaters around town. I had seen Vincent O'Neill's miraculous performance in a one-man play called Joyicity at the Pfeiffer Theater. O'Neill, blonde and wiry, dominated the stage of the Pfeiffer for one non-stop hour that combined acting and mime in a way I'd never seen before. O'Neill, believe it or not, played 40 different Joycean characters in a performance that was as much physical as it was verbal. The audience loved it and O'Neill was brought back for half-a-dozen curtain calls. It was without a doubt the most powerful theatrical performance that I'd seen in Buffalo.

After the performance I asked around about O'Neill. I'd met him briefly before but I didn't think too much more about it at the time. Now I learned Vincent, his wife Josephine and his brother Chris, were from Dublin and that Vincent, who'd studied acting at the Abbey Theater in Dublin and mime with Marcel Marceau in Paris, had come to Buffalo in 1985 to visit his brother here. While here, the brothers made their first of what eventually would become countless performances in Buffalo when they appeared in a performance of Beckett's Waiting for Godot at Kevin Townsell's old Airport Inn. In December, 1989, Vincent, accompanied by Josephine and their infant daughter Lara, moved permanently to Buffalo. Just as "dear dirty Dublin" was, along with Nora Barnacle, the love of Joyce's life, it would not be long before "dear dirty Buffalo" would become the love of the lives of Vincent and Chris O'Neill and Josephine Hogan.

Mesmerized by Vincent's performance at The Pfeiffer I sought out his wife Josephine Hogan who was starring in a one-woman show at Daemen College called "Shirley Valentine," a monologue by a middle aged, working class Liverpool housewife whose humdrum life is uprooted and transformed by a holiday trip to Greece that she takes with a friend. One-person shows are tough to pull-off, with no place for the actor to hide if things go wrong. For both Vincent in "Joyicity" and Josephine in "Shirley," they needed none. Josephine, like Vincent, was tender, funny and endearing. Imagine the power of a performance, I wondered, in which they played together!

Somehow, I don't remember exactly how, they either came to me or I went to them. Perhaps, we thought, we could do something together, at the Calumet, as part of our Sunday series. With no theater of their own and no permanent place to perform, the O'Neills were excited about the opportunity to expand their growing audience. They had in mind what they called a "two-hander," a two-character play called "The Galway Girl." We'd do it, we agreed, for three Sunday afternoon performances, the first on Sunday, January 22, 1992.

Set in the small town of Galway, the play deals with a perfectly incompatible couple who, despite a life of dispute and disagreement, never fail to squeeze some measure of joy out of their mutual irritation and discomfort. With no lighting and no set other than two chairs, Vincent and Josephine, performing within feet of the sold-out audience, were charming and triumphant.

Their performance was everything that I desired for the Calumet Arts Café: two marvelous artists, at the peak of their game, performing before a hushed and engaged audience in this intensely intimate space. (And Tony would have been pleased too: the cash register – after, not during, the performance – was ringing as loud as the applause of the audience.) A one-off turned into a four-month long run. We had a hit and we all knew it. Now, how to build on the success of the O'Neills and Galway Girl.

The timing was perfect: the O'Neills, now officially constituted as The Irish Classical Theater Company, were homeless, without a theater they could call their own while our tenant, Nick D'Aloisio at Holly Farms, was outgrowing his space. What if, I began to think, we could transform Nick's deli into a home for the O'Neills and their Irish Classical Theatre Company? What better way to solidify the "arts" component of The Calumet Arts Café? What better way, in the process, to move towards the transformation of Chippewa Street from a place where dreams were "broken" to one where they, at least mine, were realized and fulfilled. It was an extraordinary opportunity and we all embraced it.

Limited by a shortage of time (we wanted to be open by Curtain Up, 1993) and money, (the extent of public support for the theater conversion was a $25,000 low interest loan from the city) we had to make do with what we had. This was going to be a no-frills, start-up theater: a bathroom shared with The Third Room, a tiny dressing room, a box-office fit for grade school productions and a separating wall that barely muffled the lively sounds coming from the busy Third Room.

We wrestled mightily over the question of the performance space itself. Where could we put the stage? While we all favored a traditional proscenium stage set up against one of the walls, the existence of three steel load-bearing columns, each sixteen feet apart located down the center of the space would have destroyed the sight lines. Worse, this would shrink the number of people we were hoping to squeeze in. We could have removed the columns and replaced them with horizontal steel beams placed on the ceiling, but we just didn't have the money for that. What, we wondered, if the performance space could include the columns; if the columns were to become part of the "landscape" of the performance space itself? Instead of elevating the "stage" then, the floor of Nick's Holly Farms (columns and all, minus, alas, the subs) would serve as the stage while the seats, simple stacking chairs, would be placed on slightly-elevated risers. The result would be a one-hundred seat, in-the-round theater.

It was clear from the opening night in September 1993 that our "hit" was in fact a "home-run." The O'Neills had already created a dedicated following and now they came streaming to the Calumet on Chippewa Street: for dinner in the Café, for a show in the theater and for after-theater music back in the Café or the Third Room. It was all that I had imagined. With our fingers crossed, we were balancing theater, jazz, food and beverage in one conceptually-integrated and coherent space.

The conversion of the sub shop into a theater epitomized what was becoming for me a strategic approach to my efforts to foster renewal of downtown through the arts. My partnership with the O'Neills was critical to the realization of my vision and I wanted very much to create an environment that would enable them to flourish. Rent, we decided together, would not be fixed but rather based on a manageable percentage of their ticket sales. While this worked well for them, it created problems for me as the theater was open for less than half of the year. Fortunately, the Calumet Arts Café was doing well, and the Third Room, as Tony predicted, was doing great. Given my faith in the O'Neills and my belief that the Irish Classical Theater Company would add incalculable value to my work, I was willing to live with an arrangement that would help the O'Neills get off the ground.

We worked closely together on all aspects of the creation of the theater space. No issue was more challenging than monitoring the sound, mostly the music, that seeped through the thin fire wall that separated the two spaces. We had not anticipated this but knew on opening night that there was a problem.

We quickly opted for a spray-foam sound-proofing system which, in conjunction with our commitment not to start our music in the Third Room till 10 pm, helped considerably to mitigate the problems. There were occasional glitches like the time, for example, when one of our bartenders who was unfamiliar with our arrangement cranked up the music before the agreed to 10 pm start time. While blithely going about his pre-opening routine of cutting lemons and washing glasses, the music of Bob Marley and the Wailers blasting in the background, he was suddenly confronted with an irate Josephine Hogan who, fully costumed as the Marquise de Merteuil in Dangerous Liaisons, her arms akimbo on her waist, angrily berated him. Completely cowed and intimidated – "What the f___ was Queen Victoria doing in the Third Room," he later wondered – he instantly shut off the music. Josephine, with a delicious smile of success, returned to the theater and, without missing a beat, the show went on.

It went on outside too, in the fantastic outdoor space behind the Calumet Building that we now transformed into "The Garden at The Calumet." We built a deck, planted bushes and trees and retained the fabulous muralist Meg Corcoran to work her magic on the outside walls as she had on the inside. By the mid-1990s The Garden at the Calumet had become a fabulous place for outdoor dining, concerts and, yes, movies. On a gigantic screen that we hung from the wall of the adjacent Augspurger parking ramp, we projected films (in these days before DVDs and internet film access, we rented 16mm films which were shipped weekly from New York). Every Wednesday in July and August throughout the 1990s, weather permitting, 100 plus people made their way to our garden where, on a 500 sq foot canvas screen hung from the Augsburger parking ramp, they watched "Jaws," "Cinema Paradiso," "The Piano" and every other award-winning films you could think of. We held concerts there too, featuring a fantastic band from Havana called Sabor de Cuba and wonderful, jam-packed reggae concerts organized by my son Charlie, featuring Burning Spear, Bob Marley Jr, Yellowman and others. By the end of the '90s, The Garden at the Calumet had become a unique and important cultural and entertainment destination in downtown Buffalo. Who would possibly have guessed?

• • •

Something was missing though. My years in New York and my familiarity with the cultural scene there told me that jazz was the essential ingredient of cool; that jazz musicians, not alone the marvelous local musicians who played at the Calumet, but a line-up of world-class, internationally-known jazz musicians, was what was necessary to take the Calumet to the next level. That was the way, I knew, to create the kind of buzz that we needed to keep alive my hopes and aspirations for the Calumet. And so I started yet another venture and with it yet another learning experience: the booking and programming of the leading jazz musicians in the world.

By that time, the Tralfamadore, Buffalo's leading jazz venue since the mid-1970s, had discontinued its long standing jazz line-up and the jazz musicians and their agents were looking for another place to play in Buffalo. In the Fall of 1995 I stepped into that breach and launched what, for the next five to six years, became a bold and, if I may say so, intensely creative and energetic commitment to presenting some of the some of the world's best and least known jazz musicians to the Calumet. Among the former were Ray Brown, Milt Jackson, Andy Bey, Houston Person, Etta Jones, Art Farmer, John Hendricks, Susannah McCorkle, Chuck Mangione, Kevin Mahogany, Dakota Staton, Mose Allison, Richie Havens, Freddie Cole, Ahmad Jamal and McCoy Tyner. Among the latter were Diana Krall, Russell Malone, Benny Green, Christian McBride, James Carter, D.D. Jackson, Joshua Redman, Cyrus Chestnut and oh so many more.

These jazz-filled weekends were exhilarating. I and my friend and jazz aficionado, Patty Corrin, would plan the weekend ahead: when the artists would be arriving, who would pick them up and take them to their hotels; when they would do their sound-checks and rehearse. We were excited having these most extraordinary artists hanging around with us at the Calumet, having lunch, chewing the fat, running through their routines. And then there were the performances themselves: crowds of people of all shades and colors, lined up at the door, standing at the café bar, jostling each other for seats in the room. What a thrill. What an incredible sense of satisfaction, seeing in front of me the full flowering of my vision: The Irish Classical Theater with their theater patrons, the Third Room with its flock of young people and the Calumet Arts Café and their jazz fans, all filled to the brim with patrons.

Despite the excitement and the attention that jazz brought to our larger mission, transforming the Calumet into a jazz club was a decision, one that created a financial drain that weakened our whole business. For despite the reviews, the public attention, admiration and critical acclaim, not to mention all the fun that we were having, the money that we took in during jam-packed shows was invariably overwhelmed by the money that went out. The costs, most of them unseen by the public, were staggering. Fees to the musicians, plane fares, hotel rooms, meals, and ground transportation quickly added up. Then there were costs like renting a Steinway piano when musicians like Ahmad Jamal and McCoy Tyner insisted on playing one. What about advertising and promotion? Rates at *The News* were outrageous as were underwrites at WBFO. ARTVOICE was good but how many people did it really reach? Sometimes our fixed costs on a weekend of jazz ran to $5,000. So how many tickets at $20 each (we never charged more than that) would we have to sell to cover that? Could we sell 250 tickets over two nights? Maybe. Did we? Rarely. At the end of a fantastic weekend of music with Ahmad Jamal with crowds filling every nook and cranny of the place, Charlie turned to me and said "Dad .... With the amount of money you lost this weekend you could have flown to Paris first-class on the Concord and seen Jamal there." It was, he knew and I began to realize, bad business. All the "good money," he constantly reminded me, that was coming in from the doors at the Third Room, was going right out the doors of the Calumet Arts Café. Charlie was right. By the end of the 1990s, the financial stress was too much and, despite my highest hopes and aspirations, I had to finally pull the plug on our jazz programming. A wonderful, exhilarating, yet deeply frustrating and often heart-breaking chapter in my life had come to an end. I was totally drained and exhausted and when in 2001, Steve Calvaneso came to me and told me that he would like to lease the Calumet Arts Café and transform it into a restaurant he called "Bacchus," I, with great mixed emotions, reluctantly accepted his offer. The Calumet Arts Café had come to the end of the line.

• • •

In the meantime, however, I started another venture in the Calumet Building. It was 1998 and the O'Neills, their lease up in their space in the Calumet, were making plans to move their theater company to a bigger and better space on Main Street. Why not, my daughter Lydia said upon returning from a trip to Miami, open a Latin disco. By the late 1990s, Latin music and musicians like Ricky Martin, Gloria Estevan and others, were penetrating the white market. Why not here in Buffalo? It was with that in mind that we transformed the Irish Classical Theater, formerly Nick's Holly Farm, into "La Luna," Buffalo's first and only Latin dance club.

My vision was a mix of pre-Castro Havana and contemporary Miami, a place where the music of the former – boleros, son, and cha-cha would mix with the contemporary sounds of Puerto Rico and the Dominican Republic – salsa, merengue, bachata and, something new on the market called "reggaeton." I wanted to introduce these fabulous sounds to the larger population of Buffalo while at the same time, create a place within walking distance of the largely Hispanic West Side where people of that community could come and dance to their own music. I was excited, convinced that like the other programming that we had launched at the Calumet, the addition of La Luna would continue to highlight the significance of multi-ethnic cultural arts to the revitalization of the community. As the old century ended and the new one began, La Luna quickly became one of the hottest clubs in downtown.

A reporter for *Artvoice* wrote the following about La Luna:

> "Stepping into La Luna on a Saturday night, proper dress is required. It's not that baseball hats and sweatshirts are a bad thing; they just wouldn't look right amongst all the people crowded onto the dance floor of this hot spot dressed to the nines.. Entering you must maneuver through a packed house filled by a multicultural sea of people. A move to the back of the club carries one deeper and deeper onto the dance floor which shakes under the exuberant steps of experts and beginners alike." *Artvoice* November 29, 1999, p. 6)

I was proud that I had been able to create a new nighttime destination on Chippewa Street – that "boulevard of broken dreams" – where the music was Latin and the crowd, though primarily Latin, reflected a diversity that was mirrored in no other night club in the city. We were, indeed, healing and renewing the city and, in the process, as my old friends from the '70s said, "fixing this place." While we did close the Calumet Arts Café, leasing the space to "Bacchus" in 2001 the Third Room and La Luna thrived for ten more years until in 2010, in a deal that would have left even that talkative gentleman, Charlie LaRussa, speechless, we accepted an offer to sell the building that we simply could not refuse and, after more than 20 years, we moved off of Chippewa Street.

Acknowledgements

My Brother Tony: By the mid-1980's my brother's work in SOHO had triggered the unimagined revitalization of that area. By then he was onto South Beach in Miami. (For more on Tony see notes to Chapter 7 below)

Charlie LaRussa was right. A book that came out 7 years later, Shawn Lay's *Hooded Knights on the Niagara* (NYU, 1995) corroborated Mr. LaRussa.

Joanna Angie went on to create the Buffalo Arts Studio in the TriMain Building changing forever the way people in Buffalo thought about artists and the work they do. She and I have remained good pals throughout the years. In addition to Joanna, **Meg Corcoran**, an amazing art teacher and extraordinary muralist, contributed wall art that set the tone for the Calumet.

Jamie Moses: Like Joanna, Jamie's work as publisher of the free weekly *Artvoice* from 1990-2015, changed the way Buffalonians thought about and talked about the arts and their impact on public policy. For many years, it was the only professional print competition to *The Buffalo News* distributed throughout the Buffalo metropolitan area. For 26 years *Artvoice* hosted the "Arties" Awards, an event created by its theater editor Anthony Chase to celebrate excellence in local theater and to raise funds for AIDS organizations. Along with the Arties, the Give For Greatness campaign, and other Artvoice events, the paper raised and donated over $1 million to local charities. *Artvoice* also ran an annual "Best of Buffalo" competition where readers were able to nominate and vote for their favorite individuals, groups, or companies in dozens of categories including food, people, theater, fine art, and retail. All back issues of *Artvoice* can be read in the Grosvenor Room at the Buffalo and Erie County Public Library.

City Hall: The relationships I built at City Hall, though often frustrating, were a critical part of my education about Buffalo. Most helpful during those years were my old pal Joe Ryan, Mayor Masiello's Commissioner of Community Development and my former student at Empire State College, Joe Tanzella from St. Lucy's Parish, then the Commissioner of Assessment.

The Theater District Association to which I belonged throughout the 1990s, has made a huge impact on the creation and the continued success of the entire Theater District. "Curtain Up," after more than 40 years, remains, the iconic event of Buffalo's theater season.

The 3rd Room: Kevin McNamara was very helpful to us during the early days of Chippewa Street's iconic watering hole. And hats off also to Angelo Canna.

The O'Neills: Vincent and Josephine in particular (Chris moved to New York in the early 1990s) were invaluable partners to me at the Calumet. I was thrilled at the role that I was able to play in their development and proud and happy to have them both as my friends.

Thanks also to **Jeanne Donovan** who gave us permission to use her marvelous painting of the Calumet Building with the ICTC comfortably ensconced.

Jazz at the Calumet: Very helpful and supportive of my efforts to establish the Calumet as a serious jazz showcase were Al Wallack at WEBR, Bert Gambini, John Werrick and Macy Favor at WBFO, Jamie Moses at *Artvoice*, Jeff Simon and Mary Kunz at *The Buffalo News*. Patti Corrin, who as a teenager in the early '60s heard some of the great jazz artists at the time at such local clubs as The Moonglow, The Revillot and the Pine Grill, served as our jazz ambassador extraordinaire while David Sipos tuned and prepared our piano. In addition, I want to acknowledge some of the dozens of local musicians we had the pleasure of presenting at the Calumet, among them Doug "Trigger" Gaston, Abdul Rachman Qadir, Rodney Appleby, Jimmy Gomes, Al Tinney, Sabu Adeyollah, Joe Madison and oh so many more

La Luna: We worked closely with Buffalo's West Side Puerto Rican community when we opened La Luna in 1996. First among equals was Frankie Perez, my old friend from Virginia Street during the '70s. Also helpful were Ramon Rodriguez, publisher of the weekly newspaper, *Panorama Hispano*. Chito Olivenzia, scion of the influential Olivenzia family and director of the Olivenzia Family provided help and counsel. Mostly it was the musicians on the West Side that became part of our "family" at the Calumet and La Luna: the elder of Latin music in Buffalo, Juan Texidor; the old-school singer JaJo Rodriquez; Frankie Quinones and Wendell Rivera, *congero tremendo*, and Riccardo Ferrer, timbalero. In addition we worked closely with Ephraim Burgos, proprietor of the best-known hair salon on Niagara Street and a fantastic DJ.

The quote about downtown is from *City on the Edge*, p. 365.

The quote from *Artvoice* is from November, 29, 1999, p. 6.

CHAPTER 7

What Would Grandma Rosie Do?

How everyday wisdom brought sanity to downtown development plans

While there was much that I, as the owner of the Calumet, could do to make my business successful, I came to realize that the fate of my business was tied to the fate of downtown. The condition of the streets, crime, traffic, parking, zoning and the like – what was built where, who got what subsidies and how much – were all critical issues each one of which on its own had the power to derail the work I was so earnestly engaged in. Unlike the academics and policy analysts I knew, I had real skin in the game – my own money and sweat equity. I had to jump in and beginning in 1990 I did, becoming an active, engaged, somewhat pushy and opinionated participant in the often cantankerous, but vital, debates about how to improve downtown Buffalo.

Under the rubric of a straw organization I created in 1992, called "The Idea Center at the Calumet," I began to write letters and press releases which called for a new approach to thinking about urban planning and design in downtown Buffalo. My first endeavor was a call for the creation of a "Chippewa Street master plan."

While we had begun to create an entertainment destination at the Calumet, my hope for the street was that it would become a fully functional mixed-use district, integrated into a holistic concept of the entire central business district. I wanted the immediate area filled with apartments, stores, bars, restaurants, cafes, and arts and cultural activities. But to fulfill that vision, Chippewa Street needed to be understood as "a corridor, " I argued, one that joined the east side of the city with the west side, the Fruit Belt with the Lower West Side. The street was the most direct route between downtown and the airport, a direct link between the Theater District and the waterfront ("Canalside" as a term and as a place was at least fifteen years in the future). The streets of downtown, I argued at a time when Washington, Pearl, Franklin and Chippewa were all one-way, needed to be made two-way. Bring traffic back to Main Street. Think "nice" and "clean." Pick up the garbage, clean the streets, impose design standards, and, by all means, use public art – sculpture on the sidewalks, murals on the walls – to change the experience of being on Chippewa Street. Think Times Square, not Sixth Avenue.

I was confident and cocky, convinced that my knowledge and experience, plus my New Yorker's inherent sense of superiority, provided me with the intuition to know what was best for downtown Buffalo. Think big, like Daniel Burnham insisted, but don't, in the process, forget Mies Van der Rohe, who argued that "God and profit are in the details." Plus, there was always my Grandma Rosie.

Much of the wisdom in my family was, as is true for so many others, embodied in my grandmother, my mother's mother, a woman named Rosie Schwartz. Born in Russia in the early 1880s, Rosie came as a child to New York where she did the things immigrants women are often known for: she worked hard, raised a strong family and, for the more than 100 years that she lived, contained within her body and soul a wealth of wisdom that we all sought out and valued. When in doubt about marriage or divorce, business or politics, we all turned to Grandma Rosie. And when she died in 1990 and was no longer available to us, the question became "What would Rosie do?" Rooted in common sense and the mundane experiences of her daily life rather than a refined higher education, Rosie had a way of cutting through windy explanations and half-hearted defenses, a way of leading the petitioner to say, "You know, she's right. Grandma Rosie's right." As I became embroiled in issues of public policy during the 1990s, particularly those dealing with downtown development, I found that I was increasingly asking myself and others the same question that members of my family had been asking for generations: "What, would Grandma Rosie do?" (And what, too, would Jane Jacobs say!) This question was particularly relevant at the dawn of the 21st century when Buffalo faced three of the most critical development controversies in its history.

The first was the proposal for a new convention center floated by Erie County Executive Dennis Gorski in 1998. Gorski's proposal, resoundingly supported by the usual suspects in the downtown development community, called for the demolition of an eight and a half acre site between Main and Ellicott streets and Mohawk and the central library. The proposed convention center was a superblock on steroids, one that would have closed off several of the area's streets while demolishing most of the buildings on Washington and Ellicott Streets. With a project cost of upward of $200,000,000 in state and county money, the proposal for this new convention center was a slow-moving target, a *pinata* for those of us who cared about good urbanism. We jumped at the opportunity to derail it and in the process to continue our efforts to educate the public about how best to renew our city.

Tim Tielman took the first whack at it in the Spring of 1999 by dedicating a special edition of the *Buffalo Preservation Report* to the issue of the convention center. Tim's highly effective combination of dramatic written narrative and graphic illustration produced a scathing critique of the proposal. Under a large Hopperesque color photograph of the endangered Ferguson Electric Company building on Ellicott Street, Tim wrote an apocalyptic headline: "Death Star: In the Wrong Place, Convention Center Could Be A Killer." Calling it the "biggest planning mistake since the last convention center," Tim asked: "Do we demolish a neighborhood so a convention center can be attached to a hotel on the chance that it will appeal to the occasional visiting lardass from Dubuque? Or do we save that neighborhood, provide housing, services, entertainment and jobs: in other words a reason to live in Buffalo?" Luckily, Tim was not the only outraged person. Led by a Buffalo business and social icon, John Nussbaumer, a handful of us formed a not-for-profit called Citizens for Common Sense to fight the convention center.

Our argument against the proposed convention center dealt not only with its location but also with its feasibility. Simply put, Buffalo, we insisted, did not need a convention center. Therefore, we said, not one dollar of the public's money should be spent on it. Nussbaumer, a highly-regarded business-owner with an impeccable public persona, was convinced that he smelled a rat. "It seems to me," he told the press in late 1999, "that we have a small group of people trying to jam a convention center down our throats." The self-fulfilling prophecies of the feasibility studies were wrongfully based, we argued, rooted in data generated by downtown interests most likely to benefit from the project. The public subsidies were outrageous and besides, the project, by displacing over 500 people and $18 million in payroll and $60 million in sales made no sense. Nussbaumer asked incredulously: "You're replacing people making good money with part-time workers who will make minimum wages? Who would do that?" With their data credibly challenged by two outside consultants that we had hired, the proponents of the new convention center were left with little more than the argument that, if it was good enough for other cities, it was good enough for Buffalo. Keith Belanger, a vice-president at M&T Bank and long-time president of Buffalo Place, the downtown district business association, argued: "We're missing out. Our peer cities have made this kind of investment. It's time for us." Rich Geiger, the president of the Greater Buffalo Convention and Visitors Bureau, added his cheers: "We've got to start doing things to move this community forward."

Smeared with the "obstructionist" label, red meat to the development community, we argued that our ultimate goal was not only to prevent the construction of a new convention center, symbolic in our mind of an outdated and destructive way of thinking, but to advance a new, different, more sustainable form of downtown development. The eight and a half-acre "Mohawk Site," was not a wasteland of blight and abandonment as convention center advocates argued, but rather a viable district. A neon sign that read "Electric District" that hung in the window of an old saloon at the corner of Mohawk and Ellicott, provided inspiration and from then on that is what we called the area that we were trying to protect. We thought that with densely-packed buildings, small streets, low rents, and a downtown location, the district was ripe for renewal. It held promise for the kind of renewal that Jane Jacobs had written about in the early 1960s and what my brother Tony saw in SoHo in the late '70s. A mixture of uses, repeated small blocks, old buildings and high density were just the ingredients which produce urban renewal that works. Convinced that our cause was about the future, about seeding real and sustainable urban renewal, we organized a campaign. We were not willing to sacrifice what we felt was the future of downtown on the altar of a new convention center.

Our "Save the Electric District" campaign gathered momentum. Although we were opposed by *The Buffalo News*, we had support from *Artvoice* and other local groups. The capstone was a public meeting, which Nussbaumer organized at the Albright-Knox Art Gallery in January 2000. Hundreds filled the auditorium, and as many more were turned away. At a barb-filled panel discussion with Nussbaumer and me lined up against Rich Geiger from the Convention Bureau and Mark Mendell, president of Cannon Design, the architectural firm behind many of the "big projects" in the area, we went at it. What I opposed, I said, was not development but rather "bad development," the kind that turned its back on historical context, that ignored public opinion, and that required large amounts of public subsidy. I rejected the proponents of the convention center's characterization of the Mohawk site as "blighted." Suggesting that one person's "blight" is another's opportunity I pointed to my brother's efforts in such previously "blighted" areas as SoHo and South Beach, not to mention my own going-on-ten-year efforts on Chippewa Street. The characteristics that evoked disparagement from the proponents of the convention center were, I said, actually the preconditions for successful renewal of the Electric District. Because they offered opportunities to risk-taking, creative people, worn-down buildings (albeit with good bones), high vacancy rates, and low real estate values made fertile ground for rebirth.

Hearing my remarks that night, and the overwhelmingly positive response of the audience, was Republican County Executive-elect Joel Giambra who was in attendance. Shortly after he assumed office a few weeks later, Giambra announced that he was "kicking the convention center down the road." There would be another time, he said, to consider it. I'd like to think our passionate debating that night had something to do with his decision.

• • •

Those of us in Citizens for Common Sense didn't need to read Jane Jacobs to understand the importance of "eyes on the street," of high density, of old buildings and short blocks. We didn't need to read Ray Oldenburg to know that cafés, coffee shops, bookstores, bars, hair salons, and other hangouts are important in the lives of our city. We understood what Jan Gehl, the Danish architect and city planner, meant when he wrote that public spaces and public places count far more than buildings. We happily listened to urban planner Fred Kent talk about the marvelous serendipity of Bryant Park and the Union Square market in Manhattan. For us, the focus of urban regeneration was rooted in relationships, on people, on places for human interaction, and on connections. It was incredible to us that the chief policy makers in Buffalo still did not get this.

Most certainly I did. Encouraged by the bully pulpit that I was acquiring as a result of my work on Chippewa Street, I felt emboldened to broaden my attack, not just on the convention center, but on the process of planning as it was practiced by the administration of Mayor Anthony Masiello. In the fall of 1999, at the height of the battle over the convention center, I conjured up what I impishly called "The Calumet Institute." Housed, (I said, in a press release that was widely picked up by the local media,) at "The Idea Center" in the Calumet Building, "The Calumet Institute is," I wrote, "a newly formed group of people dedicated to the creation and implementation of ideas that stimulate, energize and enliven our community." Both "The Calumet Institute" and "The Idea Center" were, of course, housed only in my imagination, but as a letterhead it was impressive. Under that rubric, I began a decade long campaign of writing – of letters, of op-ed pieces and the like (remember, this was in the days before social media) – spelling out my thoughts about how best to, using a phrase that I came to embrace, "heal and renew" the Buffalo. The "Institute's" first salvo was a widely read piece that I wrote for the "My View" column in *The Buffalo News* in January of 2000 called: "Big Ideas have been disastrous; it's time to try some small ones."

Like any good battle, the one over the convention center forced me to wrestle with my own thoughts about how best to "heal and renew" our city. Mayor Masiello, despite his allegedly good intentions – "Tony's a great guy … you don't have to worry about Tone" – people said about the Mayor as if he were the head waiter at Sinatra's, a long-standing red-sauce restaurant where the politically connected hung out – knew nothing and cared less about what I understood as "good urbanism." What I considered his ignorance was reflected in January 2000 when he issued what he called a "strategic plan for downtown." Rooted in what I was convinced were outdated and obsolete solutions and strategies, I vowed to counter the Mayor's plan with my own. The Mayor had called a town meeting, a "working session," he called it, to share his master plan with the public. I meanwhile, under the umbrella of "The Calumet Institute," printed a report of my own, which I planned to hand out at the meeting. Standing in front of the old convention center, where the meeting was to be held, with an old newspaper boy's bag slung over my shoulder, I hawked my wares: "C'mon and get it. Hot off the press. Mark's response and critique to the mayor's plan for downtown." While many people accepted the handout, few, I am sure, read it. I, however, was very proud of that work and pleased with the *chutzpah* that I was able to muster to get it out there. On the cover of the twenty-odd page booklet was a reproduction of the world's best known image of public love, Robert Doisneau's photograph "The Kiss by the Hotel de Ville." Eager to strike a contrast in every way possible with the image of the city conveyed by the Mayor (his favorite was a view of the city's skyline, taken, it seemed, from ten thousand feet), I chose "The Kiss," representing as it does the importance, if not of love, certainly of human affection and connection in the revival and renewal of our downtown.

Downtown renewal, however, needed more than a kiss. With that in mind I outlined a set of ten principles which I argued should guide downtown redevelopment strategies. While recognized increasingly by planners throughout the urbanized world, the ideas that I outlined were either unknown or not cared about by local policy makers. They are:

1. History: The plans that we make and the projects that we pursue must be rooted in how our city has evolved. Be it out of respect for the city's buildings, its parks or its street-plan, our plans and projects must be rooted in our history.
2. Connectivity: Our existing downtown assets and resources – be they office buildings, theaters or neighborhoods – must be better joined so that a sense of wholeness and unity is created while enhancing opportunities of pedestrian interaction.
3. Taste: Our plan must recognize the importance of good taste. Namely, cleanliness and attention to aesthetic details must be a part of any and all ordinances created to implement this plan.
4. Street life: Without strong and vital streets our downtown will never be revitalized. No plan, no project should be approved that does not strengthen the fabric of the city at the place where the building and sidewalk meet: namely, the street.
5. Culture: Culture and the arts must be at the core of the plan. Existing cultural and arts organizations must be strengthened and new ones encouraged as a result of this plan.
6. Economic Development: No plan for downtown should be considered that does not deal with job creation and job skill enhancement.
7. Don't forget Delaware Avenue: Any plan for downtown must consider Delaware Avenue, at least from Niagara Square to North Street.
8. Question the subsidy: How much? How long? For whom?

9. Who's the customer? It is crucial that in thinking about and planning for downtown that we recognize and remember that "the end user" is not the tourist but rather those of us who live, work and raise our families here.
10. Don't be afraid of the dark!!!

Although never sure what impact my ideas were having, I was gratified that, when the idea of a new convention center had been finally put to rest by the new county executive in early 2000, Mark Mendell, the president of Cannon Design, added a post mortem to the convention center debate. "We don't have 500 Mark Goldmans in this town. I don't think that any town does … But, Mark notwithstanding, if you only make small moves you'll never make big ones." In a friendly conversation sometime later, I reminded Mr. Mendell that it was not "big projects" that I opposed, just "bad big projects." Bad big projects that violate context and history, and what I had come to regard as common sense and the wisdom learned on the streets of New York of Grandma Rosie.

Though he took it on the chin with the convention center, Mayor Masiello refused to change direction. Ever willing to do just about anything to bring credit to himself and to the city he loved, the mayor was always sweetening the pot. His deals always involved enormous public subsidies, sometimes cash, sometimes land, sometimes tax breaks, sometimes all of them together. The turn of the last century (Masiello left office in January of 2003) was filled with these projects, "deals" really, most all of which failed: the convention center; the notorious Adelphia "deal" with the Rigas family, plus all the hare-brained schemes to put something, it times it seems as if anything would do, into the old "Aud" site on lower Main Street. Of all of Masiello's efforts to bring development to downtown none was worse in my mind than the "Pact" that he and Governor George Pataki signed with the Seneca Nation in 2001 to bring casino gambling to downtown Buffalo. I was appalled at this and in a passionate chapter in my 2007 book *City on the Edge* which I called "Strange Bedfellows," I wrote in detail about this nefarious bargain. It is, in my humble opinion, well worth reading today and I urge you to do so.

• • •

The second pivotal planning battle of the turn of the new century occurred at the Inner Harbor, the area known today as "Canalside." Since the mid-1970s, there had been countless proposals to bring new life to the city's long obsolete commercial waterfront. It was not until the desperate years of the late '60s and even into as late as the '80s, however, that major publicly driven efforts were made to "renew" it. It was during this period that old neighborhoods – the Terrace and Lower Niagara Street – had been obliterated, replaced by acres of rehashed suburban notions of progress: hotels and office buildings surrounded by parking lots; picturesque, but isolated, single family water-front homes; a massive mall-like restaurant and a marina pockmarked with strange, concrete bunker-like structures. Where, many of us wondered at that time, was the history? Where was the authenticity? Didn't anybody know better? Didn't anybody care? By the late '80s and early '90s, under the auspices of an agency Governor Mario Cuomo and Erie County Executive Gorski called "The Horizons Waterfront Commission," planning for the area at the foot of Main Street – the "Inner Harbor" – was fast tracked.

While there was uncertainty about what exactly would and should be done there, in anticipation that some work was imminent, archeological excavations which had begun in the Spring of 1999, revealed significant remains from what history had known as the "Commercial Slip." However tiny, there was no body of water in the history of our city more important than the Commercial Slip at the western terminus of the Erie Canal. For it was here that the waters of the Canal met the waters of Lake Erie and in the process laid the economic foundations for the birth and development of Buffalo. By the early 20th century, however, the Slip was obsolete. In 1926 the terminus of the Erie Canal in Buffalo was finally closed, a massive sewer drain was placed down the middle of the Slip and the Slip itself was paved over. But now, in the late 1990s, the archeological project was uncovering remains of the Commercial Slip. As word spread throughout the State, devotees of Erie Canal history descended upon Buffalo to see it for themselves, making a case for its excavation and preservation.

Governor Pataki and Mayor Masiello were not impressed. In September 1999, Pataki came to Buffalo to announce the State's plan for the Inner Harbor. He'd allocated $27 million for it and could not, he insisted, afford the extra $10 or so million it would take to remove the sewer drain and restore the Commercial Slip. Over the anguished cries of preservationists and Erie Canal devotees, the Commercial Slip, the Governor insisted, would be paved over. Built instead would be a "replica slip" at which the original rocks from the wall of the slip would be displayed as "sculptural elements." The location of the original slip would be highlighted by a row of trees, which would be planted there. In addition, Pataki's plan called for the construction of a "period style bridge" to be built over the "faux" Commercial Slip. Pataki was pleased. His plan, he said was "based on history." "Too often," he said, "great communities like Buffalo turned away from the past. We will reseize (*sic*) history and build on it." Mayor Masiello chimed in: "I believe our future is tied to our past."

Well, that was all Tim Tielman and his passionate disciples at the Preservation Coalition needed to hear. A month later, in October of 1999, citing federal requirements that the discovery of significant archeological findings required that a new environmental impact statement be submitted, Tielman' s coalition filed a suit in federal court demanding that the state comply with federal law.

Buttressed by the expert testimony of leading historians, Tim's arguments before US District Judge William M. Skretney were persuasive. Mincing no words, Tim argued that the Horizons Commission plan "is firmly in the 'atomic bomb' school of planning. It, like any plan from the 1960s, believes that history must be destroyed in order to move forward. That is a signal lack of imagination and totally out of touch with public preference and national trends."

Tim's testimony was reinforced by University of Buffalo history professor David Gerber who argued that the Horizons Commission plan was "destructive of the existing city and is contrary to the public interest. It ignores the context of the surrounding city, is oblivious to the historic character of the city, destroys the Inner Harbor site that is its focus, wastes a great deal of money and is so poorly conceived that it undermines its own goals." In March of 2000, Judge Skretney found in favor of Tielman and the preservationists: the archeological findings were indeed significant and, therefore, he ruled, New York State was required to undertake a supplementary new environmental impact review.

While Tim and the preservationists won that battle, the war over what exactly should be built had just begun. It was in an effort to win that war that Tim and the Preservation Coalition launched an aggressive, ingenious grassroots campaign. Combining a variety of guerilla tactics that they had perfected over the years – a massive signature campaign, the posting of "Save Don't Pave" signs on lawns in neighborhoods all over the city and at any number of public meetings. Tim, with key support from *Buffalo News* columnist Donn Esmonde, made the case for historical accuracy on the Inner Harbor. The ruins should be revealed, the Central Wharf rebuilt, and the historic streets restored. Above all, Tim and the coalition insisted that the Commercial Slip, Buffalo's "sacred site," the exact spot where the waters of the lake met the waters of the canal, should be restored and re-watered. Maybe even, John Montague of the Buffalo Maritime Center suggested, a replica of The Seneca Chief, the original 1825 packet boat, should be built and placed in the Commercial Slip for public viewing. Tim had another idea: when asked what he thought should fill the empty spaces in an historically authentic "Canalside." Tim made a suggestion that clearly somebody heard. "In this zone," he said, "there should be an ample supply of moveable chairs. That way people can seek sun and shadow freely and congregate or sit alone."

Tielman's efforts again saved the day when in June of 2000, County Executive Giambra, who just months before had killed plans for the new convention center, ended the debate at Canalside when he convinced Mayor Masiello and Governor Pataki to sign a memo of understanding that any and all plans for the Inner Harbor must be rooted in the history of the 12.5 acre site. Momentum for an historically accurate plan grew still more, following a two-day long event in September 2000 sponsored by the Baird Foundation, which focused on the historical significance of the Inner Harbor site. Under the pressure of Judge Skretney's court order and the recently signed MOU, Governor Pataki's Empire State Development Corporation now commissioned a new master plan for the site. Prepared by the local architectural firm of Flynn and Battaglia and based largely on Tielman's concepts for the site, the 2004 plan called for the re-watering of the "Commercial Slip," building the Central Wharf, the preservation of the ruins and the historic streets as well as the construction of two historically authentic truss bridges across the Commercial Slip. In addition, the 2004 plan called for the creation and implementation of design guidelines that would maintain the historic character of what now was increasingly being referred to as "Canalside." In November 2004, Governor Pataki again came to Buffalo, this time to announce his support for the new plan and his commitment to fund it.

In the meantime, Brian Higgins, elected to the US Congress from the 27th Congressional District beginning in 2005, was playing the lead role negotiating a deal with the New York Power Authority. In exchange for a fifty-year renewal of its license to produce and distribute electrical power, NYPA guaranteed $279 million to various government entities in Buffalo and Erie County to improve their waterfronts. With Higgins' relicensing agreement with NYPA in place, Governor Pataki proceeded to create a new state entity whose primary function would be to determine how best to spend what people were now calling the "NYPA money." Created in 2005, the agency, all of whose members were appointed by the Governor, was called the Erie Canal Harbor Development Corporation (ECHDC). High on the agenda of this new State corporation was the effort, in the word of the day, to "lure" Bass Pro, the nation's largest hunting and fishing company, to Buffalo's waterfront. Suddenly, there was a new "elephant in the room," the third development challenge that those of us concerned with history faced at the turn of the century: Bass Pro.

• • •

The effort to land Bass Pro was part-and-parcel of a long-standing effort by the administration of Mayor Masiello and County Executive Gorski to use lavish large sums of public funds to entice private developers to either stay in or come to downtown Buffalo. They'd done it with the Bills and the Sabres during the 1990s, and would have done it with the Rigas Family until their company, Adelphia Communications, went broke and the Rigases went to prison. The effort to lure Bass Pro to the waterfront was simply the last, most desperate, item on Masiello's bucket list.

There had been talk among the inside set about Bass Pro for several years. The founder of the company, a man named "Johnny" Morris was good friends with Bob and Mindy Rich, the billionaire owners of Rich Products. They were neighbors in Islamorada, Florida where the Riches lived long enough each year to avoid New York State income taxes. Once the Riches began to spread the word that their friend was interested in a Buffalo site for his store, politicians and economic development hot shots from Albany to Buffalo began to tout the advantages of a waterfront location for the "mammoth sporting goods complex."

There were all kinds of offers considered and made in what seemed to be an increasingly desperate effort to "lure" Bass Pro to the Inner Harbor. From 2001 to 2003, there were myriad contacts between Mayor Masiello and Johnny Morris, each visiting the other, sometimes in Buffalo, sometimes in Islamorada. After several years of various trial balloons, by the Fall of 2004, the outlines of a deal were in place. In November, Governor Pataki made yet another of his regular "announcement" trips to Buffalo. He'd put together, he said, an $80 million package, a combination of state, federal and local funds that would leverage the coming to downtown Buffalo of Bass Pro. He would put it, he said, inside the old Auditorium, empty since 1996. As a result, he said, "the Buffalo Waterfront will be transformed." When "Bass Pro comes to town," he crowed, "they don't just open a store ... they change that town." County Executive Joel Giambra, needing to support the Republican governor, added his voice to the growing chorus. Bass Pro was, he said, "just the hook that the waterfront needs." Buffalo's new mayor, Byron Brown, concurred: "Bass Pro brings people – three million visitors a year – sales tax dollars and" ... yes, he actually said it, "hope."

The Buffalo News was, as always when it came to projects like this, a mindless cheerleader. Under headlines like "Hope Soars with Bass Pro" and "Bass Pro Key to Revitalizing Waterfront," *The News* conveyed the impression that Bass Pro was a *fait accompli*, a project which would accomplish what over fifty years of efforts to revitalize Buffalo's waterfront had not.

With the newly-discovered pot of "NYPA money," generous pledges of support from state and federal sources, plus a new state agency – the ECHDC – now ready to spend it, there was nothing stopping the campaign to bring Bass Pro to the Buffalo waterfront. Indeed, it seemed to many that the primary, if not the sole, function of the newly created ECHDC was to do just that. Why else, some wondered, would Mindy Rich, the wife of Bob Rich, Jr, Johnny Morris' Florida fishing buddy, Maureen Hurley, Executive Vice President of Rich Products, and Larry Quinn, Managing Partner of the Buffalo Sabres and ardent Bass Pro advocate, have been appointed to the ECHDC's board?

But where to put it? For years, there was talk of transforming the old Aud into a gigantic entertainment destination, a home to Bass Pro, a new hotel and an "intermodal" transportation center. But the cost was prohibitive, and Johnny Morris wanted something new, flashy and dramatic for his hunting and fishing store. So, with money in hand and the authority, through the ECHDC to spend it, Morris and the ECHDC board began "casting" around for a new location. Why not, Board member Quinn suggested, a location directly on the Waterfront, on the edge of the water itself, on the exact site that the 2004 plan had designated for the Central Wharf? Bass Pro liked it and *The Buffalo News* trumpeted the new location too. The problem was, Tim Tielman and his increasingly well-oiled machine of preservationists argued, it violated the 2004 plan which, per Judge Skretny's ruling, called for historical authenticity at that site. "Take one square foot of the Central Wharf," Tielman warned the ECHDC, and "we'll sue you." Opposition in the community was intense. Donn Esmonde, who had been writing passionately about the importance of preserving history at the site, was incensed. In a *Buffalo News* column on July 1, 2007, (the Bass Pro controversy seemed to be dragging on forever!) Esmonde called the proposed building a "Wegman's size big-box" on one of Buffalo's most "sacred sites."

Increasingly wary not only of Tielman's use of the federal courts as well as his uncanny ability to mobilize public opinion on behalf of preservation, the ECHDC began in the fall of 2007 to abandon their interest in the Central Wharf site. Without a site for their pet project, they looked at the Aud again. This time, they were interested in the site, not the building. What if, the ECHDC suggested, the Aud were demolished and then, on its site, a brand-new Bass Pro were to be built? The powers-that-be-liked the idea and, in late 2007, the City of Buffalo sold the Aud to the ECHDC for $1. In early 2008, demolition of the structure began, the $35 million cost to be covered by the state.

There was nothing good about the Bass Pro deal. It was a ghastly piece of public policy, violating nearly every principle of modern urban development. Conceived behind closed doors by a group of private citizens selected by the governor for their insider connections, funded by dollars that belonged to the public, rooted in an architectural plan that flew in the face of any appreciation for and understanding of the historical context of the site, the notion of subsidizing a privately-owned hunting and fishing store on the site of the old Aud, was unimaginably irrational. It was an insult to all the work that so many of us had been doing to heal and renew the fabric of the city. I was appalled by every aspect of the project. In mid-2009, I lent my support to the effort to derail the fast-moving Bass Pro project by joining a lawsuit to stop it.

The opposition to the Bass Pro project was overwhelming, and in response to the growing public pressure, Congressman Brian Higgins, on July 19, 2010, issued an ultimatum imposing a fourteen-day deadline for reaching a final agreement with Bass Pro. Faced with mounting hostility and continued delays, Bass Pro announced on July 31 that it was dropping out. Their flirtation with Buffalo was, we all rejoiced, finally over.

Having played a part in the demise of the Bass Pro project, I wanted to use this opportunity to present to the people of Buffalo ideas about waterfront development that I thought might point us in whole new directions. I wanted to bring additional players to the table, not the planners, politicians and developers who had always determined the rules of the game. I wanted to engage Buffalo's "creative class," the artists and the imaginative thinkers that I had had the great pleasure of working with at the Calumet. I wanted to take the discussion out of the mouths of public policy makers and put it into those of the artists and creative thinkers. These were the people with visions for the future, who I felt needed to be at the proverbial "table."

In order to bring this kind of sensibility to thinking about the waterfront in the wake of the collapse of the Bass Pro deal, I organized a conference called "Inspirations and Aspirations: Imagining Buffalo's Waterfront." I wanted to hold it in a large, public space. For this purpose, there was no place better than City Honors: a magnificent, historic building set high on a hill. With that in mind I booked the auditorium for the afternoon of Saturday, November 6, 2010.

First, I wanted my brother to come. Tony was a passionate, inspiring speaker who could bring an audience to tears with the compelling way that he spoke about cities and the role of history and art in their well-being. Tony had become a nationally-recognized leader in the preservation world, internationally known for his daring, seemingly instinctual understanding of how cities worked and what to do about fixing them. (The week before he came to our conference he was presented with the Crowninshield Award for life-time achievement, the highest honor awarded by the National Trust for Historic Preservation.) I also wanted Fred Kent, the founder of my favorite "place-making" organization, Project for Public Spaces, to be there. I'd been following Fred for years and, along with our own Tim Tielman, there was nobody who understood and thought more clearly about the problems of the city than Fred Kent.

I wanted artists too, people whose work would inspire the audience to think creatively about Buffalo's waterfront. I wanted the sounds of water to fill the auditorium, so I commissioned Brian Wantuch to create a soundscape based on audio recordings that he made of the rushing waters of the Niagara River. I wanted to make a statement of bringing new ideas to old, cast-off spaces and materials, so I commissioned Dennis Maher to create one. He built an enormous assemblage of long-lost materials in his studio, and then brought it to the City Honors lobby where it greeted people as they came in. And I wanted something elegant and balletic, combining the movements of dance and puppetry, so I commissioned Michele Costa to build a set and then perform an abstract puppet performance that she created for our event, called "Here."

I got the word out, sending emails to anybody I could. A full-page spread in ARTVOICE the week of the conference helped, but as a veteran of promoting events, I knew how hard it was to fill the seats. With no idea what to expect, we opened the doors at City Honors at about 1pm. Within minutes, people poured in. By 2 pm, the 700-seat auditorium was completely full. It was so inspiring, I said in my opening remarks that we had, "not a meeting but a movement."

The audience listened first to Brian's powerful soundscape then watched Michele's enchanting puppet performance. They were warmed up and prepared to think creatively about how to fix Buffalo's waterfront. Fred Kent spoke first. Projecting dozens of slides, not of buildings and other images "fit for aviators and birds," but rather of children playing in spray fountains, of adults sitting on benches eating ice-cream, of people watching an outdoor movie in Bryant Park in Manhattan and of hundreds more milling around the temporary structures in Union Square. In his quiet, conversational manner, Fred was showing us how successful places were made, not by buildings but by people doing things and having fun. That was the way to rebuild Buffalo's waterfront, he said. Not only did it work but it was, introducing a phrase that ten years later is still the watch word for waterfront planning in Buffalo, "lighter, quicker, cheaper." "Remember that phrase," he said: "lighter, quicker, cheaper." (Inspired by similar thinking, seventeen years earlier, in 1993, our own Tim Tielman had announced that his "Historic Buffalo Plan was "Better, Faster, Cheaper.")

And then Tony took the stage. I'd taken him that morning to the collection of massive grain elevators that stood empty just off the Ohio Street Bridge. Rick Smith, the owner of the elevators had plans to integrate them into an ethanol plant he was hoping to develop there. I wanted Tony to see them first. I knew he'd be overwhelmed by them and thought that, if anybody could get Rick Smith to think differently about them, Tony could. On Saturday morning, Rick took us through these marvelous structures. Tony said little at the time, but he was taking it all in, thinking, pondering, as we made our way through the dirt-strewn site.

If there was anybody who could champion the value of preserving an historic streetscape, it was my brother Tony. Crying out against projects like Bass Pro, he implored the rapt audience to "save your heritage. Protect it like you would your children." He then shifted gears and talked about how art and artists transform our cities. Citing the work that he was doing in Wynwood in Miami, he turned to Rick Smith's grain elevators. "These are your canvases. Your Sistine Chapel.

Treat them that way. Every one of them. All of them," he insisted, "should bear the mark of the world's best public artists." Upon concluding his talk, my brother stood there, delighted by the standing ovation that he received.

As for me, I was thrilled and exhausted. I knew we had done something good, but exactly what I knew not. By the end of 2010, with Bass Pro finally "dead in the water," the ECHDC retained Fred Kent and the Project for Public Spaces as a place-making consultant for the Inner Harbor, now known officially as "Canalside." Over the next several months, PPS staff, working with the public, developed a master plan for the area which became the template ECHDC still uses today. By the Spring of 2011, Rick Smith had given up on his ethanol plant and, working with me on a program called "Against the Grain," planned and presented a series of music and dance programs that branded what my brother called "Silo City" as an arts performance venue.

Our meeting at City Honors brought a renewed belief that the people of the city not only cared the most but knew the most about what was best for Canalside and their waterfront. Responding to the energy of the meeting, the ECHDC created a new planning process, one that promised to be far more transparent and responsive to public opinion. It was, Fred Kent said, "place making," an approach to renewing the city that was rooted not in building buildings but rather in creating programs. The function of place making is to create as many opportunities as possible for socializing in public places, for eating, for relaxing, for meeting and mingling, and for just plain hanging-out. It is programming, not big-ticket construction projects, that attracts people to places. Construction had been replaced by "place making" and "Build it and they will come" by "lighter, quicker, cheaper." It was a brand new day. Those of us who had fought so hard for so long for an organic approach to waterfront planning and development rejoiced.

Out with Bass Pro and in with Adirondack chairs. In an unspoken homage to Tim Tielman, at our insistence the ECHDC bought 200 of them. After we painted them in bright primary colors, they were placed randomly around Canalside. In July 2011, Donn Esmonde wrote a column in The *Buffalo News* called "Giving the public what it wants on the waterfront." "There's some irony," I told him, "that the major economic development success story in our community this year amounts to $5,000 worth of Adirondack chairs. It's the Adirondack chairs, stupid!" Those Adirondack chairs filled with people doing nothing more than "hangin' out," laid the foundation for the creation at Canalside of what would quickly become one of our region's most popular attractions. They had, I crowed only half in jest, done more to revise the waterfront than anything since the completion of the Erie Canal. My Grandma Rosie would have been pleased.

Acknowledgements

Donn Esmonde, intrepid *Buffalo News* reporter/columnist who brought preservation onto the front pages of the paper.

Tim Tielman: If there has been a "Renaissance" in Buffalo, it is due largely to the work of the city's preservation movement. Tim has been the conscience of that movement since he and Susan McCartney started the Preservation Coalition in the mid-1980s. For years considered an outlier and "an obstructionist," the favored term for those who questioned the development plan du jour, Tim has become the go-to-guy for any and all Western New Yorkers interested in how to do urbanism right. For a wonderful interview with Tim see this one from the Investigative Post in 2013: ***https://www.investigativepost.org/2013/01/20/interview-preservationist-tim-tielman/***

Back copies of *ArtVoice* (see particularly the articles by Hank Bromley called "Convention Center Follies" January and February, 2000 editions) and the *Preservation Report* housed in the Grosvenor Room at the Buffalo and Erie County Public Library. *Artvoice* provided the most extensive coverage of this issue.

John Nussbaumer: Not used to the spot-light, John stepped right in during the campaign to derail the plan to build a new convention center. He provided sensible, straight-forward and critical help and advice during that most significant effort.

Fred Kent: Fred founded Project for Places in 1975 which under his leadership has become one of the world's best known urban design and placemaking "think tanks." Working with Mayor John Lindsay in New York, Fred was one of the founders of Earth Day in 1970. He has been an important colleague and personal friend for many years.

Steve Halpern: "A working-class kid from the Bronx," political scientist, lawyer, community activist and first-class friend, Steve has been a permanent fixture in the landscape of my life in Buffalo. During our efforts to “sink” Bass Pro, Steve offered strategic legal counsel and sound moral thinking.

Brian Higgins: There’d be no “Canalside,” no “Outer Harbor” not much of anything on the Waterfront without the passion and dedication of Congressman Higgins.

CHAPTER 8

The Buffalo Story

History and heritage as the building blocks of community

It has been Buffalo's history and my passionate study of it that has led me to become irrevocably attached to Buffalo, wedded to the present and dedicated to the future of this city. My knowledge of our history has made me a better citizen; more committed and concerned. If the study of our history has had that effect on me would it not, I begin to think, have the same on others too? Could not the study of our city's history become a communal movement in which the people of Buffalo, themselves, became connected to their common past, strengthening their sense of citizenship and in the process tightening the ties that bound them to each other and to their community? It was with this in mind that in 2013 I formed a not-for-profit corporation which I called "The Friends of the Buffalo Story."

The initial focus of our work was at Canalside where, several years earlier Tim Tielman's efforts had resulted in a series of archeological digs that had uncovered and revealed significant elements of the original canal, particularly the Commercial Slip and The Ruins. Here, at this most dramatic and authentic historical site in Buffalo, the city's sacred site where the waters of the Atlantic Ocean were "wed" with those of Lake Erie, was, I felt, the perfect place for the Friends to begin our work by telling the story of the Erie Canal. What if, I wondered, we created for this site a performance piece that told, right here, in the exact spot where it actually happened, the incredibly important story of the completion of the Erie Canal? Would not that be a powerful way to educate and to entertain the people of Buffalo? The Erie Canal Harbor Development Corporation agreed and with their support we planned the production of a performance piece at the Ruins and the Commercial Slip for the summer of 2016. It was to be called "The Wedding of the Waters".

Since the purpose of the piece was to educate as well as to entertain, I wanted "Wedding" to serve as a model for the best use of theater as a tool to teach the city's history. We started with the cast, all amateurs drawn from different sectors of the community. For over a week we worked together studying maps, photos and other documents that would help us learn about the people and events that shaped the early history of the canal. Then, based on what we had learned, we created a plot, chose the characters and identified the significant events. Following that, we "devised" a script that was not written, nor memorized, but rather "learned."

Under the spectacular direction of James Leaf, a close family friend and noted actor/director, we actually staged a wedding. The actors, each playing historical characters in the story – DeWitt Clinton, Jesse Hawley, Samuel Wilkeson and the rest – were "guests" at the wedding, (the "groom" being Mr. Lake Erie, the "bride," Ms. Atlantic Ocean), acting out the story in a series of vignettes. The audience too, was brought into the show, prompted to interrupt the proceedings by barking questions to the "guests" that they had been given earlier. Raw and raucous, for sure, somehow, thanks to the guiding hand of director Leaf and a dedicated cast of community actors, "Wedding" worked. The show started at dusk as our large ensemble, led by a rollicking "wedding band" consisting of six "funksters," marched across the trellis bridge down into The Ruins. The upbeat, celebratory nature chronicling of the key historical events in the story was given a tense and dramatic touch when, at night's fall, one of the historical figures of the era, one of the "uninvited" guests" – the great Seneca leader Red Jacket – entered the piece as a wedding crasher. Red Jacket was perfectly played by a man named Stone Horse Lone Goman, a celebrated member of the Seneca Nation who we recruited to play the part. Goman is a ripped body builder and covered head to toe in tattoos. A student of Seneca history and culture, Goman is a descendent of the great Red Jacket and was thrilled to have the opportunity to play him in our piece. Wearing a bright red jacket designed specifically for this occasion, Goman/ Red Jacket, standing ramrod straight in the bow of a small authentic canal trawler (built and designed for the occasion by John Montague's Maritime Society of Buffalo … the Friends of the Buffalo Story was nothing if not collaborative!) was rowed across the waters of the Slip, a lantern in one hand, a rifle in the other. Amid exaggerated "oohs and ahhs" uttered by the large audience and a suddenly frightened wedding party, Goman landed at the edge of the Slip. From there he made a slow and ominous entrance onto the stage at The Ruins, taking his time, a spotlight highlighting his steely eyes as he glared at the "invited" guests and cast alternating glances at the audience. Moving among them, Goman, an accomplished performer with a cavernous voice, delivered a powerful soliloquy in which he drew on the writings of Red Jacket himself, delivering a devastating critique of the Erie Canal and its impact on the people of the Seneca Nation. Though skeptical Goman/Red Jacket did finally agree to join the wedding party and in a joyous, celebratory theatrical outpouring, the "wedding" was concluded. We had joined the waters of the Atlantic Ocean and of Lake Erie and in the process made possible the birth of Buffalo. Bottles of champagne were popped open, our band of funksters played while members of the cast and the audience celebrated together.

While some questioned the accuracy of the piece and others raised questions about its professionalism, I was pleased with the outcome of "Wedding of the Waters." We had transformed The Ruins, so recently destined for a permanent burial, into what is now one of the city's most cherished outdoor performance venues. As significantly, we had created a model of devised theater whereby the people of this city could, in ways that were both educational and entertaining, learn and tell the Buffalo Story. What a way to connect people to their past and, I hoped, to their future too.

• • •

For many years I'd thought of Buffalo as a set of distinct, largely self-contained neighborhoods, villages really, places like Black Rock, where for so many years so many of the city's residents had lived clustered, relatively isolated lives. This way of thinking has exerted a powerful influence on how the people of Buffalo view themselves and their city, leading to the existence in Buffalo of an intense attachment to places that is both nostalgic and real. Rooted in distinctions of race, class and ethnicity, the tradition of separate neighborhoods has had a mixed historical impact on the contemporary city, creating, on the one hand, a strong sense of pride and strength and, on the other, a strong sense of exclusion. It was not really until the school desegregation case (described above) that efforts were made to create a new identity for Buffalo, a pluralistic one in which, the advocates of desegregation hoped, a strong sense of neighborhood identity would exist side-by-side with a new sense of community, one rooted in the Spirit of

'76, where "out of many" there would be "one." Could we not honor, value and celebrate the strength of our local neighborhood traditions and, still, at the same time, come together as a unified, urban community? This is the question that Judge Curtin asked in 1976 and that I asked thirty-plus years later as I began to explore what I called "The Ferry Street Corridor Project."

For years I'd been thinking about creating a city-wide public history project, one that would reach into the nooks and crannies of neighborhoods all over the city. Uncertain about how to organize and implement, let alone fund, such an ambitious city-wide public history project, I was given another idea when one evening in the Spring of 2014 I attended an event called the "Well-Rounded People's Party," hosted by Barrett Gordon, the program director of a tiny, yet ingenious community arts project called "The Wash Project".

The Wash Project had its origins in a small laundromat owned by a Burmese immigrant named Zaw Win located in the heart of the emerging Burmese neighborhood on Massachusetts Avenue on Buffalo's West Side. Laundromats are natural gathering places in low-income neighborhoods, places where people spend hours doing their laundry. Eager to create a social center for neighborhood youth, Zaw wanted to put a pool table in the corner but not knowing where and how to find one, he approached my son Charlie (there were few people on the streets of the West Side who did not know Charlie). Within days Charlie had arranged to have a second-hand pool table delivered to Zaw's laundromat. The pool table was an instant success and soon, in addition to the Burmese women doing their laundry, the laundromat was becoming a popular neighborhood hang-out. A "place-making" light went off in my head. Why not expand the list of activities at the Laundromat by creating a series of arts and cultural programs and events? I talked to my friend, long-time community activist Chuck Massey about it and, instantly and instinctively he got it. And so, with a small grant from AmeriCorps in the summer of 2012 we opened The WASH project, a tiny, all-purpose arts center nestled within the confines of Zaw's laundromat.

The director of WASH was Barrett Gordon. Barrett is an extraordinary arts organizer with an instinctive sense of how to transform barren spaces into exciting places. Drawing on his contacts in Buffalo's vibrant grass-roots arts scene, Gordon recruited some of the leading poets, writers, musicians to volunteer their time, quickly creating a full menu of arts activities within the unique confines of Zaw Win's Massachusetts Avenue laundromat. Under Gordon's leadership Zaws tiny laundromat had been transformed into a dynamic store-front center of arts activities, a model of community revitalization that was doing wonders to plant new roots in a new community for these long rootless and displaced Burmese residents of Buffalo's West Side.

Barrett loves roller skating and, as one of the outcomes of his community building work at WASH, he had organized a series of roller-skating parties which he hosted at Skateland, a decades-old skating rink at the corner of Main and Ferry. Here, at what many people in Buffalo considered to be the epicenter of our city's long-standing Main Street racial divide, Gordon hosted a roller-skating party, a party with a purpose: to bring children together from both sides of that historic Main Street divide. Unconstrained by feelings of cultural, class and racial bias, Gordon's idea was, in his words, to "use roller skating to promote diversity and inclusivity and multi-generational, multi-racial, social hangouts. That's what I'm doing with skating, and it works really."

Talk about creative place-making! Barrett had nailed it and at the event, packed with children – African-American kids from the East Side and Burmese, Congolese, Bengalis and other kids from places I'd barely heard of from the West Side – all came together to skate. Fed by tables groaning with all kinds of home-cooked dishes, dozens of kids, their families basking in pleasure, skated and danced on the packed floor of Skateland. The event was a stroke of genius and led me to think further about how programs and activities – the bread and butter of placemaking – could be used to purposefully do what Barrett had instinctively done at Skateland, namely to unite, through creative programming, the people on both sides of Ferry Street.

After all, Ferry was the longest east-west street in the city, beginning on the west side at the foot of Ferry at the Niagara River and extending for miles until it came to an end at Bailey Avenue on the East Side. It was far more than a street, a corridor actually, that crossed one of the most historically significant landscapes in the city. There's Broderick Park on the edge of the Niagara River, a major point of departure on the "Underground Railroad." There's the intersection with Grant and Ferry, a focal point of refugee settlement in Buffalo, home to the fertile nesting ground of the West Side Bazaar and other emerging organizations. There's vibrant vestiges of an old Italian community: Guercio's, Lorigo's and La Nova. There's an Olmsted circle at Richmond, the "Elmwood Village," the old Albright estate, Nardin Academy, the magisterial 800 W. Ferry tower and

Canisius High School. Crossing Delaware there's the Linwood Historic District, down to and across Main Street to Cold Springs. What if we created a community driven process which encouraged and enabled the people who lived along the whole length and breadth of the Ferry Street Corridor to become engaged in the study of their own history? Would not such a process do for the people of Ferry Street what my own studies of Buffalo history had done for me? Would we not, in other words, be using Buffalo's history – the "Buffalo Story" – to strengthen the ties that bind us to our city and to each other?

It was the notion of using the Ferry Street Corridor as a model for a city-wide project that The Friends of the Buffalo Story, with the support of Mayor Brown and funds garnered from Federal and local sources, launched The Ferry Street Corridor Project in the Fall of 2014.

I had a vast and ambitious agenda for the Ferry Street Corridor Project. I wanted to transform the empty lot on the northeast corner of Main and Ferry into a great public place, a place where the people on both sides of Main Street could come together, as they did at Barrett's Skateland. I wanted to transform as well the vast, empty walls that the Niagara Frontier Transportation Agency owned across from the site where Offermann Stadium once stood, making it a gigantic canvas where the story of the Ferry Street Corridor could be told. I wanted to reimagine and reinvent the bus stops along the corridor and transform them into showcases of neighborhood history, places where people, while waiting on their buses, could learn about themselves and their neighborhoods. I believed in the power of history and the power of engaging the public in its telling. It was a very difficult and challenging task and while we accomplished much of what we set out to do, the Ferry Street Corridor Project, with neither enough time nor manpower, fell short of my transformative hopes and expectations. I still believe deeply in the power of a project like this to heal and renew our city and I welcome the opportunity to try it again someday soon.

• • •

The seeds we planted with the Ferry Street Project sprouted when the organizers of the Buffalo Slow-Roll, weekly bike rides which since the Summer of 2015 had led cyclists on tours of neighborhoods throughout the city, chose the corner of E. Ferry and Michigan as the starting-point for the ride on Monday, July 1st, 2019. Never would I have imagined when, in 1974, I organized the first ever tours of

Buffalo's neighborhoods that there'd be a time, more than forty years later, that thousands of people, (on bicycles!) would be following a path that I had charted so many years before. Whether they knew it or not, the organizers had chosen one of the most historic intersections in the city. Did they know about the cold spring (origin of the neighborhood's name, Cold Spring) that had once flowed through the neighborhood ending in a large, bubbling pool of water in what is now the middle of Main and Ferry? Did the hundreds of cyclists gathered at the corner of Ferry and Michigan know that the church behind them, the Bethel A.M.E. church, founded on Vine Alley in 1832 and located at this corner since the late 1940s, is the oldest African-American congregation in the city? Did they know that it was here, on the site currently occupied by the Buffalo Academy of the Visual and Performing Arts, that stood one of Buffalo's greatest long-lost landmarks, a baseball park known from the time it opened in 1924 to the time it was demolished in 1960 as, "Offerman Stadium?"

There are few places in Buffalo with as rich a history as Offerman Stadium, a story that we uncovered as part of our Ferry Street Corridor Project. Built by Frank Offerman, the child of a German immigrant family, Offerman Stadium, like Ebbetts and Wrigley fields, was tucked tightly into the dense fabric of the Cold Spring neighborhood. For over forty years, Offerman Stadium was a pre-eminent neighborhood focal point, a place where blacks and whites, who in those days rarely met in public places, came together to celebrate and enjoy the game of baseball. They came to watch the Buffalo Bisons, the minor league team that made their home here. And they came on those weekends when the great Negro league teams – The Kansas City Monarchs, the Pittsburgh Crawfords, the Newark Eagles and the Homestead Greys – came to Buffalo, to Offerman Stadium, on wildly popular "barnstorming" tours. With downtown hotels off limits to the black ballplayers, those giants of Negro league baseball – Josh Gibson, Judy Johnson, Satchel Paige, Buck Henry and the rest – rented rooms in the neighborhood, hanging out on neighborhood porches, eating meals at Duke's Dive and Mama's Southern-Style BBQ on E. Ferry and the other tiny cafes and bars that filled the side streets. And at night, when the games were over they went to the jazz clubs, the Moonglow, The Colored Musicians Club and the Little Harlem. But times were changing and urban renewal was replacing baseball as the great American pastime. By the late 1950s the city wanted Offerman Stadium. They wanted it for a site for a new school, Woodlawn Jr High School.

And so, in September, 1960 Offerman Stadium was demolished. But not before it played host to one last event.

And what an event it was. Sponsored by Buffalo's preeminent jazz impresario, the son of an Italian immigrant family, a man named Joe Ricco, the show, held over two days in August, featured the greatest jazz musicians in the world: Count Basie and Dinah Washington, Art Blakey and Dizzy Gillespie, Louis Armstrong, Duke Ellington, Oscar Peterson and Dave Brubeck. All of them, all right here at Offerman Stadium on E. Ferry between Michigan and Masten. For two days they played and for two days Offerman was packed and for two days the streets of Cold Spring were filled with the sounds of this most exciting music.

But then it was over. Then Offerman was torn down and replaced, sickeningly so, in 1964 by Woodlawn Jr., which, as a result of clearly and consciously drawn district lines, became the first legally segregated public school in Buffalo. The enlarged photographs that we mounted on our E. Ferry Street walls told that history. But those marvelous photographs, like Offerman Stadium, were wiped away, replaced by cliched portraits of civil rights leaders. Had they been allowed to stay, had they been left there to tell the story of Cold Springs and the Ferry Street Corridor, the thousands of cyclists who gathered here on that sparkling late afternoon of July lst, 2019, might have learned something about the history of the neighborhood they were about to explore. (For those interested, those photos can still be seen, mounted on the Ferry Street side of the School of Performing Arts.)

• • •

Nothing, not even Adirondack chairs, not even Buffalo stories, can turn a place around quicker than food. Especially hot dogs, "Noo Yawk Dawgs." It was the mid '90s and I was spending lots of time with my good friend Steve Halpern. Steve was from New York too ("The Bronx," Steve reminded everybody) and on long walks around Delaware Park, we often reminisced about the things that we missed about New York. "You know," he said, "there's no place to get a good hot dog in Buffalo. I mean a real one, a," lapsing into his Bronx accent, "Noo Yawk Dawg." Suddenly, I had an idea. How about, I asked him, we set up a hot dog stand in front of the Calumet, right on the corner of Chippewa and Franklin. Just at night. When everything is closed and people are looking for something to eat. Steve loved the idea and immediately we went to work. Steve, as eager as I was to "get his hands dirty," to transform this dark and lifeless corner and have some fun doing it, jumped right in. But it had to be special. It had to be authentic. It had, we both agreed, to be "us." And so we launched "Mawk and Steve's Noo Yawk Dawgs." Cooking on a large, custom-built charcoal grill and under a large tent with our name emblazoned proudly on it and using a sauce that we christened "Coney Island Hot Sauce," Steve, (who worked by day as a political science professor at UB) with me on the sidelines, began a second career as a hot dog vendor.

"Mawk and Steve's" took off instantly. Word quickly got around about the hub of activity that we had created on this so recently squalor-filled corner. We were slammed from the get-go. Lines formed and limos pulled up: "Is this where you get the "Noo Yawk Dogs?" We were open weekends only from 11 at night until five in the morning and Steve, who neither wind, nor rain, nor snow ("there was no "gloom of night" at Mawk and Steve's) could keep away, was there through and for it all. Hot dogs and the brains and the brawn of these two friends from New York had created a fabulous place, a place of commerce and a place of pleasure and, above all, a place of fun. Maybe, I suggested to Steve, we teach a course at the School of Architecture on "Hot Dogs and Urban Place-Making."

• • •

I was proud and pleased as well by the positive responses that the Calumet had received and the accolades that we had earned for the role that, during the 1990s, we had played in igniting the revitalization of downtown. While the flame of the downtown revitalization spread, however, the spark that triggered it, the Calumet Arts Café, overburdened by an arts and cultural agenda that we could not sustain, went out. I loved the Calumet Arts Café and the freedom that it had given me to indulge by many artistic and cultural interests and whims. And certainly I would have loved to have been able to keep it open, but, alas, I could not. But I was not done. I believed in the idea of the Calumet and the power of the arts to turn a place around and in the Spring of 2004, I began to look around for another cast-off location in another run-down location.

I found one: an empty store-front on the corner of Allen and College Street with the name "Allen Street Hardware" emblazoned on the front of the building. I'd been aware of it for weeks, looking at it from the small table in front of

Sammy's Soul Food take-out place on the other side of Allen that I sat at eating some of the best fried chicken around. Allen Street Hardware had been a neighborhood fixture for years, owned by the Critelli family for years. I had done lots of business with them years before when we were working on remodelling the Calumet, buying most of our paint and much of the other smaller things needed for the work we were doing. By the late '90s Mary, her husband Fred and Louise wanted out and sold the building to the Yemini businessman, Mugali Ali, who owned the Holly Farms down Allen Street (me and those Holly Farms stores!) and it was now that I saw yet another small hand-written piece of paper taped randomly on the window with the words "Store for rent" scratched on it. I called and then met with Ali, a quiet, gentle and very friendly man who lived with this family over the large garage that was attached to the rear of the hardware store. Ali had come to Buffalo years before settling, like so many other of his countrymen, in Lackawanna. By the mid 1990s he had acquired a significant portfolio of real estate in neighborhoods that others steered clear of, including several delis and still more multiple dwellings up and down the side streets of Allentown. He invited me to his apartment where we drank tea and watched a soccer match broadcast on an Arabian TV station. He was vaguely familiar with the work that I'd done on Chippewa Street and was eager for me (with a heavy accent he referred to me as "Soup-a-mahn") to rent the empty store-front that had for so many years been the home of the Allen Street Hardware. I liked the space and, never forgetting Tony's advice, I loved the corner, visible from all angles. We agreed to a monthly rent of $500.

I had yet no idea what I wanted to do with this old hardware store. It had pretty good bones, including two of my favorite found attributes, an intact tin ceiling and a hard-wood floor. As at the Calumet I wanted to create a space where ideas and people mattered, a hang-out kind of place inspired, I fantasized, by the old cafeterias on the Lower East Side of New York, places like Ratner's and the Café Royale, gathering places where Jewish exiles and intellectuals sat for hours grousing about the state of the world. That not being likely in early 21st century Buffalo I thought more practically about creating a store-front for my two faux think tanks, "The Idea Center" and "The Calumet Institute," a place where concerned Buffalonians could meet and together, in a phrase that I never tired of using, "fix this place."

However low the rent was it still needed to be paid and, thinking again of Tony's "cash register," I began to conceive of a small, dark and intimate spot, a cross between McSorley's Ale House, an ancient bar near the Bowery, and Lucky Strike in SoHo, the coolest, most appealing French bistro outside of Paris. I wanted to build, as always, on history and heritage, to create a new place out of the body of the old. I wanted as well to demonstrate that small spaces make great spaces. Not only are they easier to own and operate but, as Jane Jacobs had pointed out more than forty years earlier, the impact of small spaces is synergistic, particularly in small, compact neighborhoods like Allentown. And, to quote Fred Kent who's mantra had not yet been heard in Buffalo, small spaces are "lighter, quicker and cheaper." So, without too much expense and few of the kinds of large-scale construction efforts incurred on Chippewa Street, I, with Charlie on board began the transformation of the Allen Street Hardware Store into the Allen Street Hardware Café.

We started slowly, adding space incrementally, only when and if our business merited it: first the corner room, than the side; than one back room and finally another until by 2012, six years after we started there, the whole corner of Allen and College had become what soon became known simply as "Hardware."

The creation of "Hardware" embodied all the lessons that I'd been learning. It was a sound business decision, strategic and tactical. It was rooted in the history and heritage of the neighborhood, a project that reflected my values while it strengthened all of Allentown. "Hardware" was a success from the day we opened it. Everybody, including my brother Tony, loved Hardware. When I took him there after his triumphant talk at City Honors in November 2010, he ate, he said, the best fried chicken he'd ever had. (He never did eat at Sammy's.)

Then in around 2010 I was visited by a woman named Susan Chelowa who, she said, was buying some property on Amherst Street in Black Rock. Aware of my long-standing interest not only in Black Rock but in small, intimate spaces, Susan wanted me to look at a building she had just bought on Amherst Street. It was, she said, an old hardware store (another one? What's with the old hardware stores?) that had until recently belonged to the Mazorek family. Perhaps, she asked hopefully, I might consider opening a hardware café there.

I was seduced instantly by the store-front, untouched since at least the 1920s: there was a wooden floor, wooden wainscoting, lead-paned windows and, the tin ceilings more attractive and in better condition than any I'd seen. It was a wonderful room, one I thought, and hoped, would, in this long struggling, largely invisible neighborhood, make a perfect neighborhood café. I was drawn to the idea of transforming yet another abandoned hardware store, particularly in a neighborhood to which I had been so closely tied so many years ago. Susan and I quickly agreed to terms and once again I undertook the remodeling process.

With my son Charlie, my daughter Lydia, and my-son-in-law Rob as partners, we created a gorgeous, elegant little restaurant in the hard-scrabble post-industrial landscape of Assumption Parish in Black Rock – The Black Rock Kitchen and Bar. BRKB, as it became known, was, despite its popularity, an ill-conceived venture, based far more on my fantasies than on the realities of the restaurant business and after fewer than three years, we closed it. What worked against us was not, as many thought, the challenges of this frontier neighborhood but rather the structure of the business itself. Tiny businesses, particularly restaurants like BRKB, require small payrolls, a mom and pop approach in which the owners roll up their sleeves and do all they can – cook and clean, tend bar and wait on tables. Since none of us did any of that, BRKB became a money-losing proposition and sadly we decided, despite the popularity of the place, to close. We simply couldn't make it. BRKB was lighter and it was quicker but, unfortunately, it was not cheaper. I was disappointed that our efforts to turn a place around in Black Rock failed. But with Black Rock behind us and Hardware, now in its 15th year running along smoothly, I was ready, after more than twenty years of intense efforts in the café business, to turn to another kind of place-making.

• • •

Two years after his visit to Buffalo my brother Tony, of blessed memory, died. As a result of his work in Soho, in Philadelphia, in Newark and Miami, Tony had become a legend in the world of historic preservation, recognized everywhere as an endlessly energetic and innovative source of creativity and intelligence. In the last years of his life, Tony had broadened his activities and by 2010 had become a leading advocate for the integration of public art into the daily life of cities. In the early 1990s Tony had bought a wall on Houston Street and the Bowery on New York's Lower East Side and began a curating process there that led that wall, soon known as the Keith Haring Wall, to become and to remain the most recognized venue for public art in all of New York. In the early 2000s Tony expanded the frontier of public art when he turned blocks of run-down industrial buildings in the Wynwood district of Miami into "The Wynwood Walls." Under Tony's inspired leadership, Wynwood became and remains to this day the world's leading venue for public art. When my brother died in 2012 I wanted to honor him by doing, in some small way, in Buffalo, what he had accomplished in Wynwood. With that in mind, in early 2013 I formed the Allen Street Art Collective. This excerpt from *Buffalo Rising* (August, 23, 2013) tells the story about our work well:

> *"Buffalo historian, social advocate and businessman Mark Goldman is planning to create a series of murals in Allentown, while dedicating the effort to his late brother and public art visionary Tony Goldman. In an email sent out to local press, Mark made clear that the initiative would be guided by a professional acumen that would greatly enhance the spectrum of art in the city. Allentown is already known for its artistic nature, and this effort should dovetail perfectly with Tony's lifelong efforts. A few BRO readers always thought that Tony's spearheading nature to produce mind-blowing works of arts by marrying acclaimed artists with blank walls, would have been an excellent addition to Buffalo's own built landscape. It looks as if that time has finally come."*

By sponsoring and supporting the world's leading street artists, Tony gave voice to a new generation of artists while at the same time bringing unbelievable energy and art to the streets of long-forsaken parts of two major American cities. His work, though cut-short by his untimely death on September 11th, 2012, will live on, however, not only in Soho and in Miami but on the streets of Buffalo, New York. By creating the Allen Street Street Artists Collective, I did, on a smaller scale, for the streets of Allentown what Tony's work did for New York and Miami. It was as a tribute to him and to the people of Buffalo that I had undertaken this most challenging and important project. As Tony himself said: "The work that we do is not for the faint of heart."

The work of our Collective struck a chord. Recognizing the power of our work, the Albright Knox Art Gallery (following our lead now as they would with their public art project on E. Ferry Street) initiated a public arts project that in the wake of the Allen Street Art Collective has transformed the blank facades of buildings throughout Buffalo. I was proud. Tony would have been too.

• • •

There are many story collectors among us, a passionate and plentiful crew. We are motivated by the belief that by sharing, collecting and preserving stories and memories about places – the streets and neighborhoods of our past – we create a web of shared experiences that bind us to those places and to each other. The story collectors among us recognize that somehow, somewhere stored in our stories are seeds of truth and sparks of wisdom that offer us not only sweet reminders of a more gentle past but, as significantly, provide the foundation for the future. The story collectors among us know that stories and memories are powerful place-making tools. We know too that above and beyond the nostalgia that they offer an older generation, the highest value of the stories that we collect and the memories that we preserve are the source of wisdom for the next generation. Among the best of the story tellers and collectors among us is a group of Sicilian-Americans who collectively call themselves "The *Per Niente*." (Derived from the Sicilian expression "non per niente" roughly understood to mean that "what we do we do for nothing) The *Per Niente* boys were all products of Buffalo's old Italian neighborhoods – the Hooks, the Terrace, the West Side and St. Lucy's Parish on the East Side. They are proud and deeply committed custodians of their unique heritage and take seriously what they regard as their responsibility to pass it onto the next generation. With that in mind in 2005 two of these gentlemen, Joe DiLeo and Joe Giambra, both first generation descendants of Sicilians, founded a magazine that bore the name of their group, *Per Niente*.

I'd been drawn to the culture of Italian-Americans since as a kid my sister had taken me to the San Gennaro Festival in Little Italy. It was love at first sight. At college, in Boston, I could not wait to explore the packed and tiny streets of the North End. Then, back in New York, on those eye-opening walking tours led by Professor Bayard Still, I explored further the fantastic history and culture of what were in the mid-1960s, the richly textured Italian neighborhoods of Little Italy.

When I came to Buffalo in 1967 there was, despite the hideously heavy hand of urban renewal, a still lingering Sicilian presence on the Lower West Side. Niagara Street in particular retained a handful of Sicilian-owned businesses: bakeries and pastry shops like Muscarella's, Blue Bird, Balistreri's and Cristiano's. There was even a remnant of the old chicken market and the Columbia Market whose outdoor stands gave the place the look and feel of an old Italian neighborhood.

It was too late however for "the Hooks," that old waterfront neighborhood that had grown up around the terminus of the Erie Canal at The Commercial Slip. Made up of tiny streets with names like "Fly" and "leCouteux," "Maiden Lane" and "Peacock," "the Hooks" had by the 1920s become Buffalo's largest first generation Sicilian neighborhood. The local press had been fascinated with the Sicilians in "the Hooks" and there are countless articles and photographs on the neighborhood in the amazing scrapbook collection housed in the Grosvenor Collection at the Central Library. While I have reported these discoveries in *City on The Edge* there is still so much that any one of us, on our own, can learn from these scrapbooks. I implore you to visit the collection. It was here that I came across one of my all-time favorite Buffalo stories, that of Sal Rizzo the puppeteer and owner, during the early years of the 20th century of a marionette theater on Canal Street. I have revisited this story several times, first in *City on the Edge* then later in a performance piece that I devised and presented at The Ruins at Canalside.

By 1967 there was nothing left of Sal Rizzo's Hooks and nothing left of the neighboring Sicilian neighborhood on "The Terrace" where Joe DiLeo grew up. "Na-ting," "Niente." The Hooks had been replaced by the Marine Drive Apartments and DiLeo's Terrace was cleared and replaced by a hotel, a tv studio and acres of parking lots. Gone was Mt. Carmel Church and the schools, #2 and the school at St. Anthony of Padua. Gone too was the playground and baseball diamond, the clam stands and a fabulous old Italian restaurant, Andy's, known to generations of Buffalonians, on W. Genesee, above which the DiLeos, the Licatas and the Sciandras lived for so many years. And gone too was Sal Rizzo's teatrino.

Saddened, if not sickened by the loss of the neighborhoods of his childhood, Joe DiLeo decided that the stories and memories of these places needed to be preserved. "We are the last generation. We have to preserve these memories. For the kids' sake. How are they, living in their big houses with their six bedrooms, gonna possibly visualize what our lives were like. It's up to us to preserve these stories." In the meantime, Joe DiLeo was hatching his plans for *Per Niente*, a magazine that would memorialize the old Italian West Side that he and his friends talked so much about. While it started as a group of pals from the old neighborhood who met for coffee and weekly rounds of golf, DiLeo, the ambitious and imaginative custodian of memories, quickly transformed his social get-togethers into something more.

Joe believed that Buffalo old Italian neighborhoods – the Hooks, the Terrace and the Lower West Side on the West Side, St. Lucy's, Lovejoy and Edison Street on the East Side – were sacred and that it was his mission, through *Per Niente*, to connect a new generation of Sicilian-Americans to that special time and special place. At first a one page broadside, *Per Niente* quickly became a full magazine. Published quarterly today, *Per Niente* is a marvelous, perhaps unique journal of urban folklore, an extraordinary treasure trove of memory, a repository for all the stories, all the photographs, all the recipes that fill the hearts and minds of so many of Buffalo's Sicilian-Americans who still call these neighborhoods home.

The pages of *Per Niente* are a sensory guide to a long lost world. In it are stories and dozens of extraordinary photographs of growing up on The Terrace, of dances at Holy Cross, of countless parties at the Town Casino, of baseball games in the sandlot behind St. Anthony's. There are profiles of the people in the neighborhoods: of Joe Caci ("Joe the Fish") the fisherman from Porto Empedocles in Sicily; of Joe Sebastian ("Joey Nerves") who owned Scotty's Clam Bar; of Tony Maggio from the 4 Aces, of Peter Capitano who traveled from the coal mines of Pittston, Pennsylvania to Buffalo in the 1930s. There are articles about Sicilian history written by Angelo Coniglio and Frank Giacobbe; profiles of the old towns and villages: Valledolmo, Montedoro, Aliminuso, San Fele and all the rest. And there are recipes, dozens of them from Sam Arena, Russell Salvatore, Joey Giambra, Sal Maggiore and all the others for whom the sights and smells of those long-lost Sicilian kitchens are the foundational stuff of which so many of these memories are made. And there are recollections that fill the pages of the magazine, memories of specific nooks and crannies, like this one about life on the corner of Busti and Hudson written by a woman whose father Sal Butera, had a barbershop there:

> *Most of my childhood memories were of this corner. Fond memories of my uncle, Mimi Polito going off to war and returning to work in the family grocery store. My grandfather made Italian ice and sold it at the front of the store while my grandmother sat in front carefully manning the fruits and vegetables. Church bells ringing at Holy Cross on Sunday morning, smells of crabs and clams from the clam stand in front of Nick's Tavern, roosters waking up the neighbors from the chicken market, the smells from Luigi's Bakery. So filled with life and fun. The*

merry-go-round man, the knife sharpener, the fishmonger, the peanut and popcorn man, the waffle man …

Best of all, though, are the photographs. The memories of the members of the *Per Niente* group are filled with thoughts and images of places destroyed long ago, of streets and neighborhoods abandoned, demolished and covered over. While there are no traces, no remnants or ruins, not even plaques that indicate that "here," under the foundations of the Marine Drive apartments, of the Adams Mark Hotel and of the Virginia Street entrance to the New York State Thruway, lie the remains of Joe Giambra's Hooks, of Joe DiLeo's Terrace and of Karima Bondi's 7th street, the memories of these places are preserved in the pages of *Per Niente*. For what *Per Niente* is, above all, is a family album, of not one but many families from all of Buffalo's old Italian neighborhoods. Unlike the "family album" created by the Farm Security Administration during the New Deal or the misery-filled faces of Milton Rogovin's photographs of the Lower West Side, the photos that fill the pages of *Per Niente* reveal the raucous, often joy and fun-filled daily life of the first and second generation Sicilian American families who lived in these fantastic, lost-forever places.

There was no more avid contributor to *Per Niente* than Joe Giambra. A former cop, a one-time candidate for mayor, a leading jazz trumpeter and as a poet, playwright and novelist, an inveterate, tireless chronicler of Buffalo's Sicilian American story, Joey came into my life in 1996 and stayed there until his untimely death in the Spring of 2020 from complications related to Covid-19. Following his death I was asked to write a tribute to Joey which, at the suggestion of Elena Cala, I called "Cheap trumpet, lottsa brass: A day in the life of Joey Giambra." Mine is just one of the many lives touched by Joey Giambra and I am proud that he and I worked as colleagues on more than one project. I have reprinted the tribute below:

> It was in the early winter of 1996 when I got a call from him. I'd seen Joey perform many times, most memorably and powerfully in local productions of Mamet's "American Buffalo" and Miller's "View from the Bridge." I'd heard him play his music too, in fabulous ensembles that often included "Red" Menza, Lou Merino, Richie Merla and Sam Noto. Years before, when I was teaching at UB's College of Urban Studies, people were talking about an

instructor there, an ex-cop named Joe Giambra, who was teaching a course on crime in Buffalo. "You gotta sit in," I was told and sure enough I did: up close and personal with "Professor" Giambra, as he reminisced about "the wise guys" he'd busted in nooks and crannies all over the city.

"I got an idea for you, kid," a gravelly voice on the line said when he called. "A good one. You're gonna like it." I knew already that I would and we agreed to meet down the street at Spot Coffee. "Spot Coffee … What?" he shot back. "That's Holzman's Pharmacy. You wanna meet at the counter at Holzman's?" After explaining that Holzman's, that iconic drug store with its long-winding lunch counter and endless supplies of theatrical accoutrements, was no more and that it had been transformed into "Spot," Joey reluctantly agreed. "Sure," he said, "I'll meet you at Holzman's … I mean Spot. What the hell kind of name is that for a coffee joint, anyway?," he muttered under his breath.

I was waiting outside on that cold, snowy afternoon when trudging down Chippewa, his head bent slightly forward, I saw coming towards me – Joey Giambra – shoes covered in snow. In one hand he carried a trumpet case and in the other a briefcase. Nodding at each other at the door, Joey triumphantly held up the trumpet in the air. Before as much as a hello he said "I just bought this trumpet for eighty bucks, ain't it a friggin' beauty?!" Then, looking around, he said "What the hell happened to Holtzman's? You shoulda seen that store. It catered to all the theaters in downtown Buffalo. You could buy all kindsa theatrical make-up. Costumes too. What a place! The lunch counter. Where the hell did it go? All the actors used to meet there for lunch. Oh, well … Let's have a cawfee … Waddaya want? I'm gonna have a muffin an' cawfee. It's on me." I took the same: two muffins, two cups of "cawfee." "What"? Joey exclaimed in mock outrage when the waitress told him the price. "Twelve dollars? What did I do? Break a frickin' window?" And so I was introduced to Joey Giambra.

As if we'd known each other for years, Joey took hold of my elbow and led me over to a table. "I heard about you, kid. You helped the O'Neills set up the Irish Classical Theater Company. I got a play for you. I may not be Irish but it's classical, that's for sure. You're gonna love it! Sit down I'm gonna read some of it to you, he commanded. It's called "Bread and Onions."

"It's based on my youth – the people I knew, the things we did – on the Lower West Side." Putting the trumpet down he opened his briefcase and took out a sheaf of pages filled with text, some typed, some scrawled by hand. "Listen to this." Joe began reading intently, losing himself instantly in the world of his transcendent Lower West Side.

He read: "Andrews Hall; a hot summer's day … may it never end. A wedding at Bronzino's. Sam Scamacca, "Jabber" Calabrese, a four-piece band, an abundance of rhythm; the windows dressed in black. Draft beer in glasses; pop, Queeno, Oscar's, Nehi. Ham sandwiches in wax paper wrapped, cold pizza, homemade cookies. Who could ask for anything more. Agnes Alessandra, their sons and Luisa lived upstairs. In front of the store children wait religiously to board Mike's carousel: miniature horses, colorful moments of happy, galloping abandonment, innocent faces, thrilled, turning, always turning clockwise."

I couldn't resist: the language, the rhythm of his writing, the characters he had created and the passionate energy of his involvement with the material. I was enthralled. "Are you kidding," I exclaimed. "Put this on? You bet we're gonna put this on. It's fantastic. We're gonna kill it!"

We left Spot and walked down Chippewa towards the Calumet. "I shined shoes on Chippewa as a kid you know. We lived right around the corner on Georgia Street. I walked over here every afternoon with my shoe box. Made a good buck doin' it. Wish I had that shoe box now. I could use the extra dough."

We came to an instant agreement: we would present "Bread and Onions" for two Sunday evenings, see how it went and then go from there. As much as Joey loved to write, to act and to play music he, as we all know, loved to cook. "I'll tell you what," he said, "I'll make dinner – bread and onions, pasta and meatballs – for everyone, we'll serve it before the show and then … boom … "Bread and Onions." Now talk about an offer I wouldn't refuse. What could be better than an evening like that, a whole event dripping in the red sauce Italianness of Joey Giambra's Lower West Side?

The show was fantastic. Six actors, each reading different parts, punctuated by the plaintive wails of Joey's recently acquired and prized $80 trumpet. The colorful characters who peopled Joey's script jumped off the pages: Johnny Dit-em, Frank the Clam, Jebber Calabrese and the others. The audience, alternatingly laughing and nodding familiarly, loved it. The two Sundays quickly became four, which became eight as dozens of people, many of them Joey's old West Side friends and neighbors and many other curious Buffalonians of all stripes who knew a good thing when they heard about it. They all flocked to the Calumet week after week to immerse themselves in the irresistibly colorful world of Joey Giambra. It was at the Calumet in 1996, that I was invited into that world – a world that I joyfully inhabited until the very last days of his life.

Joe's countless contributions to *Per Niente* have helped to keep the memories of these long-lost neighborhoods alive. By doing so, Joe Giambra and Joe Dileo have helped to shape the "collective unconscious " of Buffalo's Sicilian-American community, imbuing the words "The Hooks," "The Terrace," "the Lower West Side," "St. Lucy's Parish" and the others with a magical meaning. Tied to each other through their shared past, the Sicilian-Americans of the Per Niente group remain connected today. Indeed, so many of the faces that appear in the photos published in *Per Niente* – the young boys playing baseball in the sandlot behind St. Anthony's and basketball at the Butler-Mitchell club on Massachusetts; the girls, posing in their dresses on a Myrtle Avenue porch and in their bathing suits on the beach at Crystal Beach – can be found today, having coffee at Bagel Jays, having dinner at Marco's on Niagara Street, celebrating St. Joseph's Day at Rocco Termini's "table" at Tappo and dancing at the *Per Niente* Christmas dinner dance held annually at Salvatore's Italian Gardens. While the places that they have made sacred no longer exist, memories of them most certainly do. By keeping them alive and by consciously passing them on to the next generation, the creators of Per Niente, the club and the magazine, are performing a service to their community that, though hard to quantify, is incalculable and invaluable. With their roots in the old West Side, via Sicily, these second and third generation Italian Americans are working diligently and successfully to maintain their traditions. In the process they are tightening the bonds that tie them, their children and grandchildren to the home that adopted them, Buffalo, New York.

The members of Per Niente, many of whom were baptized at St. Anthony's Church on Court street and still attend a weekly Italian mass there, are committed to the future of their old neighborhood as much as they are to its past. Concerned about the spiritual needs of the growing number of Italian immigrants in America, Giovanni Battista Scalabrini, the Bishop of Piacenza, founded the Scalabrini Brothers in 1887. Within a few years they were in Buffalo and it was here in 1891 that they founded St. Anthony of Padua Church on Court Street whose mission was "to maintain the Catholic faith and practice among the Italian immigrants in Buffalo." (St. Anthony's maintains a small, marvelous museum in the basement, a testimony to the congregation's commitment to heritage, that tells this most interesting story.)

The men and women of Per Niente who grew up as beneficiaries of the Scalabrini brothers are dedicated to perpetuating the Church's original mission and have created a Christmas Fund which, with money raised from the members (close to $40,000 in 2020) they use to "clothe, feed, provide cheer and assistance to the new settlers among us in need." The pages of the *Per Niente*, (and indeed, even *The Buffalo News* which during the Christmas season of 2017 and 2018 did several articles about their work) are filled with stories and photographs that describe and depict the generosity of the members of Per Niente. Sometimes it's food and clothing for refugees and victims of Hurricane Maria; sometimes it's help with tuition; sometimes it's furniture and help with the rent. The Sicilian-Americans of Per Niente, who have never forgotten who they are or where they came from, are building the future as well as conserving the past. I am proud to be one of them, their one and only Jewish member!

Acknowledgements

Peter B. Dow: There would be no Friends of the Buffalo Story without Peter Dow. Peter has been an inspiration to me since, when I met him for the first time in the 1970s, he was ardently suggesting that a museum of industrial history be created. As founder of First Hand Learning, Peter works everyday to bring history and the sciences alive through a hands-on inquiry based methodology. In 2015 Peter was one of the founders of the Charter School of Inquiry. I wouldn't consider undertaking a project without the wisdom of Peter Dow. Peter remains active in our efforts at the Friends to bring our city's history alive to those of us who live here.

Scott Wood: Scott, a thinker, inventor, graphic artist, designer, all-purpose problem solver, Renaissance man extraordinaire, Scott has had his fingers in just about all of the work that we have done at the Friends.

NYS Erie Canal Harbor Development Corporation: The work of the Friends at Canalside has been generously supported by the ECHDC where **Tom Dee**,

Steve Ranalli and **Sam Hoyt** have been so significant in transforming that most historic place.

James Leaf: An old and much loved family friend, James came to Buffalo via New York and Ann Arbor to help shape and create the "Wedding of the Waters" at Canalside during the summer of 2016.

The support of **Mayor Byron Brown** was critical to the success of the Ferry Street Project as was the work of **Michael Breen**, City of Buffalo grant writer, **Margaret Kaiser**, **Barrett Gordon** and **Marissa Lehner**, our arts administrators.

The Wash Project evolved from my many visits to New York City where, in Harlem, I saw a neighborhood laundromat transformed into a community arts center. Through my son **Charlie** I'd come to meet **Zah Win**, a recent Burmese refugee who owned and operated a tiny laundromat on Massachusetts Ave on the West Side. Working closely with **Chuck Massey** who was as close to grass-roots community work on the West Side as anybody, we arranged for an Americorps grant to hire **Barrett Gordon** to open and operate an arts center in Zaw's laundromat. While closed for repairs and reconstruction, we are looking forward to the reopening of WASH in 2021-2022.

Offerman Stadium: There is much information on Offerman on the internet. I was fortunate that Frank Offerman's son **Paul** was so eager and willing to share with me some of his recollections. The story of Offerman which opened in 1924 and was demolished in 1960, is one of the great untold Buffalo stories. I first heard of the 1960 jazz festival by none other than the magnificent **Joey Giambra** who was there and gave me a poster from that event. Leave it to Joey!

Allen Street Hardware: My son **Charlie**, with his unmatched managerial skills, has been critical to the continued success of "Hardware." Thanks too to **Clayton Perry**, **Pat Gilmartin**, **Tracy Volker**, **Laura Latona**, **Carlos Villaneuva Cruz**

and **Teddy Collins** who have worked with us since the beginning. Thanks also to **Meg Corcoran** whose murals helped define Hardware in the early days.

Allen Street Art Collective: Key figures here were local artists **Ian DeBeer**, **Max Collins**, **Julian Montague** and **Patrick Gallo** who came back from New York to work on these murals.

Per Niente: Joe DiLeo's group and magazine of the same name are one of the great "Buffalo stories". **Richard Gioia**'s stories of working at Gioia Macaroni have provided an invaluable context for understanding the Sicilian-American experience in Buffalo. In addition I received help from many others, including **Lucy Ederer**, **Angelo Coniglio**, **Peter LoGiacono**, **Jeanette** and **Ralph Delmonte**, **Peter Tasca** and dozens of other members of this fabulous group. Sal Butera's memoir is from (*Vol. IX, III, Summer 2013, p.2*) Of all the characters in the life of Buffalo's Italian (Sicilian) American culture there was no one quite like Joe Giambra. A cop, a jazz musician, recording star, playwright, film-maker, Joey, endlessly energetic and creative, devoted his life (in addition to running for mayor and owning and operating two restaurants) to chronicling the story of his people in his city. He loved the Lower West Side and he loved Buffalo. His song, "I love You Buffalo" is the best musical tribute to Buffalo extant.

A piece in *The Buffalo News* chronicled the work of *Per Niente* at the time of Hurricane Maria."Free From Hurricane Maria, a warm Per Niente landing in Buffalo," *The News* on December 9, 2017)

LOOKING BACKWARD:

ERIE COUNTY SAVINGS BANK, AUGUST 11, 1967

"A Buffalo duchess will soon return to the dust. Arched of brow (windows), ornamental of coiffure (turrets), and buxom of figure (granite walled), the old Erie County Savings Bank Building will bow to progress." —Ellen Taussig, 1967

The Erie County Savings Bank was perhaps Buffalo's most beloved building. Built from 1890 to 1893 and designed in the Romanesque Revival style by acclaimed architect George B. Post, the nine-story building was often referred to simply as "The Castle." In this 1967 photograph, the 74-year-old building is chipped away by the wrecking ball. The elevator shaft of the Main Place Tower, to be the bank's new headquarters, is under construction to its north. Harlan J. Swift, Erie County Savings Bank president, made the decision to demolish the old landmark. The bank went out of business in 1990. - THE PUBLIC STAFF

Erie County Savings Bank coming down. August, 1967.

TOP: Karima Bondi and friends in front of their 7th Street home, c. 1955
BOTTOM: Joan Bozer's Humboldt Parkway.

V.F. CITY PLANNING

What's going into Buffalo's "Hour Glass"?

(other than 35,000 cars a day)

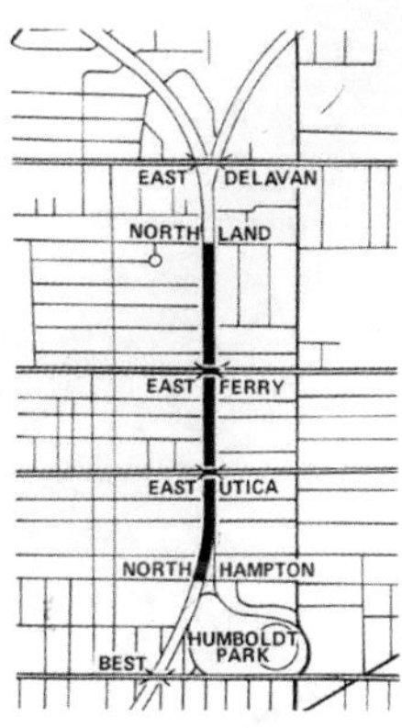

For completion, this is what will be required:

Excavation: more than ¾ miles long, 120 ft. wide, up to 20 ft. below existing grade.

Sheet piling: 280,000 sq. ft.—half of it to be withdrawn and re-driven for second phase of job.

Concrete: 35,000 sq. yds.,—for paving, retaining walls and sidewalks.

Stone curbing: 35,000 lineal ft. (over 6½ mi.)

Pipe: Relocation of 42,000 lineal ft. (nearly 8 mi.), up to 84" dia., for diverting sewer and water lines.

Conduit: 18,000 lineal ft. (over 3 mi.) for street lighting.

Steel railing: 7,000 lineal ft. (over 1 mi.)

Construction: storm water pumping station; 2 overhead bridges.

Reconstruction: Rebuild 1½ miles of service roads, curbing and sidewalks.

In a few words, – ingenuity in engineering, experience, modern equipment and 2½ years of skilled work to complete. In one word, – DARLING!

What was known as Humboldt Parkway in July 1968 is now a complex of construction that will provide 5 lanes of traffic in each direction, must be completed on schedule in December 1970 . . . and traffic must be maintained in the meantime!

Humboldt Parkway, June 1968

The "Hour Glass", November 1968

Solving Heavy Construction Problems
Above or Below Ground or Water Level

HERBERT F. DARLING INC.
ENGINEERING CONTRACTORS
131 CALIFORNIA DRIVE BUFFALO, N. Y. 14221
PHONE 632-1125 (Area Code 716)

TOP: Advertisement for Darling Construction Company.
BOTTOM: Darling's vision for Humboldt Parkway.

The Spectrum . Friday, October 8, 1971

TOP: Dan Montgomery's Restaurant on Exchange Street, 1968.

BOTTOM: Campus interviews for Bethlehem Steel announced in the UB Spectrum.

On location with historian/narrator Goldman, producer Dan Healy and cinematographer Bob Lehmann.

Mark Goldman.

6

"On the road" in Black Rock, 1974.

Bill and Carol Ostendorf Hoyt and family, c. 1972. Whitney, Carolyn, John, Sam (who is William B Hoyt III). Courtesy of the Hoyt family.

First 'Cause' Convention Takes Psychedelic Bent

By RICHARD E. BALDWIN

The new social action group 'Cause' conducted its first convention Saturday, but it was more like a psychedelic "happening" than a business meeting.

Before the meeting, each of the more than 500 delegates threaded his way through a series of tableaux calling attention to urban problems.

They began with an "Apartheid Registration Station" where suburbanites were segregated from city dwellers by the "commissioner of de facto segregation." Another booth depicted living conditions in a ghetto room, with its bare light bulb and decrepit furniture. Tainted meat was available in another booth.

Pollution Dramatized

Other exhibits dramatized the water and air pollution in Metropolitan Buffalo, and showed a replica of a public schoolroom where more emphasis was being placed on discipline and regimentation than on education.

A humorous display pictured the Buffalo Common Council, complete with a trash can labeled "received and filed." In the council, action to "receive and file" amounts to taking no action at all.

Another booth was selling a chemical spray used by police in riot control, and still another was a representation of a jail cell in which police were beating a prisoner and forcing him to declare that he would "Vote for Wallace."

Books on Sale

Nearby, a photographic slide presentation was under way of scenes in Metropolitan Buffalo, and a selection of books on urban problems was on sale.

Inside the convention hall in the Canisius College Students Center, the meeting was called to order with the announcement, "Metropolitan Buffalo now will come to disorder!"

The darkened room immediately was filled with brightly-colored, psychedelic, flashing lights, a motion picture, two slide presentations and some live actors, all performing at once.

Urban Problems Filmed

The movie focused on problems of air and water pollution, decaying housing, city government, police, politics and other aspects of life in the inner city.

The live actors, like many suburbanites, appeared more interested in discussing which television program to watch that evening than in the problems being depicted all around them by the movie and slide programs.

Among the pictures were photos of some of Buffalo's councilmen, taken during council meetings. They drew laughter and boos from the nearly all-white audience.

Cite Growth in Rolls

During the business meeting which followed, it was announced that 16 existing organizations in Buffalo and its suburbs have joined 'Cause' in addition to 505 individual, dues-paying members. The organization's name is an acronym for Coalition for Action, Unity and Social Equality.

Among groups which became members of the federation on Saturday was 'I Can,' a group of clergy, religious and laity operating under the full name of Independent Catholic Action Now.

A long list of strongly-worded resolutions on social issues had been prepared for the convention, but only one resolution was taken up Saturday. Action on the rest was postponed to a future meeting.

The resolution which was adopted committed 'Cause' to "exercise careful and continuous scrutiny over the actions of public officials, administrative agencies and legislative bodies in the interest of maintaining responsive and responsible government" and dedicated the group to "exposing racism where it exists and applauding positive actions for social equality when they occur."

Mrs. William Hoyt, a delegate from the newly-formed Westminster Action Group of Westminster Presbyterian Church, was elected president for a one-year term. Norman Goldfarb and Charles H. Weston were elected executive vice presidents; Roger Squire, treasurer, and Raymond E. Owen, secretary.

Other Officers

Thomas Roycroft was named assistant treasurer, and Mrs. Peter Bright, assistant secretary.

Ten "area representatives" were named — five from various sections of Buffalo, and five from the suburbs.

They are the Rev. Robert Wilson, the Rev. Herman Cole, Mrs. David Eslick, the Rev. Robert Moore and Dr. John Medige, all of Buffalo; Albertus Secor of Kenmore, Mrs. Edgar Mayer of Williamsville, Mrs. William Thayer of East Aurora, John Bailey of Hamburg, and the Rev. Randall Niehoff of West Seneca.

Mrs. Hoyt R. E. Owen N. Goldfarb C. H. Weston

Officers elected at first 'Cause' convention

Article on Carol Hoyt's Cause Convention.

TOP: Harold Cohen, c. 1975.
BOTTOM: Joan Bozer, c. 1980.

Jesse Kregal runs through Buffalo, Skylon Marathon, 1974.

Michael Morgulis 1977 iconic "City of No Illusions" design.

TOP LEFT TO RIGHT: Federal Judge John T. Curtin, c. 1990.
Joseph Murray, c. 1975. Eugene T. Reveille, c. 1980.

BOTTOM: At our Empire State College Neighborhood conference, 1981.

TOP: Calumet Building at the time of its completion, c. 1910.
BOTTOM: Calumet Building at the time we bought it, 1988.

TOP: Fisherman's Wharf, c. 1988.
BOTTOM: Interior of Calumet, 1988.

TOP: Joanna Angie and Perry Young working at The Calumet.
BOTTOM: Charlie and Pat Gallo working on the facade of The Calumet, 1989.

TOP: Meg Corcoran's fabulous murals inside the Calumet Arts Cafe.

BOTTOM: One of six "characters at the Calumet", lithographs created by Michael Morguls, 1990.

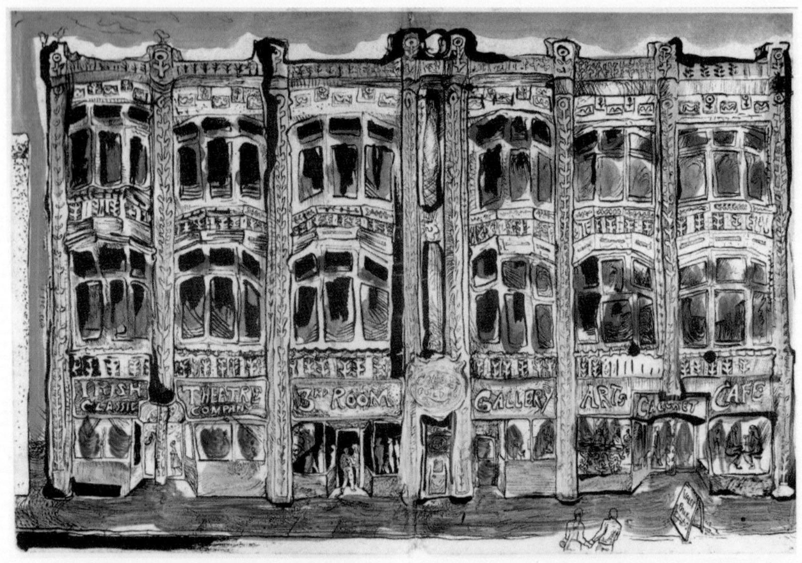

TOP: Jeffrey Paul Lane's conception of the Calumet Building, 1992.

BOTTOM LEFT TO RIGHT: Sukie Payne in front of The Third Room, c. 1993. Charlie in front of The Third Room, c. 1997.

TOP: Line-up to see Burning Spear in The Garden at The Calumet, 1996.
BOTTOM: Crowd preparing to watch an outdoor movie in The Garden, 1996.

"On Tour", 1994.

TOP: Charlie and Kevin "Mac" behind the bar at The Third Room, 1992.

BOTTOM: Pat Gallo and Charlie transforming Holly Farms into the Irish Classical Theater Company, 1995.

TOP: Jeanne Donovan's painting of the exterior of the Irish Classical Theater Company.
BOTTOM: Poster for Irish Classical Theater

TOP: With McCoy Tyner, after his gig at The Calumet, and friends at the Colored Musicians Club, 1996. Me on the far right standing over "Pres" Cutter, our fabulous photographer. Charlie standing over WBFO's Macy Favor on the left.

BOTTOM: Frankie Quinones performing in the window of La Luna, 1999.

TOP: Saturday night at La Luna, c. 2000.

BOTTOM LEFT TO RIGHT: Diana Krall trio at The Calument, 1997. Transforming the Irish Classical Theater into La Luna, 1997.

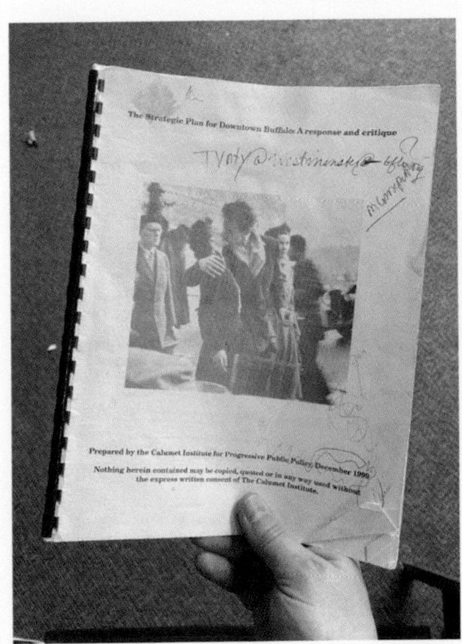

TOP: Flyer announcing our transformational meeting at City Honors, November, 2010.

BOTTOM LEFT TO RIGHT: Cover for our "strategic plan for downtown Buffalo, 1999.
Tim Tielman (2020) holding with his transformative sign used at the time of his epic battle to save the Commercial Slip, 2000.

TOP: Friends of the Buffalo Story logo.

BOTTOM: "Lighter quicker cheaper" at Canalside44.

TOP: Wedding of the Waters, 1. The Ruins, 2016.

BOTTOM: Wedding of the Waters 2, The Ruins, 2016. Stone Horse Lone Goman, far left.

TOP: Allen Street Hardware Cafe, 2010.

BOTTOM: Hardware at Night.

TOP: Black Rock Kitchen and Bar, 2012.

BOTTOM: Steve at the grill at "Mawk and Steve's Noo Yawk Dogs," 1997.

TOP: The Walls of Allentown, 2013.

BOTTOM: Brother Tony on the walls above Hardware, 2013.

Per Niente cover.

TOP: Capraro's Clam Stand, from the pages of Per Niente.

BOTTOM: The Per Niente boys, Bagel Jays, 2019. Joe Dileo is third from right.

Joey Giambra and his trumpet, 2019. Photo by Brendan Bannon.

Photos from our Ferry Street mural project.

Photos from our Ferry Street mural project.

TOP: Offerman Stadium from the air, tucked into the heart of Cold Spring, c. 1945.
BOTTOM: Lining up for a Buffalo Bisons game, Offerman Stadium, c. 1950.

TOP: "Slow Rollers" at the corner of Main and Ferry, 2018.
BOTTOM: Opening of Wash Project, 2012.

TOP: Mark and Steve, c. 1996.

BOTTOM: Halpern-Stanton Seder, 2014.

TOP: "Temple Beth Mr. Pizza".

BOTTOM: Tom McDonnell at Dog Ears Book Store, 2021.

TOP: Karen Lickfeld Murray at the Firefighters' Memorial.

BOTTOM: The Mount Mercy Girls at Dog Ears, Fall, 2019. LEFT TO RIGHT: Kathleen Crowley, Jeannie Cronin Cassidy, Barb Kelleher Fitzgerald, Grace Gannon

TOP: Mural on the outside wall of the Buffalo Irish Center.

BOTTOM: Rince Na Tiarna dancers performing at Buffalo State College, 2020. Photo by Bill Faught.

TOP: Rehearsal of Greater Buffalo Firefighters Fifes and Drums at the Buffalo Irish Center, 2019.

BOTTOM: Marge and Tom Ryan in front of their home on Coolidge.

TOP: Dianne Kam and friend at the "cardboard cottages", 1988.
BOTTOM: Classic home in the First Ward.

OTOWEGA CLUB, BUFFALO, N. Y.
Green & Wicks, Architects.

TOP: Parkside Lutheran Church, 2021.
BOTTOM: Otowega Club.

TOP: Back cover, Max Meets the Mayor, 2014.
BOTTOM: Five Corner kids, Fall, 2019. Photo by Steve Gabris.

TOP: Don Morris coaching at Shoshone. Photo by Bill Snyder

BOTTOM: North Buffalo Blaze at Shoshone, Summer, 2020 (that's Max, standing third from left). Photo by Steve Gabris.

Burke's Green. Photo by Steve Gabris.

TOP: Pandemic storm, Delaware Park, April 2020.
BOTTOM: Sunset, Broderick Park, Fall, 2020.

Charlotte, Eli and Max on their bench in Delaware Park.

TOP: Murray Levine leading a discussion of our Jewish Men's Reading Group.
BOTTOM: Family fun at Shoshone Park.

CHAPTER 9

Next Year in Jerusalem

What? A New Yorker finds his Jewish Identity in, where? Buffalo?

It was easy for us to be Jewish growing up in post World War Two New York. While our family did not live in any of the old Jewish neighborhoods like the Lower East Side, the Bronx, or Brownsville, our world, the world of middle and upper-middle class Jews on the Upper West and East sides of Manhattan, the world I grew up in, was heavily Jewish. My parents' world – my father's in the garment industry, my mother's among the political and cultural left – was almost entirely Jewish. So was mine, including: all of my friends and my teachers at the Walden School on West 88th St.; all the kids and counselors at Camp Androscoggin in Maine, and just about all of the people I met at Brandeis University.

As thoroughly Jewish as it was, our lives had almost nothing to do with the Jewish religion. Though both my mother and father were raised in Orthodox Jewish homes, they abandoned those traditions years before I was born and for as long as I can remember, formal religion played no part in the life of my family. We did not keep kosher. We never set foot in a synagogue. I did not go to Hebrew school; neither me, nor my brother, nor any of my friends celebrated a bar or bat mitzvah. Indeed, I cannot remember ever having gone to any Jewish religious services as a child. Christmas was for us a wonderful secular holiday, which we celebrated annually with a large party to which my parents invited all their Jewish friends. We were not trying to hide or pass. The Goldman family was not trying to pretend that we were anything other than who we were. Growing up in New York, the largest Jewish city in the world, we simply felt secure in our identities as Jews. I took it for granted and gave it not a thought. That is, until I moved to Buffalo in 1967. For here, for the first time in my life, the landscape was not Jewish. Here, where barely 3% of the population was Jewish – c. 25,000 of the approximately 900,000 who lived in metro Buffalo when I moved here – I suddenly found myself part of a real and distinct minority.

Had I been willing to join a synagogue it would have been easy but since that was not a path I had taken before, I had no interest in pursuing it now. In the absence of being affiliated to a religious congregation how could I, in a city where Jews were a relatively invisible part of the landscape, was I to find a meaningful way of being Jewish? I would, I quickly decided, have to do it on my own.

My efforts to find some Jewishness in the diaspora of Buffalo began in earnest with the birth of our son Charlie on December 7, 1972. While we opted out of a *brit milah* choosing instead to have a doctor at the hospital perform the circumcision, I quickly regretted that decision and I now, in the weeks after Charlie's birth I began to search for a ritual substitute.

My quest led me to the wonderful library at Temple Beth Zion on Delaware Ave. There, I came across an ancient Jewish religious tradition which required that a family's first-born male child be given over to "the priesthood." Charlie in the priesthood? At the age of one week, I wasn't ready to commit him to a lifetime of service. But there was, the tradition said, a way out. At a ceremony called a "*Pidyon Ha'ben*" held thirty days after the first born's birth, the child, in this case Charlie, could for a mere five silver coins, be "bought back." Well, this sounded like fun. It sounded like theater and it sounded like a party. We were going to have a *Pidyon Ha'ben*, a blast of a redemption party for Charlie. And we were going to have it at Temple Beth Zion.

Well, not, as it turned out, so fast. Temple Beth Zion was the largest Jewish congregation in the area. Founded in Buffalo in 1850 by German Jewish immigrants from Germany, the congregation early on became dedicated to the then-new practice of Reform Judaism. Even in 1972, TBZ was still a bastion of German-Jewish propriety; still not a place comfortable with traditional, more conservative, religious practices. While prayer shawls and yarmulkes were no longer banned as they had been when Reform Judaism started in Germany in the nineteenth century, if you wanted to wear them during services at TBZ in the 1970s, you'd better bring your own. When I approached the rabbi about my idea for a *Pidyon Ha'ben* ceremony, I was unceremoniously dismissed. This is not something, he said, that was done at Temple Beth Zion.

Surprised and disappointed, a little bit hurt and a little bit angry, I walked across Delaware Avenue from Temple Beth Zion to the Montefiore Club, a prestigious Jewish town club then still in existence. Might they, I wondered, understand? Indeed they did. So, a little more than thirty days after Charlie was born, we staged a rollicking "redemption" ceremony, replete with costumed relatives, prayers, songs, silver shekels (we used Kennedy half-dollars) and plenty of food, music and drink. I was thrilled, proud, and happy that Charlie had been forever redeemed.

While learning next to nothing of the Jewish religion as a child, I had been exposed to Israel and to all aspects of Jewish history and Jewish culture. Rooted in relationships that were both personal and political, my parents had deep ties to the kibbutz movement in Israel. They had visited Israel immediately after the founding of the State in 1948. In 1956, in the wake of yet another war there, my brother Tony (was it an accident that Tony and I both bore the names of Catholic saints?) and I, accompanied by our grandmother, Rosie, went to Israel too. My older sister Barbara influenced me as well. Barbara had an anthropologist's interest in Jewish history and it was through her that I became acquainted with the YIVO Institute in New York City. Founded in Vilna, Lithuania, in 1925, YIVO – whose letters in Yiddish stand for "Institute for Jewish Research" – was comprised of Jewish anthropologists, historians and sociologists who, with a premonition that the days of Jewish life in Poland were on the verge of becoming extinct, committed themselves to the collection and preservation of any and all documents, photographs, and other records of Jewish life in Poland. Following the Nazi occupation of Vilna, YIVO's massive collection of manuscripts, rare books, and diaries and other Yiddish sources, were packed up and secretly shipped to New York where they formed the foundation of what is, with its collection of over twenty million documents, photographs, recordings, posters, films, and other artifacts, the world's largest collection of materials related to the history and culture of Central and Eastern European Jewry. YIVO was an incredible place. Housed in a down-in-the-dumps former mansion on Fifth Avenue and 86th (YIVO is now headquartered on W. 16th while its building on 86th is the elegant home of the Neue Gallerie) YIVO was operated by a small staff of dedicated Yiddishists, each one of them, like the institution itself, a survivor of the Holocaust. By the mid-1960s my sister, preternaturally inquisitive, was producing radio documentaries using the massive audio archives at YIVO and it was through her that I was introduced to the incredible world of Yiddish music, art and theatre. Through YIVO, with the passionate encouragement of my sister, I was discovering both sides of the world of Yiddishkeit, the tragic one of the Holocaust and the incredibly uplifting one of Jewish cultural life. These interests were part of the rich legacy of treasures that I acquired in New York, and that I took with me to Buffalo.

The success of the *Pidyon Ha'ben* ceremony for Charlie turned out to be an important starting point. The seeds of my interest in Jewish matters, which had been planted in New York, began to grow and to flourish in Buffalo. What was going on here? Was there some powerful *ruach* (spirit) here in my adopted city, some special convergence of forces that was allowing me to connect with my roots in a way that I had not done before?

I began to think that maybe there was when I met Donald Zisquit, because it was through him that I was introduced into the world of traditional Judaism. Donald was a remarkable guy. Born and raised in Miami Beach, he moved to Buffalo following his marriage to a Buffalo girl in the early 1970s. Donald was blonde, blue-eyed with a big smile and a superb tennis player. Educated at both Harvard Law School as well as at a yeshiva in Jerusalem, Donald, the first observant Jew I ever knew, had his feet planted firmly in two different worlds.

I met Donald at the day care center at the Jewish Center where his daughter Daria and our son Charlie (no longer destined for the priesthood) were in the same group. Before long, Donald and his wife Linda had us over to their home for Shabbat dinner. As dark as it was that night in early 1974 their apartment glowed warmly. There was nothing pompous, formal, or too ceremonial that night as Donald and Linda led us gently through the Sabbath rituals: lighting candles, and then blessings over the wine and challah. Donald was a proud, energetic and upbeat celebrant of Judaism. He made the evening fun, interesting and exciting. I was hooked and wanted to know more.

Donald, like all Orthodox Jews, took very seriously the commandment to "honor the Sabbath and keep it holy." He was, I then learned, "shomrei Shabbos," a person who "guarded the Sabbath." What this meant in practical terms was that the world of the week and the world of the Sabbath were separate and different, the former being "normal," the latter being "sacred." At sunset on Fridays, be it at 4:30 in winter or 9:30 in summer, everything stopped for Donald and the observance of the Sabbath began. Even in a court of law where, one late afternoon in December, Donald, at the behest of his boss, was dutifully sitting, taking notes. Looking up at the clock, he told me later, he suddenly put down his pencil and stopped writing. "You're kidding," I asked him later. "What did

Manny (referring to his boss) say?" Donald looked at me with a slight grin and a confident shrug of his shoulders: "What's he gonna say? It's Shabbos." Later that afternoon, after court, Donald, as he did on so many winter Fridays when an early sunset meant an early Shabbat, began the long walk back from downtown to his home on Lexington Avenue.

Donald's synagogue was a tiny Orthodox shul (a "school house," in Yiddish) on Elmwood Avenue, located flush up against a large pizza joint called "Mr. Pizza." Donald paid little attention to aesthetics and cared not a bit where his house of worship was located. What mattered was that it was there and that he could walk to it. And so he went, every late Friday afternoon with his daughters Daria and Yael perched haphazardly on his shoulders and Linda on his arm. Rain or shine the four of them went to Beth Abraham, Donald joyously in the lead.

Well, if Donald didn't drive on Shabbat and he didn't use the telephone and he didn't carry anything (no keys, no money, no wallet and the like), how was he possibly, I asked him, going to compete in the finals of the MUNY tennis tournament on a Saturday afternoon in June 1975? No problem, his look suggested. "It's all about the *eruv*," he said. "It's a wily, but kosher way 'round the Sabbath rules. I save it for special occasions." So, in an imaginative way that was uniquely Donald, he created his own personal ritual enclosure around the area between his house and the courts in Delaware Park. Morphing into a more rabbinic demeanor, he explained that that way the public space becomes an extension of the private space. So, he said to me, "If you bring the racket to the courts, I can play inside the eruv around the courts." I did and now, while others watched the match at what they thought was the McMillian Courts, I knew that we were really watching it in the middle of Donald's sacred space, his "eruv."

Of all the concepts and rituals that I learned from Donald, the one that I cherish most is Havdalah. Performed at the end of the Shabbat right after sunset on Saturday nights, the purpose of Havdalah, which means "to separate," is to distinguish between the sacredness of the Sabbath and the normalcy of the week. With a bright double-wicked candle, the sweet smell of cloves and cinnamon, the ritual glass of wine, and singing, Havdalah, particularly when performed on a cold, dark Saturday night of deep winter in Buffalo, is a powerful and stirring ceremony. Donald and Linda's house is where I first entered the magical place in time that is Havdalah.

As long as Donald was around, we didn't have to worry too much about Charlie's (Lydia was still an infant) Jewish education. He loved Charlie, telling us that if he only came to live with him for a month, he'd make out of him a real "Yeshiva bocher" (a serious disciple of Judaism). But Donald and Linda wanted to live in Jerusalem and, in 1977, they moved there permanently. Abandoned by my "rabbi," I was on my own, left to wonder how, here in the diaspora of Buffalo, our family would ever learn the traditional Jewish customs and values that I was becoming increasingly interested in.

• • •

By the late 1970s, suburbanization had sucked the air out of Jewish life in Buffalo. While a sprinkling of Jews still lived in the Jewish enclave of North Buffalo, and a handful of older, wealthier Jews still lived on the streets of the Delaware District, virtually all of the families with children had moved to the suburbs. When Charlie entered City Honors in the early 1980s, and Lydia joined him a few years later, they had but one Jewish kid between them in their classes. But, I wondered, did that really matter? The experience of exile, of living in strange and different lands had been an integral part of the Jewish history for centuries. Charlie and Lydia did not, I felt, need the presence of other Jews in order for them to feel safe and comfortable in Buffalo. This remained true even when they, looking for new and different educational experiences, transferred schools, Lydia to the Buffalo Seminary in her sophomore year, and Charlie to Canisius, the Jesuit-run high school on Delaware Ave.

The "Sem" had long ago lost all traces of its historic anti-Semitism. During the 1950s, when Lydia's mother, Kitty went there, there were a dozen Jewish girls in her class. What kept the number of Jews in Lydia's class to just two was not a quota but rather simple demographics. By the mid-1980s, the Jewish population of the Buffalo metropolitan area had dropped in half – from c. 25,000 to c. 12,000 – and there simply were not enough Jewish girls to go around. The Buffalo Seminary, however, like City Honors, was a warm, homey and very welcoming place and not once during her three years there did Lydia feel the slightest hint of anti-Semitism. This was not the case, however, for Charlie at Canisius High School. Charlie was pretty thick skinned. Only once, when his art teacher suggested that he, like the other Jews, might, if he continued to misbehave, end up in the gas chambers, did he report (did he keep other experiences to himself?) feeling anti-Semitism at the school.

I'm still not sure if Charlie liked Canisius, but I do know that he loved playing soccer on the school's varsity. (He never liked saying the Lord's Prayer in the huddle before the game and refused to join in, when at the end of it everyone else shouted "St. Peter of Canisius pray for us.") Charlie may not have been good at praying to St. Peter, but he was a very good soccer player. At the end of the season of his senior year, he came home and announced excitedly: "Dad. Guess what? I'm all Catholic!" (referring to the All-Catholic league soccer team) "What?!?!," I responded with playful shock, "You're what? All Catholic? For over two thousand years, the Jewish people have suffered persecution, torment and exile so that my son could come home and tell me that he's 'all Catholic!'"

Charlie and Lydia, despite the relative absence in their world of other Jewish kids, were exposed to gulping quantities of Jewish life and lore at home. Unlike me, they each had their *b'nai mitzvot.* Under the watchful eye of their mother, Kitty, each learned Jewish prayers and songs and each attended Jewish summer camps. They learned still more when we retained two extraordinary Jewish educators – Ticktin Back and Rabbi Shay Mintz – to work with them. Between them, their home life and the strong Jewish blood that ran through their veins, we had nothing, even here, even in the *galut,* (Hebrew for "diaspora") to worry about.

• • •

My own interest and engagement with things Jewish continued to grow. Despite Donald and his family making *aliyah* to Israel, I remained involved with Beth Abraham, that funky, little *shul* next to Mr. Pizza on Elmwood at Bird. ("Temple Beth Mr. Pizza," we called it.) Beth Abraham was a tiny congregation, composed largely of old Jewish men with loyal ties to the synagogue. It was hard then, as now, to find parking on Elmwood. One Saturday morning two of the members parked their cars (these Jews drove on Shabbat!) in the small lot in front of Mr. Pizza. After services, as these two elderly men walked out of the shul to their cars, two burly guys wearing "wife-beaters" stained with tomato sauce rushed out of Mr. Pizza, hurling abuse and profanities. I did some swearing of my own, vowing that I would never buy a pizza from these guys.

Luckily, most of the neighbors were friendly. One, even, helped to make a "minyan." At least in the case of one of them, they were willing to help out.

Jewish law requires that no prayer service can take place unless and until a gathering of ten Jewish men, a *minyan*, are present. Beth Abraham was very small and it was never easy to get a minyan. Often, late on Friday afternoons, I'd get a phone call from Harry Weinrib, the *shul's* president: "Hey Mendel," he said using my Jewish name, "we need a *minyan*." On one Friday November 1996, we could not, despite my presence, gather a *minyan*. "Wait," I said to the eight other guys huddling in the cold of the barely-heated house of worship, "I'll be right back. I'll find one."

So off I went, crossing the street to the Elmwood Print-Out, where my old friend Larry Patti, an Italian kid from the West Side, was closing up shop for the weekend. "C'mon, Larry. Let's go. We gotta make the *minyan* at Beth Abraham. Just don't tell 'em you're not Jewish." Larry and I were friends and, though not at all sure what I was talking about, Larry, buttoning up his coat, said that sure, he'd come along. So off we went, "Mendel" and Larry, crossing the street, past Mr. Pizza and into Beth Abraham. Larry made the *minyan* and our Kabbalat Shabbat service could begin..

• • •

Even more than Beth Abraham, it was my ties to the Jewish Center that did the most to strengthen my Jewish identity. Following the birth of Charlie and Lydia, not a winter weekend went by without the three of us going there, to play in the large gym and enjoy the family swim time. By the early 1980s, I was increasingly interested in the many events and programs that the Center sponsored and, encouraged by the cultural arts director Susan Langer, I became particularly involved in the annual Jewish Book Fair and the International Jewish Film Festival. At first, these events were held at two venues, the Delaware Center and the new one in Amherst, the Benderson Building, which had opened in 1973. But by the end of the 1980s, as the number of Jews living in the city continued to drop and long-standing communal ties to the downtown center dwindled, the Amherst building became the full-time location of the book fair.

Although the Jewish population in Buffalo was waning, a new group of Jews started coming to the city and I was among those happy to welcome them. In the mid-1980s, the government of Mikhail Gorbachev allowed increased Jewish emigration from the Soviet Union, several hundred of whom, as a result of active recruitment efforts by Buffalo Jewish Family Services, settled in Buffalo. The migration of Jews from Russia was my story, the story of my father's and most of my mother's family. Now I, who had been consciously making an effort to create a Jewish home away from home for myself, wanted to do nothing less for these recent arrivals.

What if, I wondered, we had a *seder*, a Passover dinner with and for these new Buffalonians? With that in mind, I reached out for help to a social worker at Jewish Family Services named Janice Friedman. Like me, my friend Janice had come to Buffalo from somewhere else and now, together we planned a large, communal seder to be held in the gym of the Delaware Avenue Jewish Center.

Word in the Russian-Jewish community spread quickly, and within days over fifty people had committed to coming. We engaged our families and enlisted the help of other volunteers in the community. Sylvia and Bess Ozarin made the matzo ball soup; Phyllis Smukler the gefilte fish. Large tins of kugel were made by Sophia Rossman and Rose Goldstein and so it went until, finally, on the afternoon of March 22, 1988, we were ready. There were a handful of musicians among the immigrants ("How do you know if the Russian Jew getting off the plane is a pianist?," a joke at the time went. "He's the one not carrying a violin!"), and we enlisted two marvelous violinists, both veterans of esteemed Soviet orchestras – Max Zeligman and Semyon Ziskind – to provide musical accompaniment to the seder.. Sunlight poured through the large windows of the Jewish Center gym. The haunting music from the violins of Max and Semyon and the grateful, joy-filled faces of the seder's celebrants, led by Rabbi Shay Mintz director of Hillel, the Jewish student union at the University, created a magical moment for all of us, an experience which, I hoped, would bind the celebrants of the seder to their new home in Buffalo.

Despite the welcome influx of Russians, by the mid-1980s, the Delaware building was emptying out. Younger, suburban members were more interested in state-of-the-art work-out facilities and the brand-new pool at the Benderson Building than they were in connectedness to their Jewish communal roots. The contrast between the suburban facility and the increasingly drab Delaware building was stark and obvious. Many of us who called the Delaware building "ours" began to wonder if in fact the aging facility was, like so much else in the city, being "red-lined."

The most consistent users of the Delaware building were a core of seniors who attended the Center's free kosher lunch, which was served on weekdays on the first floor of the Center. I sensed something special about this group and, when invited to join them for lunch, I did so. (Perhaps, I wondered, was I searching for the elders I did not have in Buffalo?) I was intrigued by them, drawn to their life stories and their warm, sympathetic faces. What if, I asked Karla Wiseman who ran the program, I were to offer a weekly discussion group on current events? Let's try it, she said, for a month, and see what happens. And so, one day in Spring 1982, our month-long experiment began. Soon the months rolled into years and for over a decade (when finally in 1997 our meetings came to an end when death and illness took their toll) there was not a topic of significance – four presidential elections, the collapse of the Soviet Union, the disaster at Chernobyl, the implosion of the space shuttle Challenger – that we did not discuss together.

They were an extraordinary group of people who, as you can imagine, over the course of many years, became deeply connected to one another. And, indeed, as I had hoped, not only did I learn their story, but they, too, came to learn mine. The members of our group fluctuated but there were a handful of regulars whose stories, at least in outline, are worth recounting here. For example, Lily and Otto Popper, both born in Pilsen, Czechoslovakia before World War I. Both raised in highly-assimilated and well-educated families, both Lily and Otto were headed for futures as academics when their lives and aspirations were ended with the annexation by the Nazis of the Sudetenland in 1938. Following a valiant escape by boat from Norway, the Poppers made it to England, living out the war years in London. By 1949, with the support of the resettlement efforts of Jewish Family Services, the Poppers arrived in Buffalo. A year later, Otto and Lily were both working as social workers at the newly opened Delaware Avenue Jewish Center.

Otto, who always wore a sport-coat and tie and Lily, always well-dressed herself, were elegant, warm and very kind. One day, in Spring of 1983, when I, with a great deal of mixed emotion, told the group that I was getting a divorce, Lily walked over and gently, without saying a word, kissed me on the cheek and then just as quietly sat down.

Then there were the Ozarin sisters, Sylvia and Bess, both from immigrant families in The Bronx, both school teachers who, unable to find work in New York during the Depression, came, on a wing and a prayer, to Buffalo. They were sisters – "spinster" sisters, they were called then – Sylvia, a music teacher, Bess a history teacher – and they found a flat on Norwalk Avenue off Hertel in North Buffalo (where they still lived when we met in 1982). Soon, they both had jobs, Sylvia at Lafayette High School, Bess at Bennett, each teaching until their retirement in the mid-1970s.

The Ozarins were full of life and energy. They loved their work in the Buffalo schools and they never tired of regaling our group, despite its alleged focus on "current events," with endless tales from their days in the classroom. There were others too: Ed Falkenstein, a Communist community organizer who had moved to Buffalo after World War II to infiltrate and organize the workers at M. Wile, the Jewish-owned men's clothing manufacturer on Tupper Street. Falkenstein, originally from Oakland, California, was a veteran of the Abraham Lincoln Brigade and talked passionately about his experience in Spain. Growing up, I'd heard tales of the Spanish Civil War from my mother and father and it was thrilling to hear them here, in Buffalo, from Ed.

There was a non-Jew too, an African-American named Frank Crawford, proof that you didn't have to be Jewish to be a member of the Jewish Center. Crawford, like the rest of us, had come to Buffalo from somewhere else, he from New York where he'd been a highly regarded jazz pianist. Frank had played with some of the greats of modern jazz and began many of our discussions knocking out all kinds of tunes on the broken-down upright that stood in the corner of the room. He couldn't stand the drugs in that New York scene, he said. He had to get out. He came to Buffalo where he raised his kids, working as a music teacher at School 81.

By the end of the 1980s, hardly a week went by without our meeting. Our get-togethers had become an important part of a Jewish communal life I was building for myself in Buffalo. Together, I and my loyal and loving group of Jewish seniors had created something special. When in the early 1990s it was threatened, we fought together to protect what we had built.

The fate of the Jewish Center on Delaware Avenue can best be understood within the context of the decades-long suburbanization of Buffalo's Jewish population. By the early 1950s, sooner than any of Buffalo's other second generation immigrant groups, Jews began moving to suburban Amherst, an extension of their earlier settlement in North Buffalo, in large numbers. The Jewish Federation, the largest Jewish charitable group in the city, responded by urging that a new Jewish center be planned and built in Amherst. Hardly had the cement on the Delaware Building dried when in 1955, a mere six years after it opened, the Center's Board of Directors began to consider a new suburban location. The modern exodus of the Jewish people was clearly inexorable.

Other Jewish institutions responded to the same population trend. In 1961 Temple Beth El, the oldest synagogue in the city dating back to the 1840s, moved their entire congregation from Richmond Avenue to a new location in Amherst. Temple Beth Zion also wrestled with the suburbanization trend. Indeed in 1958, TBZ built a suburban annex in Amherst. But, in 1961, following a disastrous fire which destroyed their magnificent facility on Delaware Avenue, a slim majority of the congregation voted to rebuild and created a new modern home for the temple next to the Jewish Center on Delaware Avenue.

Jews were moving out of not only the city but the entire Buffalo metropolitan area. By 2000, the Jewish population of metropolitan Buffalo (the city and its surrounding suburbs in Erie County) had fallen from approximately 25,000 in 1967, the year I arrived, to under 12,000. In the face of these staggering numbers, what could the Jewish community possibly do? How could Jewish institutions, historic places like Temple Beth Zion and Temple Beth El possibly survive, whether in the city or the suburbs? And what about my special place, the Jewish Center on Delaware Avenue, the place that I first came to during the early days of my arrival in Buffalo?

Meanwhile, conditions in the Jewish Center continued to deteriorate. Was the leadership of the Jewish community convinced that if Jewish Buffalo had any future it was only in the suburbs? Were they intentionally "red-lining" the Delaware building in favor of the Benderson Building, which had opened in Amherst in 1973? By the early 1990s, it certainly seemed that way. Everything in the building was falling apart and nothing – the broken floor tiles, the rusty lockers, the leaking pipes, the missing lights, even the ever-out-of-balance scale – was ever repaired or replaced.

As the younger families flocked to the Benderson Building, and as programs like the book fair and other cultural enrichment programs moved there too, the Delaware building, with only a few die-hards in the gym and pool left, teetered on the brink of abandonment. Among them were the dozen or so seniors who came to the center every day for a free kosher lunch and who, once a week, stayed on to meet in our more than decade-long discussion group. Yet now, in the Spring of 1992, this too, was threatened when, one week before Passover, the Jewish Center Board of Directors announced that it was going to shut down the Delaware Center.

What? On *erev Pesach* (the "eve of Passover") they made this announcement? Closing the center was bad enough, but now, to tell us on *yontif*? (Yiddish for "holiday.") That was a *shanda* (more Yiddish, this time the word for "disgrace"). The decision to close the Delaware building was, like those that I'd fought in downtown and on the waterfront, though deserving of discussion given the demographic realities, arrived at and announced in an arrogant manner, one made by a board of directors disconnected from the lives of the people they were supposed to serve. Don't worry, we were told, we'll (inadvertently using a frightening word from the recent Jewish past) "transport" them (the seniors in the kosher lunch program) to Benderson. We were shocked, but like others who have appeared in the pages of this book, and armed with a love for our community and a faith in our ability to "fix this place," we fought back.

We pulled out the stops: lobbying and letter writing, organizing meetings and, in a demonstration of guerilla theater, the seniors in the lunch bunch picketed in front of the center on Delaware Avenue. There were many battles in this war, but the war was won when in the early 1900s Ann Joyce Holland Cohn, one of the center's great supporters, donated funds enough to renovate and thereby save the Jewish Center's Delaware Building. As a result, the building was renamed in honor of Ann's family and since then has been called the "Holland Building."

The effort to save the Delaware building was for me a powerful experience. We, a small group of Buffalo Jews, people who'd come here from far-away places, had taken and made our stand. We helped to save a critical institution in the lives of our people. It was a victory that not only salvaged the dignity of my elderly Jewish friends, but it was also a victory for our Jewish values and for our whole community.

Despite the growing identity of the Center as an athletic facility where fewer than half of its members are Jewish, the Center remains in 2021 committed to its traditional function as an incubator of Jewish life, values and culture. Here, in a building that stood at the threshold of sale or extinction, are signs printed in Hebrew as well as English that indicate direction and place – in the locker room, gym and elevator. The tee shirts the trainers wear are also emblazoned with words and names in the ancient Hebrew language. The highly popular early childhood program fills the building with the sweet sounds and smells of the Jewish experience, while poetry, reading and discussion groups fill the meeting rooms of the now vibrant Holland Building. And, today, more than fifty years after I first set foot in the Center in June of 1967, three generations of my family remain active members.

• • •

Seeking the comfort, support and stability of the familiar, many people upon moving to a new community affiliate with a religious institution. For me however, who'd had no formal religious training nor any institutional affiliation, this was not a path that I chose to take. While I was drawn to Donald Zisquit, it was his personality and the fervor of his faith, more than the tenets and ritual practice of Orthodox Jews that attracted me. Nor was I interested in Reform Judaism which seemed bland and uninspired. Like many similarly displaced Jewish souls, I was drawn to the exoticism of Hassidic Judaism. When two Lubavitcher rabbis from Brooklyn showed up in the mid-1970s, I sought them out. Working out of an old store-front across from UB's Main Street campus, Rabbi Nosan Gurary and Rabbi Heschel Greenberg, wearing *kapoteh* (long, black overcoats) and spritzing a combination of Brooklynese and Yiddish, were exotic, authentic, and very appealing. I was moved by the sincerity of their efforts to appeal to the lost Jews of Buffalo, their entreaties to "lay *tefillin*," to "*daven lulav*" and say the "*baruchas*." While attracted to the ecstatic side of their faith, the substance of it had little appeal to me. Finding no home in any quarter of Jewish life in Buffalo, I, like at least fifty percent of American Jews, remained unaffiliated with any synagogue. My quest for belonging, as a Jew and as a Buffalonian, continued.

By the early 1990s, I had become friendly with Steve Halpern, a self-described "working-class Jew from the Bronx," my partner in "Mawk and Steve's," the political science professor at UB. Though our backgrounds were different, we were both intense New Yorkers. Despite our attachment to Buffalo, we bonded as we debated what we liked about the Big Apple and what we missed. We bonded, too, over our shared Jewish roots and our often ambivalent desire to be more connected to them.

What we were looking for was not so much faith but rather friendship and beyond that, connection to our traditions. We wanted, in other words, "to belong." There was nothing that we wouldn't try. Together we went shul-shopping – *Rosh Hashanah* at Hillel, Y*om Kippur* at Temple Beth Zion, *Simchat Torah* at Chabad – but nothing resonated and clearly nothing stuck. We created services and celebrations of our own: annual *Tashlich* services for the Jewish New Year at a spot on the Niagara River; *Havdalah* at the foot of Ferry Street, *Sukkot* under a tent in Betty and Steve's backyard, and wonderful, inspired, free-form seders in their dining room. We wanted more. Luckily, inspiration hit us while walking one day (as we did when we "stumbled" upon "Mawk and Steve's) around Hoyt Lake in Delaware Park. What if we formed a Jewish men's book club, a small group of guys who would, together, explore topics and themes dealing with questions of Jewish culture, religion and identity. With this in mind, we gathered a wonderful, diverse group of older Jewish men, some natives, some, like us, outsiders.

Among them was Murray Levine, a product of the Depression-era Bronx, a retired and highly esteemed psychology professor at UB. Another member was Joe Masling, also a UB psychologist, who was born in Rochester. He was a Freud scholar and a skeptic who took nothing on faith. We had a psychiatrist, too, Gary Cohen, born and raised in Jewish North Buffalo, a Bennett High School grad. There were several doctors and a Yiddish-speaking businessman from St. Louis who became the owner of more McDonald's franchises than anyone else in the country. Here, in the company of these Jewish men, most of whom like me had come from somewhere else, I felt safe, comfortable and content. It was another way to strengthen the structure of my life in Buffalo..

Ruach, the notion that the Holy Spirit lives among us, is a core principle of Judaism. So, too, is *Tikkun Olam*, the belief that our primary work in this life is to heal and renew our global community. I believe in both these principles and feel that, in fact, it is both of them – *Ruach* and *Tikkun Olam* – that have motivated me to do the work that I have done in my fifty-plus years in Buffalo. By bringing *Ruach* into the public sphere, by infusing the landscape of our daily lives with the Holy Spirit, I could, we could, create *Tikkun Olam*, and in the process heal and renew our city and our world. If we could not make it a sacred landscape, we could try at least to make it an enchanted one.

Acknowledgements

Donald and **Linda Zisquit** have led rich and full-filling lives in Jerusalem where they have raised a family of five children and seventeen grand-children. Donald has worked as an attorney, Linda as a poet.

Kitty Friedman Goldman for her recollections of growing up Jewish in Buffalo.

Steve Halpern for his steadfast friendship and all the members, past and present of our Jewish men's book group.

Harry Weinrib, of blessed memory, single-handedly kept Beth Abraham alive during its most challenging years. His work laid the foundation for the renewal of the synagogue today.

Karla Weissman, Director of Senior Services at the Delaware Avenue Jewish Community Center, supported all of our efforts to serve the seniors there.

For background information on Bennett High School and its role in the life of Buffalo's Jewish community I have relied on the help and friendship of **Lenny Katz**, **Steven Greenberg**, **Ginger** and **David Maiman**, **Gary** and **Michael Cohen**, **Bob Dickman**, **Don Gilbert**, **Marilyn Whitman**, **Neil Lange** and others.

CHAPTER 10

Discovering the Power of Faith, Family, and Friendship

In South Buffalo, I learned, you are never alone

My first real introduction to South Buffalo came in the mid-1980s, when I was immersed in researching and writing about the Buffalo school desegregation case for my book, *City On the Lake*. It was then, while studying the impact of Judge Curtin's decisions on the structure of community life, that I became aware of the devastating impact of the decline of the industrial economy. It started in 1959 when the completion of the St. Lawrence Seaway swept away thousands of jobs on the waterfront – in the grain elevators, on the ships and railroads – that for more than one hundred years had pumped blood into the veins and arteries of South Buffalo. That, followed in the late 1970s and early '80s by the closing of both the Bethlehem and Republic steel companies, were, so many people thought, the final nails in the neighborhood's coffin. While these blows were cushioned somewhat by the large presence of so many South Buffalonians in the police and fire departments, even that long-time source of stability, the ease of access that South Buffalonians had to these jobs, was threatened when during the late 1970s and early '80s South Buffalo's own, Federal Judge John T. Curtin, John Curtin of Pawnee Place, of Seneca Street and St. Theresa's Church, ordered that they be integrated.

But it was at this time too that I learned something else about South Buffalo and the people who lived here, something that I would stay with me for the thirty years that passed until 2018 when I finally made it back there. My "epiphany" occurred at Bay Beach, Ontario, where in July of 1988 I took my daughter Lydia to visit Kristin Kam, her friend from school. Lydia and Kristin met at City Honors which, like so many of the magnet schools created by Judge Curtin and school superintendents Gene Reville and Joe Murray, drew together children from all parts of the city, in this case Lydia from North Buffalo and Kristin from Belvedere Road in South Buffalo. Kristin's parents, Charlie and Diane Kam were Buffalo public school teachers, both products of First Ward and South Buffalo families. By the late 1970s the Kams had joined a large group of their friends and neighbors at a small summer colony in Crystal Beach just across the Peace Bridge in Canada known to them and their neighbors alternatively as "the South Buffalo Riviera" or "the cardboard cottages."

Lydia and I crossed the Peace Bridge, drove up the Dominion highway, over to Sodom Road, then onto Erie Road where, Charlie Kam told me, in about a mile or so "you'll see the entrance to Bay Beach. Drive right past the entrance. You'll see a collection of cottages. The 'cardboard cottages,' we call them. Park right in front. I'll be looking for you." Well, sure enough there they were. Haphazardly arranged around a central area filled with sand and scruffy grass, there stood a dozen or so tiny cottages, nothing more than shacks really, all of them wood, all painted white, many with large shamrocks painted, like talismans, on their doorposts. There were any number of families: the Higgins, the Canaans, the Barretts, the McMahons, the Lickfelds, the Keanes, the Dargavels – names which, when I actually began to study the neighborhood in 2018, would come to roll off my tongue like water.

Many of the people whom I later came to meet in South Buffalo had ties to this tiny, humble beach resort, a place which, in spirit at least, resembled the crowded, friendly and familiar streets of the neighborhood that I would subsequently become so familiar with. Here, on Bay Beach, eating fries and drinking Loganberry from Eli's beach front snack stand; playing football and spending hours of so many endless summers, several dozen families all from South Buffalo, many from the same parish there, had created for themselves and the extended members of their family, a summer paradise. At "the cardboard Riviera," as in South Buffalo itself, the ties of ethnicity and neighborhood, faith and family ran deep creating a place where, I would soon be told, "you are never alone."

In subsequent years, South Buffalo receded from my mind until one day in the Fall of 2018, I ventured for the first time into the Buffalo Irish Center. I was intrigued by a flyer announcing an evening of traditional music sponsored by a group whose name I'd never heard and certainly could not pronounce – "Comhaltas Ceoltoiri Eireann." Located on Abbott Road, the Irish Center is an extraordinary place, right out of *Brooklyn*, that fantastic film about an Irish immigrant young woman making her way in New York in the early 1950s. The Pub Room of the Center is a large, open space with a small, raised stage on one side and a big, rectangular bar on the other. It was packed with people of all ages, older ones with walkers, many men wearing tweed caps and a contingent of men and women, selling food from folding tables, wearing red tee shirts proudly displaying their membership in "The Greater Buffalo Firefighters Pipe and Drums." Helping to serve the food and beverages and acting as ushers for the growing crowd, was a large contingent of teen-age girls each wearing costumes that identified them as members of the Rince Na Tiarna School of Irish Dance. The concert was held in the Emerald Room, a square hall with 32 large, colorful flags, 26 of them representing counties in the Irish Republic, six representing the counties in Northern Ireland, which the people gathered here naturally assumed would be joined with the Republic sooner rather than later. Sitting with an audience of 200 or more, I watched and listened to this extraordinary performance. The show opened with a *shanachie*, an Irish storyteller who embodied what I soon learned was an ancient Gaelic oral tradition. Who was this large and bearded man, I wondered, with his broad brogue, dressed in a tweed coat and cap, spinning these touching, riotous tales of pain and loss, laughter and love? Where was he from and what was his story? Another performer followed, Tom Callahan, a white-bearded man sporting a tweed cap, who sang a lilting version of a 19th century song, "Arthur McBride." I'd heard Bob Dylan sing that song years before, but his version was no match for Callahan's, whose powerful Irish brogue dramatized McBride's haughty resistance to the English officer who tried to press him into His Majesty's Royal Navy. Callahan's performance was followed by an acoustic duo, a fiddler and a pipe player who played not the breath-powered pipes that we are accustomed to, but rather Uillean pipes powered by the players' right arm. These sounds and rhythms were new to me. The crowd however, was tapping and clapping along to music that it seemed they'd known all their lives.

I was overcome by my experience at the Buffalo Irish Center, the rapt attention of the audience, and the passion of the performances. I knew right away that I had entered a new world. "Come back next week," the bartender told me on the way out, "if you want to see something really special. The Greater Buffalo FireFighters Pipes and Drum Corps are having a rehearsal." Eager to know more, I called my long-time friend Brian Higgins, the South Buffalo born and bred congressman from New York's 26th District, and told him about my experience at the Irish Center. "Call Mary Heneghan," he said. "She'll tell you the whole story." I did. "Come down on Friday," Ms. Heneghan said, making me an offer I could not refuse. "We can talk and then go to the Fenian Fish Fry," named, Mary told me, for those Irish patriots who, I would find out later, loom large in the historical memory of the neighborhood.

The Buffalo Irish Center has a library filled with a staggering collection of books, magazines, and ephemera dealing with Irish history and culture. It was here at a long wooden table that Mary Heneghan recounted the story of how the Irish Center was created in 1970. The effort was led not by the earlier generation of Irish immigrants, men and women who'd come to Buffalo as long ago as the mid-19th century, but by immigrants from Ireland who came to America in the years after World War II. While many went to New York, to Boston, or Chicago, many came to Buffalo, too. Hundreds found work and a home in South Buffalo's still-robust industrial economy. Seeking out the familiar, this new generation of Irish immigrants filled the taverns and social halls of the neighborhood. Unlike the far more assimilated earlier generation of Irish-Americans who made up much of the neighborhood, this just-off-the boat generation wanted a place of their own, a cultural and community center where the ties of faith, family and tradition strengthened and reinforced the ties that bound them to their neighborhood and to each other.

By 1970, a small group had acquired the necessary funds and were now able to purchase an empty YMCA building at 245 Abbott Road. Raising the money and then, relying on the talents of the skilled laborers among them, they renewed the old Y, transforming it into the Buffalo Irish Center. Now, more than fifty years later, the Buffalo Irish Center is the epicenter of the Irish-American cultural and political life of Buffalo, a dynamic hive of Irish and Irish American cultural and heritage activities, home to among others the Buffalo Comhaltas, devotees of Gaelic music; the Celtic Angels, a young girls singing group; the Gaelic Youth Choir; The Rince Na Tiarna Irish Dancers; the School of Irish Culture and Language; the Buffalo Irish Genealogical Society, the Daughters of Erin, the Knights of Equity and an athletic club known as the Fenians of the Gaelic Athletic Association.

For many years, Mary Heneghan has led the Center. Born in St. Teresa's Parish on Seneca Street, Mary met the man who became her husband, Tom, a new immigrant from County Mayo, at an Irish picnic held at Schiller Park in 1964.

Much of Irish American life in South Buffalo is now a Heneghan family affair. In his shop, the Tara Shop right across the street from the Center, Mary's son Tom sells the finest Irish linen and imported woolen clothes. Meanwhile, Mary and Tom's daughter, Mary Kay, who learned Irish dance as a child, founded and still directs the Rince Na Tiarna Irish Dancers which is located in the Center itself.

After talking in the Center's library, we moved to the Pub Room, where the Fenian Fish Fry was about to begin. A mix of people of all ages, made their way to the dozen or so picnic tables, ready to place their orders. On the stage a man named Kevin O'Neill began reciting "The Child's Poem" by W. B. Yeats that he'd set to music:

We foot it all the night,
Weaving golden dances
Mingling hands and mingling glances
Till the moon has taken flight.
To and fro we leap
And chase the frothy bubbles,
While the world is full of troubles
And is anxious in its sleep.

The bar was busy and Mary, who knew everybody, pointed out the local celebrities who were sitting around it. There was Margaret Keane. ("She's a Whalen," Mary knowingly told me.) I'd known her husband Jim, long before he died in 2014, a scion of the great South Buffalo Keane clan, when he'd been a councilman from the South District. Margaret, like so many members of the Keane family, had been a Buffalo firefighter. She rose to become the first woman in the country to serve as the department's Deputy Commissioner. Though she is retired now, two of her daughters, Katy and Meg, are both lieutenants in the Buffalo Fire Department. I wanted to talk with her more but she told me that I'd have to wait. She was going to Florida and would not be back for five months. "Five months," I exclaimed. "How can you leave South Buffalo for five months?" "I'm not," she replied. "Half of them are coming with me. Remember the cardboard cottages? It's the same down there."

The bar was packed with chatty and very friendly South Buffalonians, some I knew, others Mary introduced me to. She pointed out Bobby Doyle, a short, redhead "from Belfast." He was active in NORAID, the Northern Irish Aid association in Buffalo during "The Troubles" of the 'eighties and 'nineties, Mary said: "He told us the money was for the women and children." Then, with a sly smile at Doyle, she said: "But we know what it was really for, don't we, Bobby?" Getting up from their bar stools near-by were Jack Doyle and his wife, Jane. They had to leave early, they said, their daughter was coming home from a college trip to Ireland and they had to collect her at the airport in Toronto the next morning. Chris Scanlon, South Buffalo's young representative in the Buffalo Common Council, set down his Guinness and, smiling ruefully, said: "That's something that never happened in our house. No Ireland for us. Not with seven kids. We were lucky to get to the skating rink in Caz Park." Bonnie Kane Lockwood, "Bonnie Kane of the Seneca Street Kanes," a "Crick rat" (a term of endearment for one who hails from the Cazenovia Creek section of South Buffalo) who'd "crossed the Crik for love," for her husband John, was there too. She'd been a council member from the South District and for years worked as a key administrative aide to Congressman Higgins in his Buffalo office. I'd known Bonnie from our struggles over the Waterfront but never did realize just how deep her roots in South Buffalo were. Her family, filled with judges and politicians and even a hockey star, Pat Kane, is very big here. Like Judge Curtin, she told me over a Guinness, she too grew up on Pawnee Parkway, off Seneca Street, on the other side of "the Crik." There were eight Kanes in that one house on Pawnee, she told me. "I never really did go anywhere else. There was no reason to really. Never alone? You got that right. Where would we go … maybe to Hillery Park and the cardboard cottages. That was it."

At that point Mary Heneghan took me aside. "I want you to meet him," she said pointing to a man across the bar from us. "That's Tommy McDonnell … he owns the Dog Ears Book Shop and Café. Don't miss Dog Ears. Trust me."

Several days later, I met Tom at the Dog Ears, a book-store-cum café and a "literary arts center" all under one roof. Tom's roots are firmly planted in South Buffalo. His mother, Margaret Reilly, grew up on Indian Church Road, in St. John's parish, just around the corner from the old Seneca Indian burial ground on Buffum. She remembered seeing her mother uncover bones in their backyard. "We always wondered," she said, "if they were not the bones of Red Jacket." Tommy grew up on Carlyle, off Abbott on the other side of the Cazenovia Creek. "We travelled in packs then. And we still do now. The Carlyle Cougars that was us. I'm still good buddies with most of the "Cougars": Teddy Nagle, "Dinker" Gallagher, the Mulligans and the Hillerys." Like so many of his old neighborhood friends, Tom went to Bishop Timon High School. He loved books and he loved learning and thought about teaching. But he was restless, uncomfortable with the structure of the classroom. "I like freedom," he says. "I like being my own boss. So, what did I do? I became a bartender … there's not a bar in South Buffalo I haven't worked: Mudd McGrath's, Charlie O'Brien's, Houlihan's. I still do work at one … every Saturday night at O'Daniels just down Abbott." But books were his passion and, in 2008 McDonnell opened Dog Ears Bookstore and Café. Dog Ears is Tom's life and he has created here a veritable community center around books: story hours for toddlers, poetry nights, weekly book club meetings and a movie night, all held in a second floor room that is part library part living room – The Enlightenment Literary Arts Center. While Tom focuses on the kids and the programs, the book store itself is staffed by volunteers, people from the community like Jack Coyle.

Jack Coyle's story, I learned, is the story of South Buffalo. Tim Bohen, the great historian of the old First Ward, was right. The roots of South Buffalo are planted firmly in the First Ward and it is there, on Perry Street, that Jack Coyle's mother was born. His father, who worked two jobs, one as a cop, the other as a railroad engineer, was from South Buffalo and it was there, on Bridge Street, "right behind St. Martin's," Jack says, that he was born. There's not a job, it seems, that Jack hasn't done, always, like so many of the men in South Buffalo, working two concurrently, as a scooper in the grain mills and, like his father, as a railroad engineer on what until recently was known as the South Buffalo Railroad. "It was easy in the 'fifties," Jack told me. "There was work everywhere." And if you didn't want to work in a plant or on the railroads, there was always the Aud where all the jobs, Coyle says – the security guards, the ticket takers – were filled with South Buffalo boys. "That's because of Jim Keane's father, Dick. He controlled that union and saved all the jobs there for his kids' friends. We all worked, all the time. That's just what we did." There was a similar pipeline, Jack says, for the girls in South Buffalo. "So many of the girls I knew growing up had aunts who were either Mercy nuns, Mercy nurses, or Mercy teachers. Retired now, Jack, who served on the Buffalo School Board for more than ten years, volunteers at Dog Ears. "I read to the kids, upstairs, every Thursday afternoon after school."

Dog Ears is a hang-out as well as a bookstore and a coffee shop and there's no better place to meet the people and to hear the stories that are the DNA of South Buffalo than this café. Dog Ears is packed on Saturday mornings and on one in December of 2018, Brian Higgins and his brother-in-law, Dennis Dargavel were at one table; the two Redmonds, father and son, Dan Sr and Dan Jr., both retired police officers, were at another. The Redmonds are an interesting family who, like so many of the people I met in this neighborhood, have deep ties and connections to it. Like others, the Redmonds have lived all, if not most, of their lives in the neighborhood, Dan Sr. on Dundee, right around the corner from Dog Ears, where his daughter and her family also live. Dan Jr, who, while he did follow his father into the police department was, he says, "the rebel. I moved around the corner to Downing."

I was drawn to the six women sitting together at a round table in the center of the room. "Oh, you're the writer," one of them said, with a very warm and friendly smile, "the fella' writing about South Buffalo." "I'm Grace Gannon, this is Jeannie Cronin – she's Peggy Cronin's sister." "I'm Barb Kelleher," said the woman at her side, "and she," pointing across the table, is Kathleen Crowley." "Those are our maiden names. Most of us girls, we all use our maiden names. That's how everybody knows us." Known as the "Mercy girls," they meet at Dog Ears every Saturday morning at nine.

"There were over 200 girls in my class, the Class of '76," Barb Fitzgerald said. "There's not a woman in my family, going back to the 1920s, who didn't go to Mount Mercy. The Mount was just a part of our blood," she declared, adding that three of her aunts were Mercy nuns and Mercy nurses. Grace Gannon chimed in: "One of those aunts was Sister Mary Annunciata Kelleher. She was the real founder of the Catholic Health System. Nuns or nurses, that's what they were." "Hey, just a minute," interjects Grace Gannon, who is a partner at a downtown law firm: "Yes I did work at Mercy as a kid but then I went to law school." "And I," adds Barb, "am a Buffalo public school teacher in Hamlin Park." Our meeting breaks up. Barb wants to get home. Her son is taking the police exam and she is dying to know how he did. We promise to meet next Saturday, same place, same time. "You've got to meet my sister, Peggy," Jeanne Cronin says on her way out. "She's the president of Mount Mercy on Abbott Road. She'll tell you everything." When later that week I called Ms. Peggy Cronin, she, like everyone else that I'd met here, was warm, friendly and eager to talk. I met her at her office at "the Mount" on Abbott Road in early January 2019.

Peggy Cronin, born and raised on Edgewood around the corner from the Mount in a home her parents still live in, wasted little time. We were together for a few minutes before she showed me a book. "I want you to read this," showing me a worn tome, a history of the Mercy nuns. "The author, Sister Mary Gerald Pierce, was my great-aunt, you know." She continued, "it was Bishop Timon who brought the sisters here from Dublin in the 1850s but it was the Sisters – themselves – who built and sustained the entire infrastructure of parochial education in Buffalo." We studied the book together: the Sisters started in the old First Ward, at St. Bridget's Church on Fulton Street, where in 1854 they founded Buffalo's first Catholic elementary school. As Buffalo's population pushed south following the opening of Lackawanna Steel at the turn of the century, the Mercy Sisters followed. In 1904, right across the street from the recently opened Holy Family parish, they converted an old home into a thirty-bed hospital known then, and still, as the Mercy Hospital of Buffalo. Later that year they opened Mt. Mercy Academy, on Abbott Road and Red Jacket Parkway where it remains today.

The Mercy Sisters excelled at education and soon it was the Sisters of Mercy who ran the elementary schools in all of South Buffalo parishes. By the mid-1920s the schools in all of them – St. John the Evangelist, St. Agatha, St. Martin's, St. Thomas Aquinas, Holy Family and St. Teresa – were staffed and managed by the Sisters of Mercy. By the mid-1940s even the school at St. Anthony's, the old Italian parish on Court Street, was run by the Sisters. "You simply cannot," Ms. Cronin insisted, "begin to understand the culture and the values that we here in South Buffalo live by without knowing just how deep and how strong has been the influence of the Sisters of Mercy."

Mount Mercy Academy is a fascinating complex. Housed in an impressive brick and sandstone structure built in 1911, "The Mount" sits directly across from the entrance to Cazenovia Park. The school and the Mercy Hospital (in 1928, the Mercy Sisters moved their tiny hospital here) dominate the landscape of this part of South Buffalo.

For generations, Peggy tells me, the girls of South Buffalo poured into "The Mount," particularly after World War II. The years of the great baby boom were on; in Catholic neighborhoods like South Buffalo, young couples heeded the countless priestly admonitions to "go forth and multiply."

There were, she continued, in those halcyon years of the baby-boomers during the 1950s and'60s, more than enough kids to fill the schools. All the Catholic schools in South Buffalo were jammed, she told me, pulling out numbers from the late 1970s that supported her claims: St. Ambrose, 1200 families; Holy Family, 1775; St. Agatha, the smallest, with 812 families; St. Martin's, St. Theresa's and St. Thomas Aquinas each had over 1700 families .... Altogether there were 20,000 families, all Catholic, almost all Irish ... and oh how so many children! You know how many baptisms and first communions that meant," she asked rhetorically? "How many weddings? How many wakes? How many kids we all had to play with?"

Peggy, like so many Buffalo baby-boomers, recalls a time when neighborhoods were strong and happy places, where there were zero degrees of separation, where everybody knew everybody, where mailmen and crossing guards, teachers and priests, bus drivers, firefighters and cops knew two and sometimes three generations of the same family. Despite the depth of her ties, marriage took Peggy to live in Los Angeles for over twenty years. She returned to Buffalo in 2014 and became president of her alma mater, Mt. Mercy Academy. "Imagine," she says, "in LA if I went to three wakes a year it was a lot. Here, I'm at three a week." What she missed most, she said, pressing the three fingers of her right hand against her thumb, a gesture more associated with Italians, "the *this* of South Buffalo." Raising the four compressed fingers of her hand to her face for emphasis, she reiterated: "It's *this*. *This*," a quality of life that started in large families, spilled out on and into the street, then to the block, around the corner to the church and the school producing a neighborhood where public and private lives merged, a place where so many felt an overwhelming sense of comfort and belonging. "I'm not sure that you understand," she said sympathetically. "You see, in South Buffalo we were never alone. Who wouldn't have wanted to grow up here! Who wouldn't want to live here?"

Things were getting complicated. I was in way over my head. I needed guidance and so I called my old friend Marge Ryan, a long-standing and highly respected community leader, the go-to- gal for anybody who wants to get anything accomplished in South Buffalo. I'd met Marge at my first South Buffalo go-around in the 'eighties and in the years since had followed her work as an outstanding community leader. "Come with me," she told me on the phone one day in March of 2019. "Meet me here, at my home on Coolidge Road. I'll show you around."

I'd first heard about Coolidge Road from Anne Gioia, the wife of one of my close friends, who, as Annie Driscoll, grew up on the street during the late-1950s and early 1960s. Coolidge, she said, was "the Middlesex Road (the toney neighborhood in North Buffalo) of South Buffalo," which, with its large, single family homes on each side of a road divided by a tree-filled median, was the street of choice for neighborhood doctors, lawyers and judges. Marge has lived here for years and now, the week before St. Paddy's Day 2019, she was waiting for me in the driveway of her home there, flanked on one side with the American flag, the other with the Irish flag. "We bought this house fifty years ago from Judge James Kane. "It's hard to believe," she says pointing out the modest exterior of her home, "but the Kanes raised twelve kids in this house. We raised six of our own here. Our seventeen grandchildren might just as well have lived here. There's lots of South Buffalo roots in this house, that's for sure." Marge was eager to show me around. Things were looking good in South Buffalo, she said, and with a little break in the weather, "we'll be ready to go for the garden walk." Yesterday, she told me, she had what she said was "a perfect afternoon" in South Buffalo. Biking up and down the streets of her neighborhood, up Coolidge to McKinley, then over to South Park Avenue, she checked on all of the gardens that she maintains along with a small cadre of other volunteers. Then, she biked home, took a shower and "it was off to the four o'clock mass at St. Tommy's."

"Let's have another one today, in the car," she said. "You drive and I'll lead." There's not a person of any importance to the people of South Buffalo that Marge does not know: every business owner along Seneca Street and Abbott Road, the head of every department in City Hall, the principals and most of the teachers in all of South Buffalo's schools. She is greeted everywhere; even the firefighters blast their horns in respect and recognition.

Marge, tall, thin red-headed, is a remarkable force of nature, omnipresent in the streets of South Buffalo. In 2000 she, along with a handful of neighbors and friends like Donna Curry and Kathy Cunningham, founded the South Buffalo Garden Walk and "South Buffalo Alive," now an influential business and neighborhood association. She began our tour with some background, about how South Buffalo is divided by the Cazenovia Creek, with the Seneca

Street neighborhood on one side, the Abbott Road neighborhood on the other. She nodded familiarly when I told her that I'd already heard about the "Seneca Rats" and how Bonnie Kane had "crossed the Crik" for the love of John "Locks" Lockwood. Marge was born on that side of the "Crik" too, on Sage Street, right around the corner from Pawnee, birthplace of both Bonnie Kane and, remember, Judge John Curtin. She, too, was a St. Teresa's girl. We drove down Sage, a narrow tree-lined street with both single and double homes. Sage ends at the banks of the Buffalo River and it was here along these river banks and the woods that filled the landscape of her youth, that Marge came to fully appreciate the importance of the natural environment. It was her childhood on Sage, she says, that years later inspired her to organize the South Buffalo Garden Walk.

We proceeded to McKinley Parkway, a beautiful boulevard, the Olmsted-designed showcase of South Buffalo, and stopped in front of Bishop Timon High School. Someday, Marge said, "you've got to get in there. For the men of South Buffalo, for people of my husband Tom's generation, Timon **is** South Buffalo. You can't write about South Buffalo without writing about Bishop Timon." We drove down other streets: Tuscarora, Pawnee, Peconic, Niantic, Minnetonka named for Indian tribes, testimony to the place of the Senecas in the history of South Buffalo. We went to Buffum Street, site of Marge's childhood school #70, but more significantly, the site of the old Seneca Burial Grounds and the original resting place of Red Jacket, who, along with several hundred other members of the Seneca Nation of Indians lived in this area until they were removed in 1842. (Red Jacket's remains were removed as well when in 1884 his body was exhumed and, in defiance of his last wishes, reburied in the white man's cemetery at Forest Lawn.) All that is left of his original burial site is a bronze plaque affixed to a boulder in the middle of a tiny, shady park. Its fading letters tell the sad and haunting story: "In this vicinity from 1780-1842 dwelt the larger portion of the Seneca Nation of the Iroquois League. In this enclosure were buried Red Jacket, Mary Jemison and many of the noted chiefs and leaders of the nation."

We drove down other streets that filled the conversation of so many of the people I met in South Buffalo: Karen Lickfeld Murray's Strathmore, Terry Schuta's Lilac, Peggy Cronin's Edgewood, the Redmonds' Dundee, Tommy McDonnell's Carlyle and so many more. Marge pointed out the sights as we drove along Abbott Road: her church, St. Thomas Aquinas, a landmark at the corner of Abbott and Strathmore for almost a century. "There, in that empty store-front across the street, was Sullivan's Ice-Cream Parlor. We all hung out there. They had a juke-box in the back where we danced. That's where I met my husband, Tom." We continued just past Dog Ears BookStore ("don't miss Reddingtons Funeral Home across the street," Marge advised. "You know how many wakes have been held there, and at Canaan's and McCarthy's, over the almost one hundred years that they've been here.")

We turned on Warren Spahn Way, named for the great South Buffalo-born pitcher, then Red Jacket Parkway, and entered Cazenovia Park. Designed by Fredrick Law Olmsted in the early 1890s, Caz Park has been a focal point of community life since. Marge is passionate about Caz Park and serves on a citizens' group that advises the Olmsted Conservancy. She, like so many others here that I met and spoke with, reminisced about her childhood in the park, a time when both the ice skating rink and the swimming pool were still outdoors and open to the fresh air; when there were so many kids in the pool, she said, that they were afraid to jump in. Driving through the park on Jacket Parkway, we stopped and looked at the "bowl," home to the Cy Williams baseball diamond, a place where generations of South Buffalo boys played little league ball. We exited the park on Seneca Street. "See that corner," she said, pointing to St. John the Evangelist Church. "It was just bought by the Hook 'n Ladder Development Company. Hook 'n Ladder is turning all of Seneca Street around." She pointed out just some of the work that they have done: the transformation of St. John's into a mixed-use commercial and residential building, the restoration of "Bob's Barber Shop," an iconic wooden building from the early 1920s, a magical, wood-frame mixed use building at Seneca and Kamper, and their own offices across the street. Marge is intensely proud of the Hook and Ladder Company and talks about the men who own it as though they were her children. "Three of the four of them are from South Buffalo, you know. All four of them firefighters, all working out of the same firehouse on Jefferson Street on the East Side. And look what they're doing for South Buffalo."

We continued down Seneca where, at the corner of Kingston and Seneca, Marge had me stop. "That's where the Keane house was," she said. Repeating a foundational piece of South Buffalo lore which I'd heard years before, she told me the Keane Family saga: "Sixteen Keane children were raised in that house. Five of them," she told me passionately, "were firefighters: Jim, his brothers Dick, Mike and Neal, a battalion chief. Then there was Bill Keane, known to everybody in South Buffalo as "Puff," who was killed in the line of duty." Marge continued: "Jim's wife Margaret came from a family of firefighters – ("a Whalen," I'd remembered from the Irish Center!) – on both the Whalen and the Healy sides. Two of Marge's uncles were firefighters too: "Whipper" and R.J. who, like Jim's brother "Puff," was killed on the job. In 1983, Jim's wife Margaret joined the fire fighting force and would soon become, Marge proudly reminded me, one of the first female deputy fire commissioners in the country. Hard to believe but true," she continued. "If you count the Keane's and the Whalen's, there's thirty-five of them who have served in Buffalo's Fire Department."

Marge took me over to meet Jim Keane's older sister, Mary Alice O'Neil, who lived in a small house on Tuscarora Road between Abbott and Potters Road. Mary Alice, though diminutive, had a big personality, a woman, I was told, "who curses in Gaelic and prays in Latin." "Imagine," she said shortly after Marge introduced us, "what it's like to live in a family with sixteen kids. We were all friends with each other's friends and their families too, some of them as big as ours. Even before any of us got married and had families of their own, we moved in circles of several hundred people." I told her how Peggy Cronin described the "this" of South Buffalo. "Exactly," Mary Alice said. "Our tribes were big ones but they were close ones. Those big families in tiny houses, filling the streets of the neighborhood, filling the churches and the schools .... She's right. We never really were alone."

The Keane family remains intensely close today. Mary Alice can't walk out of her house on Tuscarora, she says, without bumping into a family member. On the morning that I was there with her, her son "Stitch" stopped by with his son, both, by the way, members of the Buffalo fire department. Meanwhile, Mary Alice's brother Mike called to check in, while her daughter Patty, who owns a beauty shop around the corner on Potters Road, stopped by to see if her mom would go with her to a wake in Angola. Seven of her children live in South Buffalo, as do all 17 of her and her late husband's grandchildren. There are no degrees of separation in the Keane-O'Neil family: two of Mary Alice's granddaughters in fact, work at South Park High School, where Terry Schuta, one of South Buffalo's finest, is the principal. Just to make sure that no one was missing, Mary Alice, who knew of my friendship with Bonnie Kane Lockwood, told me that one of her granddaughters is married to Bonnie Kane's son. (Sadly, Mary Alice died in early 2021.)

"You want to know just how important fire fighting is in the life of South Buffalo?" Marge asked as we left Mary Alice's house. "I'm going to take you," she said, "to the firefighters memorial at the triangle where Abbott meets Potters."

The memorial has intense, personal meaning to her and to so many of her friends and neighbors, all of whom are proud of the generations of South Buffalo men and women who have served in the Buffalo Fire Department. Marge tends the memorial as she would the grave site of a dear family member, and when we got there she began picking up pieces of stray garbage that had collected, raking the leaves and fussing with the flowers. The fire department in general and the firehouses in particular, were, I began to realize, like the neighborhood itself, warm, friendly and familiar. In the sometimes yawning, sometimes fatal world of the firefighter, the ties that had been formed in the streets, the neighborhood and the parish, were bound tighter still in firehouses throughout Buffalo. Particularly following the propane fire tragedy of December, 1983 – "South Buffalo's 9/11" she called it – that Marge now described to me. I took notes as the story, told in Marge's still sad voice, unfolded. It all happened at 8:23 p.m. the night of December 27, 1983, when Ladder 5 on Seneca Street received a call that propane tanks, illegally stored in a warehouse on N. Division Street, were leaking. A full assignment was dispatched and within seconds of their arrival, were met with a horrific explosion. The block had become a war-zone: Houses in the neighborhood were instantly destroyed when a fire truck that was blown across the street crashed into them; firefighters screamed for help, neighbors ran for their lives while the division chief, with a 5-inch stake sticking into his neck, did his best to command the scene. The damage was frightening. The fire had leveled the entire four-story warehouse and the ensuing fireball demolished many buildings throughout the neighborhood. A large Gothic church, one block away, had a huge section ripped out of it as if a great hand had carved out the middle. Worst of all, five firefighters, four of them from South Buffalo, were killed: Michael Catanzaro, Michael Austin, Matty Colpoys, Tony Waszkielewicz and James Lickfeld. The propane fire of that year created a deep scar in the heart of South Buffalo and at "2020 hours" on December 27 every year, dozens of neighbors gather here at the memorial while the Buffalo Fire Department rings out the "1-9-1" alarm in honor of the men who died there. Among them is Karen Murray, nee Lickfeld, daughter of Jim Lickfeld. Pointing to the names on the monument. Marge Ryan singled out Lickfeld. "Everybody called him "Red," she said. "Even before the fire, he was a legend in the neighborhood. One of those guys who everybody loved. You know," she continued, "his daughter is the principal at Public School 67, just down Abbott Road."

Now there was an irresistible South Buffalo story if ever there was one: the young woman whose father, a legendary neighborhood fire-fighter killed in the line of duty, returns to her childhood neighborhood to serve as a school principal. Marge got it immediately and within days she had arranged for me to meet Karen Lickfeld Murray in her office at Public School 67 on Abbott Road.

Marge told me that Karen was raised on Strathmore and before our March 2019 meeting, I visited the short tree-lined street that runs between Abbott Road and McKinley Parkway. The street is a tableau of intimacy, filled with one and two family homes, each with those inviting front porches which, if they could only talk, would repeat a thousand conversations and tell a thousand stories. Strathmore is shadowed by the imagery and symbolism of Catholicism: the façade of St. Thomas Aquinas Church on the Abbott Road side and Bishop Timon High School on the McKinley Parkway side. It was clear from the time I spent here that Strathmore was a place, like so many in South Buffalo, where, as Peggy Cronin said, "You are never alone."

We met in Karen's office at Discovery School 67 where, stuck prominently onto the bulletin board behind her desk was a large sign that read: "Thank the Lord I was born in The Ward." She was getting ready, she told me, to march with her father's brother, in the annual First Ward St. Patrick's Day parade. Tim Bohen said it: the list of South Buffalonians with roots in The Ward is long and filled with many familiar names.

Like everybody else I spoke to in South Buffalo, Karen Lickfeld Murray grew up with tons of kids, a pack of girl-friends – "the witches of Strathmore," they called themselves, with whom she is still close today. Today she lives, along with many of those same "witches of Strathmore," around the corner on Cushing. Here's how she describes her Cushing Street community. "Well, there's my best friend, Bridget McMahon who married Jim "Doler" Dole, a Buffalo firefighter. "Doler," she says, "grew up with my uncle Butch, in The Ward. Bridget though grew up right next door to me on Strathmore. We play golf with some of the other 'witches' all summer long at South Park." Karen continued enthusiastically: "Next to the Dole's is Mark and Amanda Scanlon, Councilmember Chris Scanlon's older brother. His wife, Amanda, was in my class at St. Tommy's. Chris is only a first generation South Buffalonian, you know. His dad – "Scanoots" – like mine, grew up on Mackinaw in The Ward. Lots of us who live on Cushing today went to St. Tommy's together: Chris Shanahan, Kevin Lalley, Kara Scanlon, Joy Carney. And there's lots of firefighters on the street too, just like my Dad: Matt Hayes, Kathy Gall, John Otto, Pat Britzzalaro, Jim Coughlin and Jimmy Basil." When I suggested to her, again citing Peggy Cronin, that she was "never alone," she laughed heartily: "Never alone? We never were. And still aren't."

Karen Lickfeld Murray's story is a compelling one. I was moved by her passionate commitment to family, to faith and to the traditions of her neighborhood. And while rooted to that history, Karen Murray, as an educator is looking to the future, working to transform Discovery 67 into a "school of inquiry" where first-hand and experiential learning will someday replace the test-based approach that Karen so strongly questions. It was her ties to her neighborhood and to the memory of her father's service and his tragic death in the propane explosion of 1983 that inspired Karen to come back to South Buffalo, to live and to work. She wanted to be here, in this neighborhood, close to where her father died, to continue the Lickfeld family's commitment to South Buffalo.

One of the last people I met with in South Buffalo was Gene Overdorf who, as an historian, honors the area's past; as a teacher, lives vibrantly in its present, and as a grandparent is deeply committed to its future. On a beautiful summer's morning in late July 2019, Overdorf led me and my friend Tim Bohen through the grounds of Holy Cross Cemetery, just down Ridge Road from Our Lady of Victory Basilica, on the border where South Buffalo meets Lackawanna. Overdorf, like so many South Buffalonians of his generation, has his roots deeply planted in the First Ward where members of his family have lived since the end of the 19th century. Gene was born in The Ward in 1953 in a house on Mackinaw Street that had been in his family since the 1890s. Indeed, his sister Peggy Overdorf, one of Buffalo's great grass-roots community leaders, still lives there. Overdorf, who has taught for years at Bishop Timon, is an avid historian deeply knowledgeable about Buffalo's Irish American history as well as the history of Ireland. Like so many of his South Buffalo friends and neighbors, the Overdorfs have made several trips back to the Emerald Isle, visiting libraries and archives, old friends and family. It all comes together, he tells me, at Holy Cross Cemetery.

On monuments and gravestones, some that date back to the middle of the 19th century, Holy Cross contains the stories and the secrets of the foundational story of South Buffalo, the history of Old First Ward. Like Tim Bohen, Overdorf is particularly drawn to the fantastical 1866 story of the Fenians. In their passionate commitment to Ireland, the Fenians invaded and tried to conquer Canada so they could swap it to the British in exchange for a free Ireland. The stories about the Fenians that had captured my imagination years before were here, in the silence of Holy Cross substantiated in the cemetery's several monuments to the veterans of that fascinating event. For example, the gravestone of Edward K. Lonergan, a 21-year-old lieutenant in a regiment called "The I.R.A." (Irish Republican Army) who "fell gallantly fighting Ireland's enemies on the famous field of Ridgeway, Ontario on June 2, 1866." Many of the Fenians, Overdorf told me, were veterans of the New York State 155th Regiment, organized in Buffalo by an Irishman named Colonel John E. McMahon. Drawn from the growing number of Irishmen who, by then were all living in the First Ward, the 155th was dispatched to New York City. They wanted to stay together, Lonergan and the other boys from The Ward, to fight together as they'd lived together. Alas, that was not to be and in October,1862, Buffalo's Irish soldiers from the First Ward were incorporated into a much larger Irish unit, "the Corcoran Brigade." It was there that Lonergan and his pals from the neighborhood learned how to fight and at the War's end, hearing the calls of the Fenians, they joined yet another war for freedom, the glorious crusade to conquer Canada, and then swap it for a free Ireland.

The names of the Irish families that are buried here are legion: Connors, Kennedys, Brennans, Sheehans, O'Days, Driscolls, Cronins, Crottys and more. As a historian with deep ties to the First Ward, Overdorf knows everything about most of them. But it's not all about the past. "My family's future is here too. Right here in South Buffalo. All four of my kids and all of my grandkids live right around the corner from me in South Buffalo. Three of my boys are police officers … all working at the C-District. Like the members of that old 155 regiment. Except my boys stayed together."

In South Buffalo there were simply no easy endings. It never stopped: one after another, the cascading stories and memories – all of them filled with the power of family, of faith, of history, of place. There were still so many people to talk to, many stories to learn and many places to go. I wanted to know what it was like to meet after school at Sullivan's Ice Cream Parlor across from St. Tommy's on Abbott and Columbus. I wanted to know what it felt like to skate on the outdoor rink and to swim in the outdoor pool at Caz Park; to sit on the beach by Eli's Snack bar at the "cardboard cottages"; to watch the Timon Tigers play baseball on a lazy summer afternoon in "the bowl" in Caz park; to sit on the porch on Strathmore Avenue waiting for Karen Lickfeld and the other "witches of Strathmore" to come home for the night. I had discovered in South Buffalo an incredibly rich tapestry of a tightly knit community which, rooted in a common faith, a common ethnic identity and a shared and heightened sense of place, a place where family and faith, street, neighborhood and parish created a structure of daily life that was warm, closely-knit and supportive, the kind of place that on a personal and intellectual level, I found so appealing. The countless hours that I've spent in South Buffalo have revealed to me an unimaginably layered and carefully structured way of life, one so richly rooted in faith, in family and in neighborhood that to me they seemed to be never alone. They were people who, like the Sicilian-American members of *Per Niente*, had journeyed through life together: in families, on streets, in neighborhoods, in schools and in churches and beyond. Years later they were still together, meeting regularly for meals and holidays and traveling to ancestral towns and villages in Ireland and Sicily.

But time, at least for now, was running out. I was spending too much time in South Buffalo. I had other work to do. But I knew I'd return, just as Peggy Cronin and Karen Lickfeld had. The stories were too rich, the people too compelling. But now, at least, other areas of the city were calling and I was off to North Park and to Central Park, where the people who lived there, like those in South Buffalo, I would soon find out, were also never alone.

Acknowledgements

A great archive whose focus is the Old First Ward is housed at the Mutual Rowing Club at Hamburg and South. Inspired by the MRC clubhouse built on South Street in 1881, this homage to the Club, which opened in 2012 contains, in addition to boat storage, a fabulous archives of any and all kinds of material related to the First Ward and South Buffalo. Under the aegis of the Valley Community Association, the "Waterfront memories and more museum" is staffed by a dedicated trio of women, First Warders all: **Peggy Szczygiel**, **Bert Hyde**, **Joan Scahill**.

Tim Bohen is the historian of the First Ward. His book, *Against the Grain*, (Buffalo, 2012) which has sold widely throughout Buffalo, a compelling and irresistible history of this most fascinating neighborhood. Tim, along with a hand-full of his close to fifty first cousins, was an invaluable resource in my efforts to learn not only about the ward but about the dos and don'ts of neighborhood history.

Peggy Cronin grew up on Edgewood, the daughter of a South Buffalo mailman. She spent most all of her childhood in South Buffalo, graduating high school from The Mount. Peggy started at Mercy Hospital at the age of 16 working there alongside her sisters. While she spent considerable time in Los Angeles, she returned to Buffalo in 2014 and became President of Mount Mercy Academy in 2015. Her knowledge of the neighborhood is vast and her insights invaluable.

The Buffalo Irish Center located at 245 Abbott Rd in South Buffalo: The BIC is a great and unique Buffalo treasure. It has been headed by **Mary Heneghan** for many years and under her tireless leadership the Center, which celebrated its 50th anniversary in 2020, continues to be central to everything Irish in Buffalo. I have attended countless events here: performances of the Rince Na Tiarna Irish Dancers, under the direction of Mary's daughter, **Mary Kay Heneghan**; (Mary's son Tom Heneghan, Jr, presides over the marvelous Tan Tara shop across the street) performances of traditional Irish music as well as the more raucous programs of Irish fighting music. In addition I have watched rehearsals of the Greater Buffalo Fire Department's Pipes and Drums Corps; heard Irish poetry read here and have sat in on one of **Margaret McGrath**'s Gaelic language classes. Above all of the events that I have attended here, nothing is more fun than the Fenian Fish Fry, held every Friday at the BIC.

Gaelic heritage also is being celebrated as well a few blocks away on Tift Street. Here, at the historic neighborhood church, Holy Family (now known as Our Lady of Charity) are a series of unique wall and ceiling frescoes painted, like none other in the United States, in intricate Celtic style, are being restored. Painted between 1915-1920 by a Danish painter, these unique frescoes were covered over in the 1960s when decades of grime and industrial waste rendered them all but invisible.

Over the past few years, however, Holy Family parishioners, on their own, have raised sufficient funds to have their fabulous frescoes restored. Under the direction of Swiatek Studios, a Buffalo company known nationally for its work restoring churches and theaters, three large murals have been fully restored. The people of South Buffalo, many of them ardent advocates of Celtic art and culture are intensely proud of this which, like so much that happens here, strengthens the ties that bind people to their neighborhood.

The Dog Ears Book and Coffee Shop. Located at 288 Abbott Road since its opening in 2008, Dog Ears, under the energetic and visionary leadership of Tom McDonnell, has become a neighborhood institution. Dog Ears is really a community center, a place to buy a book, have a great snack and, upstairs in the Enlightenment Literary Art Center, to enjoy the world of books. It is a fantastic place to meet and greet "anybody who is anybody" in South Buffalo. Among the people I met and talked with here are:

Jack Coyle and I met when he was volunteering at the Dog Ears Book Store and Café. Jack, a former school board member, a veteran of both the railroads and the grain mills, knows as much as anybody about the fabric, the essence and the history of the South Buffalo neighborhood.

Dennis Dargavel. I had the great pleasure of taking a one-on-one driving tour of South Buffalo with Dennis Dargavel. Like so many of my South Buffalo journeys, this one began and ended at Tommy McDonnell's Dog Ears Book Store. There's not an inch of concrete or a blade of grass in South Buffalo that Dennis does not know and what I learned from him was invaluable. Dennis was born on Tift Street in Holy Family Parish. He has raised his family here and has lived his whole life in South Buffalo. He has, he says, no plans of moving … anywhere!

Brian Higgins: Congressman Higgins told me that he "grew up in the shadow of the elms, on Milford Street." A product of neighborhood schools – St. Thomas Aquinas, School 27 and South Park High School – Brian is steeped deeply in the history and lore of South Buffalo. His roots are planted firmly in Irish blue-collar South Buffalo. His father was Daniel J. Higgins, a proud union bricklayer, Local 45, as was his grandfather, Patrick. Brian's Uncle Jim, meanwhile, was President of the Buffalo Federation of Labor (AFL-CIO). Like his father, Brian, who was the South District councilman from 1969-1976, Brian chose public service as his career, serving as South District councilman, New York State assemblyman and since 2005 US congressman representing the 26th congressional district. There are few initiatives that have occurred since then, not only in South Buffalo but throughout the entire city, that do not bear the Brian's significant fingerprints. Brian's Buffalo office is made up of a staff of South Buffalonians including Megan Corbett Rizzuto, Chris Fahey and recently retired Bonnie Kane Lockwood. Bonnie's stories about growing up on Pawnee Park, with Hillery playground behind their house and Butler park in front, of "crossing the Crik for love" and others, have been invaluable.

Bob Doyle: Bob, a native of Belfast, was active in South Buffalo during "the troubles" of the 1980-90s and was one of the several neighborhood people involved in raising funds for the shattered Catholic children of Northern Ireland.

The "**Mt. Mercy Girls**": Grace Gannon, Barbara Fitzpatrick Kelleher, Kathleen Crowley, Jeannie Gannon.

Most of the research for this chapter was based on my uncountable hours hanging out and meeting people. In addition to those mentioned above, others are:

Charlie and Diane Kam: the family that in the late 1980s introduced me to the "cardboard cottages." Both life-long Buffalo school teachers and avid South Buffalonians, the Kam's were the first to make me feel that South Buffalo was a special place.

Margaret Keane: "the Whalen girl." I was a great fan of Margaret's late husband Jim of the extraordinary fire-fighting Keane family. It was Marge Ryan who took me to their family home, a two family flat on Seneca Street across from St. Theresa's, where sixteen Keane children were raised. It was from Jim himself when he was serving as Deputy County Executive, that I learned about their family's deep connection to the Buffalo Fire Department. Both Jim and his brother Mike were firefighters. Another brother Neal was a battalion chief while yet another brother, the legendary Bill "Puff" Keane was killed in the line of duty. Then of course there's Margaret herself, one of the first female battalion chiefs in the nation. Her family too, The Whalen's, have equally deep ties to South

Buffalo's firefighting tradition: her brother R.J., like "Puff" Keane, was killed while fighting a fire and her cousin Ray and Dennis Sullivan and Danny and Jack Corcoran were also proud members of the BFD.

Mary Alice O'Neill: The recently deceased older sister of Jim Keane, Mary Alice was a fount of information about growing up on Seneca Street with fifteen brothers and sisters.

Margaret McGrath: Irish born teacher of Gaelic and all things Irish at the Buffalo Irish Center, helped me to better understand the language and culture of the Emerald Isle.

Karen Lickfeld Murray: Her passion for her neighborhood, her dedication to the memory of her father, her leadership of School 67 on Abbott Road, all left me with an powerful, indelible memory.

The Redmonds: Dan senior and and junior, are fixtures in South Buffalo. Dan Sr, though he came from a fire-fighting family made his mark as a Buffalo police officer until he retired in 2001. His son Dan Jr, recently retired himself had a distinguished career as a Buffalo police officer as well. Like so many families in South Buffalo, the Redmonds maintain their closeness by both their career choices and their residential choices. Dan Sr lives today on Dundee in a home he's occupied for many years, across the street from his daughter and her family.

Gene Overdorf: He, along with Tim Bohen, are the go-to experts on the history of the Old First Ward. For both the First Ward is a family affair. Gene's sister, the director of the Valley Community Association, is the preeminent and undisputed grass-roots leader of this neighborhood. And for Tim, who knows how many of his 51 first cousins have their roots in The Ward. Gene, a teacher at Bishop Timon-St. Jude High School led me and Tim Bohen on a magical tour of South Buffalo's Holy Cross Cemetery.

Jim Pace, president of the West Seneca Historical Society. It was Jim who introduced me to the 18th and 19th century Seneca Indian settlements of South Buffalo. His museum, housed in a building on the grounds of the original Ebenezer settlement, is yet another hidden gem. In addition to having a great deal of material on the Ebenezers, the Society has terrific information on the Senecas and their settlements in what became South Buffalo and West Seneca.

CHAPTER 11

In the End

The enchanted landscape of North Buffalo and Central Park

I have been married twice, both times to women from Buffalo. My first marriage, to Catherine Friedman, brought me to Buffalo. Later, I married again, to Cricket Gordon. Both women, whose ties to family and neighborhood extend back generations, have very strong memories of growing up in Buffalo. Their attachment to place has influenced and inspired my own.

Kitty grew up on Lafayette Avenue between Delaware and Elmwood, where extended families lived next to each other in closely connected single and double homes. Kitty was surrounded by a large coterie of aunts, uncles, cousins and friends. For Kitty, like so many of the people I met and friends I made in South Buffalo, her street, like theirs, was an extension of home, a place where she, like them, was rarely, if ever, alone.

For Cricket, home was on Lexington Avenue between Elmwood and Delaware Avenues. Descended from a family whose roots on both her mother and father's side were planted firmly in mid-19th century Buffalo, Cricket's Lexington, like Kitty's Lafayette, though not an ethnic neighborhood, did in many ways resemble one. Surrounded by friends and family with decades-long attachments not only to the neighborhood but to Westminster Presbyterian Church, Cricket's memories – of biking with friends to the Campus School, of ice-skating in a neighbor's back-yard, of a street-filled with children – are detailed and compelling. Raised in families with intimate, multi-generational ties to small, well-defined neighborhoods, both Kitty and Cricket's coming-of-age-stories in neighborhoods like these inspired me as I sought to create a similar sense of connectedness and belonging for my children and then, later, for my grandchildren.

• • •

Some of my earliest ties to Buffalo were forged during my first years in Buffalo when, with my infant son Charlie tucked safely in a baby seat, I made my initial explorations of the streets and neighborhoods of the city. Charlie helped me to experience the city sensuously, responding to the sights and the smells around us. He loved the smell of Cheerios near the General Mills plant at the foot of Michigan Avenue. He liked seeing the long freight trains clanking across the railroad crossing at Tonawanda Street in Black Rock. He enjoyed the sound of the fast-running waters of the Niagara River at Broderick Park. His pleasure became mine and it was through him that my attachment to Buffalo grew.

Both Charlie and Lydia were adventuresome kids, wandering out beyond the immediate confines of their childhood neighborhood in North Buffalo. By the time he was 12, Charlie was hanging out on Lancaster Avenue where his best childhood buddy, Patrick Gallo, lived. Pat, the youngest child of a large Italian-American family, had a buoyant, outsized personality. Raised in a warm, protective family, Pat was a street kid and there was no better place to be a street kid in Buffalo than on Lancaster Avenue. Developed like the other side streets in the Delaware District at the turn of the 20th century for the city's booming middle-classes, Lancaster is a beautiful street, filled with trees and elegantly constructed large, wooden homes. What makes Lancaster particularly appealing, the glue that holds it together, are the front porches. Walk down the street and you will understand the value of these porches for the life of this street.

But it was more than porches, trees, and the proximity of Elmwood Avenue that made Lancaster Charlie's favorite place to be. A lot had to do with Pat's mother, Lucille. While her husband could be the macho Italian, Lucille was the warm, hysterically funny, and incredibly welcoming "Mama." Lulu, as we all called her, became a central figure in Charlie's youth, doting on him, teaching him how to play poker, and above all, cooking meals for him the likes of which he'd never had at home. Charlie was awed by the home environment of the Gallos: late night poker-games played in bathrobes and underwear; mounds of home-made Italian food, and lots of laughter and yelling. But the primary attraction was Pat: the wonderfully garrulous, ever-up-for-fun kid who made Charlie laugh like no one else could.

He loved the Gallo family and he loved Lancaster Avenue. Charlie said that there was no better place to watch a Bills game, where the groans of defeat and the cries of success could be heard erupting from every house on the block. While

Pat now lives in Brooklyn, all the others Lancaster kids have stayed in Buffalo. Almost forty years later, Pat and the other members of their Lancaster Avenue gang remain together, still the closest of friends. Charlie, meanwhile, lives around the corner on Highland with his wife Meghan and their daughter Charlotte.

Lydia, younger than Charlie by four years, too, had an Elmwood Avenue gang of her own. The focal point of her teen-age years was right around the corner from the Gallo's, at the DiCarlo's house on Auburn near Elmwood. The DiCarlos had three wonderful daughters and Lydia became friends with all of them, particularly the oldest, Aurore. Enticed, to a certain extent, by their exotic, French-speaking mother, it was the warm embrace of the three sisters that most appealed to Lydia. And, perhaps still more, there was the excitement of Elmwood Avenue, which was just steps from the DiCarlos' Auburn Avenue front porch, where "Willy's," the Playground, Circular Word Books, the Captain's Table Restaurant, Positively Main Street and Preservation Hall Bakery offered an irresistible lure.

My son Jonathan also helped me become further bound to Buffalo. Although we did not come into each other's lives until Jon turned 13, we did, in subsequent years, spend many afternoons and evenings exploring the hidden crannies of the city. Jon loved the off-beat; a Niagara Street botanica, a funky West Side clothing store, and an Arab food market on Hertel. His willingness to explore fueled my desires to do the same. Jonathan's sense of adventure and taste for the exotic serves him well in New York City whose every nook and cranny he seems to have discovered and made his own.

I wanted my kids to engage energetically with the daily life of the city. We walked the snowy streets after the Blizzards of '77 and '85. We watched the July 4th fireworks at LaSalle Park. We went sledding and played golf, baseball, and tennis in Delaware Park. As a result of these very conscious efforts on my part, Buffalo became for them a place of warmth, friendship and stability. It was a world where they, like those I'd heard about so many years before in "The Erie Canal Song," "would always know their neighbors and always know their pals." And a world in which they would stay. "Home," we knew, "is where the heart is" and "our hearts," clearly, were in Buffalo. Ties to my children and ties to my city were becoming intertwined and indistinguishable, producing an ever growing sense of belonging for all of us. I felt it. My children felt it and, I hoped, my grandchildren would too.

In fact, Max Langer, Lydia and Rob's oldest child, was no more than four when he, like his Uncle Charlie before him, started to join me on my never-ending trips of discovery around Buffalo. One time, driving around Niagara Square, Max, then aged 7, pointed at City Hall and asked: "What's that, WaWa ?"s (Max's term of endearment for me.) "That's City Hall, Max. It's an amazing building. That's where the Mayor works. Want to go inside?"

As we approached City Hall from Niagara Square, Max was awed by the size of the building. His eyes fixed on the sculpted frieze that spanned the front of the building and he wondered about the characters that were depicted on it: the Michelangelo-like female with a book in one hand and her pen in the other; the stevedore; the ship captain; the electrician; and the iron worker. Upon entering this magical building, we were struck by four columns, each inspired by Native American symbols depicting the Four Winds. Under the three-story-high barrel vault, where every surface is ornamented with brightly colored tiles, we felt an air of drama and mystery. What an amazing place: gigantic murals with surreal titles – "Frontiers Unfettered By Any Frowning Fortress" and "Talents Diversified Find Vent in Myriad Form" – cover the walls. With their Herculean men and Amazonian women, cascading waterfalls, stupendous ships, and towering grain elevators, the murals at City Hall are a thrilling sight for children. Were the figures that filled these massive murals monsters or superheroes? And could it really be that it was here, in this enormous fantasy-filled lobby that, Max wondered, the mayor actually worked?

He was about to find out. I'd known Mayor Byron W. Brown for years and had been drawn to his sincere manner, particularly with children. "Of course," he said, when I called him from the lobby. "C'mon up. I've got some time right now."

Up we went to the second floor. A friendly guard welcomed us. "You must be Max," he said, ushering us through the large, carved wooden doors. The mayor's suite of offices are an Art Deco marvel. The vestibule has polished, wood-paneled walls on which hang oil-painted portraits of each of the city's mayors. A bronze railing with elegant details separates the waiting and the working areas. Mayor Brown came out to greet us and, placing his hand gently on Max's shoulder, led him to a large fish-tank set up against the bronze railing. Kneeling so as to be at Max's height, Mayor Brown identified each of the fish, telling Max how as a child, it was his fish tank – "this very one" – that was his prized possession. Mayor Brown led us into his office, a large space radiant with sunlight. Leading him to his desk, Mayor Brown said, "Here's where I sit. Right there on that big chair behind the desk. Want to try it? You will sit there too, when you are Mayor."

My memories of our short visit to the Mayor's office will last a lifetime. I was moved by the Mayor's sincere interest in my grandson. I valued the working relationship that I had established over the years with the Mayor, and now cherished the personal connection that he made with Max. The ties that bound me and my children to the city of Buffalo would now, I felt, begin to bind my grandchildren, too.

"That's a perfect children's book," my friend Irene Sipos said when I told her about our visit to the city hall. She was right. Later that year, working with a marvelous artist named Elizabeth Leader, I published my favorite book about Buffalo, *Max Meets the Mayor.*

• • •

In 2014, Lydia, Rob, Max and his younger brother, Eli, moved from Auburn Avenue on Buffalo's West Side to live in a larger house on Beard Avenue in the Central Park neighborhood. I'd been aware of the area since my first years in Buffalo but it was not until the Langer's moved here that I became fully familiar with its incredible hidden treasures. While I had noticed the beauty of the tree-lined streets, I never explored the neighborhood in my early years and it was not until the Langer's moved onto Beard that I became fully familiar with it.

The key to appreciating Central Park is its history, a story lovingly told in *Central Park: A Neighborhood of History and Tradition*, a book written and published by neighborhood residents in 2010. Much of the land in the neighborhood Buffalonians know as Central Park was bought in the late 19th century by a concrete magnate named Lewis J. Bennett. Bennett, who'd been raised on a farm near Schenectady in the early 1830s, came to Buffalo in the 1860s and soon after founded the Buffalo Cement Company, located on an enormous tract of land that extended from what is now the intersection of Main and Amherst streets as far east as Bailey Avenue. Bennett was a visionary, deeply influenced by the work of Fredrick Law Olmsted in New York's Central Park and soon devised a plan for the development of a new residential neighborhood in the vicinity of his concrete business at Main and Amherst. By the early 1880s Bennett had begun to acquire large tracts of land on the west side of Main Street and it was here that Bennett began to plan the brand new neighborhood which, in honor of Fredrick Law Olmsted's great creation in New York City, he named Central Park.

Bennett set out to create a new residential neighborhood for the city's wealthiest residents. It was with this in mind that he imposed stringent deed restrictions and land use covenants which continue to determine land use in Central Park to this day. There would be no commercial uses and only single-family homes were permitted. (Bennett did allow a barn in the rear!) Bennett also outlined the minimum costs for all residences based on which streets they would be located on. Homes on Depew were to cost a minimum of $4,000, those on Main $3,500 and those on Linden $2,500, significant sums for that era. To ensure that only large houses would be erected, he laid the foundations, at his own expense, on each of the lots.

Like Olmsted, Bennett's vision for his Central Park was rooted in trees. Bennett wanted elms and chestnuts planted everywhere. By 1900, he had imported from Canada over 1,200 elms. These, complimented by row after row of American chestnuts, are what today provide the trees that envelop the streets of the neighborhood. By 1910, the streets of Central Park had become the newest and most desirable neighborhood in Buffalo. A school followed when in the early 1920s Bennett donated the land on Main Street which in 1925 became Bennett High.

There is a manicured elegance to the streets of Central Park and with Max and Eli in tow, we have biked them all starting from the Langer Family's Beard Avenue home. It is the best way to view that most extraordinary neighborhood. Bennett was drawn to interesting intersections. Several streets in the neighborhood converge in triangles. These small public spaces feel enchanted to me. There's one at Linden and Starin, a large lot where once stood the neighborhood clubhouse, The Otowega Club. There's another triangle at the convergence of Depew, Linden, and Wallace, where Parkside Lutheran Church was dedicated in 1925. There are countless other evocative places as well: the circular Duane Place, named for Bennett's hometown in Central New York, the vast lawn in front of Parkside Lutheran, the incredible beauty of Morris, Linden, Woodbridge and Depew, the old railroad station that once served the Belt Line, now converted into one of the most unusual homes in the city.

My favorite spot in Central Park is at the intersection of Depew, Wesley, and Morris, a small triangular park known today as Burke's Green. Named in 1969 after F. Brendan Burke, a passionate neighborhood leader, Burke's Green is maintained by the Central Park Homeowners Association. Their efforts have resulted in the creation of an outstanding public space. With benches around a bubbling fountain, beds of flowers, a cluster of shade trees, and the Central Methodist Church as a backdrop, Burke's Green is a transcendent part of our family's collective memory, a go-to destination for us twelve-months of the year.

For so many families in Central Park, our's included, there is no more quintessentially important place than Shoshone Park. Opened during the boom years after World War II, Shoshone has, since 1954, been home to an institution that is essential to the DNA of the neighborhood, a fantastic, volunteer-run organization known as Hertel-North Buffalo Youth Baseball. Baseball is the life-blood of this neighborhood, fundamental to the lives of hundreds of families who live here. Games at Shoshone are a family affair, attended by parents and grandparents many of whom themselves grew up playing baseball here. For the close to one thousand boys and girls who play ball here, Max and Eli are very much among them, baseball is, as Eli says, "my life." It is through baseball at Shoshone that Max and Eli, like so many of their friends and neighbors, have developed ties to this neighborhood that will last a lifetime.

Max and Eli love Shoshone, their summertime home-away-from-home. Even during the long winter months when Shoshone is closed, the three of us go just to check out the fields and to "see how Shoshone is doing." For several years, the boys have played on the same travel team, each year with the same group of teammates and dedicated coaches. Shoshone has become an integral component of our Buffalo.

Adding further to the glue that holds this neighborhood together are the churches, Parkside Lutheran and the three parish churches: St. Margaret's on Hertel, St. Rose of Lima on Tacoma and St. Mark on Woodbridge. Bound together by ties of church, family and yes, baseball, the streets of North Park and Central Park are filled with families many of whom have lived here for three generations. As a result the atmosphere and the aura, the *ruach*, if you will, is one of continuity and stability. It is palpable just around the corner from Shoshone Park where Voorhees, Tacoma, and North Park come together at an intersection known to everyone here as "The Five Corners." The streets of the Five Corners are filled with children. Go some school-day morning to this intersection and see gathered there dozens of kids waiting for buses that will take them to St. Mark, City Honors, and Olmsted. If you stand near the green fence and listen carefully, you can hear the bells of the Carmelite Monastery just around the corner on Carmel ringing at nine in the morning, at noon and again at six in the evening, tolling the Angelus prayer. I can hear the bells of the Carmelites in other parts of the neighborhood, too. I listen for them over the din of a Shoshone baseball game and among the gentle sounds as I sit quietly at Burke's Green.

These ties of family, faith, friendship, and place were on full display over the course of the first weekend of May 2019. After weeks of rain, the sun came out to greet the hundreds of kids, parents, and coaches who had gathered in the parking lot at St. Margaret's Church on Hertel to march in the annual parade to kick off the 65th season of the Hertel North Buffalo Youth Baseball League. Led by siren-blaring fire trucks and police cars, the uniformed players and coaches marched proudly down Hertel Avenue, past their cheering friends and family, they were greeted by Mayor Brown as they entered Shoshone Park. Hundreds gathered around the flagpole as the Mayor led the recitation of the Pledge of Allegiance. All joined in throaty communion to sing the Star Spangled Banner. It was not until the next day that an umpire would call "Play Ball!" and the first pitch would be thrown.

That Sunday morning was the day of first communion for children all over Buffalo. By noon, celebratory families poured out of St. Margaret's, St. Rose and St. Mark, the churches of North Buffalo and Central Park, their kids, meanwhile, scurrying home to change from their Sunday best into their baseball uniforms. By afternoon the growing crowd again gathered at Shoshone where, accompanied this time by the Pipe & Drum Band of the Buffalo Fire Department, again we sang, a shrill but enthusiastic rendition of "Take Me Out to the Ball Game." Another season of baseball at Shoshone had begun, and I, here in the city of my heart, was right in the thick of it.

Acknowledgements

The Gallo Family: Our family and the Gallos remain tied at the hip. When my mother, aging and alone in New York City, needed help towards the end of her life, we called on that fantastic caretaker, Lucille Gallo. Lulu picked up and moved to New York, providing help and comfort during her final years. Charlie's life-long pal Pat, married Lydia's life-long pal, Laura. They live today with their son Lucca in Buffalo.

The vivid memories and stories that I have heard from **Kitty** and **Cricket** of their childhoods in Buffalo have merged with mine.

Franklin LaVoie: I am indebted to the unique vision of Franklin LaVoie and his perspective on the symbolism embedded within City Hall.

Mayor Byron B. Brown: I cannot say enough about the warmth of the greeting that we received from our mayor. The idea for *Max Meets the Mayor* came from Irene Sipos. The marvelous illustrations were done by Elizabeth Leader.

James Arnone's *Central Park, Buffalo. A neighborhood history and Tradition*, 2010, is a must-read. A marvelous example of grass-roots history, this book was written and produced largely by residents of Central Park.

Brendan Burke's son Christopher, is a Central Park/North Buffalo lifer with a home at The Five Corners where North Park, Voorhees and Tacoma intersect.

Maeve Barton, one of six Barton girls who grew up here, helped me to visualize the early days of Burke's Green.

All baseball caps off and kudos to **Don Morris** and the men and women who make the Hertel North Buffalo Youth Baseball League and Shoshone Park what it is. And to Bill Snyder, the great free-lance photographer whose images of baseball at Shoshone fill the pages of the *North Buffalo Rocket*.

Still more kudos to three men, coaches and fathers who dedicate countless hours to the young ball players who people Shoshone and in the process strengthen the ties that the boys have for this enchanted place that: Kevin Mahoney, Ryan Gallivan and Dave McKendry.

Rick Ganci, Sr., schooled me on the intergenerational connections at Shoshone. Indeed, the mother of his grandson Jack, Max's great baseball buddy, is the daughter of Chris and Mary Pat Burke from Burke's Green fame.

Others who helped me to understand the strong sinews of the North Buffalo and Central Park neighborhoods are Tom Beecher, his daughter Megan Beecher Cavanaugh, Laura Corrin Gallo, Liz Sheehan, John Hornung, Mike Schmand and Rev. Joseph S. Rogliano, aka "Father Joe." Father Joe, an ebullient and much loved pastoral leader, has been at St. Mark and St. Rose since the churches were joined in the Fall of 2010.

Epilogue

A healing heart: Buffalo, 2020

Monday, March 2, 2020, was a typically rainy early Spring day in Buffalo. It was chilly, with temperatures in the high 30s. I started the day as usual, by reading *The Buffalo News*. The lead story dealt with the ongoing crisis within the Diocese of Buffalo, which had declared bankruptcy just days before. Over 250 alleged victims of sexual abuse had sued the Diocese and now, *The News* reported, they were outraged at what appeared to them an effort by the Diocese to cover-up and avoid responsibility for the misconduct of priests. The front page included coverage of the seemingly endless battle over who would succeed Western New York's disgraced congressman, Chris Collins. Collins, the representative for New York's 27th District, had recently been convicted of insider trading. Another story dealt with Buffalo's emergence as a location of choice for film-makers and the shooting here of Guillermo del Toro's film "Nightmare Alley" starring Bradley Cooper. A story on the bottom of the front page reported that the Corona 19 virus had come to New York State. The story noted that, while announcing that there was one confirmed case in the entire state, Governor Andrew Cuomo said, "There is no reason for undue anxiety." Indeed, his statement was fairly reassuring. "It's deep breath time. The general risk remains low in New York. We are diligently managing this situation and will continue to provide information as it becomes available."

Dr. Gale Burstein, the Erie County Health Commissioner, seemed to feel otherwise. Indeed, in the same *Buffalo News* that quoted Governor Cuomo's soothing response, Dr. Burstein issued a sobering warning: "We may," she said, "have to take extreme measures to protect ourselves. There's no reason to think that we can keep it out forever." (fn1.BN 3/2/ C1) Nevertheless, buoyed by the reassuring words of my cousin and the Governor, I was when I began my day on that Monday morning of March 2, 2020, still in the "What, Me Worry?" camp.

That Monday was a typical day for me. I'd been working with Peter Dow, my colleague from the Friends of the Buffalo Story, on creating a summer-time performance piece celebrating the history of the Erie Canal. That morning, we met at Canalside with Vincent O'Neill, artistic director of the Irish Classical Theater Company, to discuss our plans for a collaboration. We all shook hands and agreed to meet again after St. Patrick's Day.

From Canalside, Peter and I went to Arthur Street in Riverside, where we met with John Montague in his office at Buffalo Maritime Center. John was pleased with the progress that was being made on The Longshed, the large warehouse being built by the Erie Canal Harbor Development Corporation on the Central Wharf. It was here, in the Longshed, that John and his colleagues were planning to build a replica of the Seneca Chief, the first boat to ever make the trip from Buffalo to New York City along the Erie Canal. John wanted to talk with us about how we could coordinate our performance piece with the ceremony celebrating the unveiling of the Longshed that was planned for August 2020.

Next, I went to The Golden Cup, Larry and Jackie Stitt's coffee shop on the corner of Jefferson and E. Utica. I had met the Stitts several years earlier while working on the Ferry Street Corridor Project. Larry had served for years as the recreational director at the old Michigan Avenue YMCA. In early March, I was still trying to bring the marvelous history of Offerman Stadium to life, and Larry had the names of people he wanted me to contact.

That afternoon, Chuck Massey, Don Ingalls and I met at the Community Foundation of Western New York with Bridget Niland, Director of their Youth Sports Initiative, and Delia James, their Racial Equity Initiative Assistant. We were appalled by the recent decision by Section VI of the New York State football federation and the Erie County Interscholastic Conference to exclude the City of Buffalo's five high school football teams from competing against the Conference's suburban schools. We saw the move as a blatant effort to remove Buffalo's overwhelmingly African-American teams from the predominantly white metropolitan-wide conference. While the decision had been postponed for a year, thanks to the intervention of Mayor Brown, the Buffalo Public Schools and the Buffalo Teachers Federation, we saw this issue as an opportunity to broaden the discussion around race relations, "a teachable moment" for our community, and an opportunity to build bridges between our city and suburban schools.

That afternoon, I picked up my grandsons at their schools and took them to their home on Beard Avenue. The boys did their homework, and we talked about one of our favorite topics – only six more weeks till the start of baseball at Shoshone. Shortly after, Lydia came home and I left for a 6 pm meeting at Hardware with Samantha Rosen, a radio documentarian from Detroit. She'd been drawn to the story of Negro League baseball in Buffalo. She wanted to produce a documentary about the history of Offerman Stadium and its role in the life of Buffalo's East Side and, given my long-term interest in that topic, I was eager to talk with her about the project.

The next day's headlines in *The News* were now suddenly different. "School districts," one declared, "are preparing for the worst as they work to avert corona virus outbreak." (Barbara O'Brien and Tom Precious, BN 3/3 A1) Meanwhile, Governor Cuomo held the first of what would become over 100 consecutive daily press briefings. In a tightly packed room filled with reporters, absent any of the social distancing protocol that would soon become a way of life, Governor Cuomo and New York's Mayor Bill de Blasio, surrounded by public health officials, promoted a "stay calm" theme. Cuomo stressed that New Yorkers should not be afraid to shop in stores or take public transit. He noted that 80% of positive virus cases get "self-resolved" and that the mortality rate of coronavirus is estimated at 1.4%, compared to a 0.6% rate for the seasonal flu. And besides, "New York has the best health care system on the planet." (Press conference, March 3, 2020)

Meanwhile, life in Buffalo went on pretty much as it always had. On Wednesday, March 4, Shea's Theater announced its upcoming fall season. It was extraordinarily ambitious, a glorious schedule of plays and musicals: "To Kill a Mockingbird " in September, "Tootsie" in October, "Hamilton," in November, "Pretty Woman;" in March and, as a finale "My Fair Lady" in May of 2021. Michael G. Murphy, Shea's Performing Arts Center president, was thrilled. "We are ecstatic for this upcoming Broadway series and what it means for our community to be launching our fifth and sixth national tour from Shea's …." Estimating that a typical one-week run at Sheas had an average economic impact of $3 million, Murphy said that "The launch of these tours brings artists and crews to our region for weeks leading up to opening night." Life continued in the Old First Ward, too, where fair weather greeted thousands of runners in the 42nd Annual Shamrock Run, on Saturday, March 7. Following the race, many celebrated by cramming into the Old First Ward Community Center for a raucous beer blast.

For me too, life went on as usual. On that Saturday, my grandchildren and I celebrated our 110th consecutive weekly Saturday Muffin Day. On Sunday, there was basketball at the Jewish Center. On Tuesday, I met with Marti Gorman to finalize a September l, 2020 release date for *City Of My Heart*. (The best laid plans!) That evening, I joined over one hundred Buffalonians at a community meeting, where we were briefed on the plans for Ralph Wilson Centennial Park, including presentation of a state-of-the art design for a pedestrian bridge that would cross the Thruway into the heart of the new park.

Despite our best efforts to go about our business as usual – keeping our appointments, sending our kids to school, planning for Spring break – *The Buffalo News*, despite the official absence of any cases of Corona virus in Erie County, reported a torrent of bad news during those early days of March 2020:

> **March 4th:** A front page article written by chief Albany Correspondent Tom Precious, featured a "question answer" piece about the virus. Precious reported that although there were still no cases in Western New York "The CDC does not expect the United States to succeed in containing the virus because of the rate at which it is spreading."
>
> **March 5th:** The State University of New York, "Out of an abundance of caution," suspended their overseas study programs. All students were told to return to New York where, Governor Cuomo said, they will be quarantined for 14 days.
>
> **March 6th:** Amherst High School students and one teacher were quarantined after returning from a trip to Italy.
>
> **March 7th:** "Restaurant operators are praying for virus to pass Buffalo by," *The News* reported, adding that Rite Aid, Dollar General, 7-Eleven and others had run out of supply of hand sanitizers.

By March 10, the mood changed rapidly when Cuomo, announcing that there were now 32 new cases in New York for a total of 76, all of them downstate, declared a "state of emergency." No one knew what exactly Cuomo's declaration meant as there were no restrictions or requirements imposed. However, the writing, to anyone who could read, was clearly on the wall.

That same day, Sandra Tan's story in *The Buffalo News* included a litany of scary items: the day before, the Dow Jones Industrial Average New York stock market dropped 2000 points and New York State with 142 cases, 90 of them in Westchester County, now surpassed Washington as the state with highest number of cases. Meanwhile, Tan reported, the global death total had reached 3,900. Though Boston and Dublin had cancelled theirs, Buffalo's St. Patrick's Day parades were still on for the weekend. "Go, but be cautious," Mayor Brown advised. "I'm encouraging people not to shake hands but just do the warm, friendly elbow bump." Niagara University coach Greg Paulus and Canisius College coach Reggie Witherspoon, took the Mayor's advice and, in what I thought was a telling gesture, did not shake hands at the conclusion of their final basketball game of the regular season.

Two days later, *The News* proclaimed, "Virus reaches pandemic status." County Executive Mark Poloncarz insisted that the continued absence of cases in Western New York meant nothing. "We are going under the assumption that there are people in our county that have it," said Poloncarz. Adding her concerns was County Health Commissioner Burstein. "This is a scary time," Dr. Burstein said. "None of us has lived through a pandemic. The last one was over 100 years ago."

Thursday, March 12, was worse. *News* staff reporter Maki Becker reported a growing list of cancellations: both of the city's St. Patrick's parades were cancelled, as were all performances of "Hello Dolly" at Shea's. In the meantime, one sporting event after the next was nixed. The National Hockey League, the National Basketball Association, Major League Baseball canceled games. The NCAA even cancelled "March Madness."

Perhaps more than anything, the cancellation of so many sporting events caught the attention of the people of Buffalo. "The Games Have Stopped," *News* sports writer Mike Harrington wrote. "We have no idea what's happening, no idea when the teams are returning."

On Monday, March 16, at a time when a mere seven people in Erie County had tested positive, (all of them people in their 20s-30s who had traveled out of the area) all schools in the county were closed and all visits to nursing homes and jails were suspended. By the end of the day Governor Cuomo had extended the state of emergency to both the City of Buffalo and the County of Erie.

When one reporter asked Erie County Executive Poloncarz "So what are people to do?," he replied: "Don't panic. Understand, we will get through this."

Erie County Health Commissioner Dr. Gale Burstein added her highly respected voice: "If you are thinking about going out to a restaurant or working out at a gym, don't do it. Stay at home." (*News* 3/16, Page A4) Both Poloncarz and Burstein knew exactly just how serious the situation was. Testing labs at Roswell Park, ECMC and Kaleida Health were opening and they knew that testing would dramatically expand the number of confirmed cases. Dr. Burstein said, "So it's all hands on deck. We're training people every day to come work with us."

• • •

Suddenly, all of us were struggling to adjust to what people were calling "the new normal." In this brand-new world, you couldn't touch anyone, go to school, attend a sports event, or visit a museum. You couldn't go to a barber for a haircut or get a tattoo. You couldn't go to work, unless you were considered "essential." Playgrounds and basketball courts were shut; even swings were removed to keep kids away. What could you do? Take a solo walk, go grocery shopping if you dared, grab take-out food – that was about it.

What was "safe," Poloncarz told us, was to assume that the virus was widespread in Western New York. "We know there's probably hundreds, maybe thousands of cases at this point." He was right. On April 9, 10,795 new cases were announced in the State, the most to date. Five days later, Erie County reported forty deaths from Covid, the deadliest day so far. Among those affected were two dear friends, both a part of my Buffalo story. One was Joey Giambra, the writer, raconteur, musician, film-maker whose work had enriched so many of our lives. Another was Murray Levine, a beloved psychology professor at UB, and a long-term, poker playing member of our Jewish men's group. Governed by Cuomo's restrictions on hospital visitations, both Joey and Murray died alone.

It was even worse, of course, in New York City and I was worried sick about the impact of the virus on my home town, the "city of my soul." I was particularly struck by the photographs published in the *New York Times*, stark and harrowing views of the empty parks and streets in the neighborhoods throughout the city that I knew so well. No photo affected me more than the one taken on fields of Central Park, those same fields that I had played on as a child growing up there. The photo, taken in Central Park against the backdrop of the Fifth Avenue skyline, showed fourteen white hospital tents that had been erected to manage the overflow of Covid-19 patients from Mt. Sinai Hospital. The photo's caption, "Central Park Field Hospital," said it all.

• • •

Some photos transmitted pain. Others, taken by Sharon Cantillon for *The Buffalo News* transformed it. On April 15th when the news about the Corona virus could not have been worse, *The Buffalo News* published Cantillon's extraordinary portraits of forty Buffalo hospital workers. Her montage, called "Faces on the Front Line," is an unforgettably powerful statement of strong, sad, tired, warm, happy, resilient, kind and loving heroes. Taken at the peak of the crisis, Cantillon's portraits were a testament to our community's strength and the power of love, a sign of hope and faith when we needed it most. I was strengthened and fortified by the promise of transformation that I saw in Cantillon's photos and now I too picked up my own camera and, looking for faith and hope ventured forth from the confines of my home into the streets, neighborhood and parks of the city I loved.

I took my first pictures on a beautiful clear day in mid-April, made clearer by the sudden drop in carbon emissions. The air was crisp, cool and a bright yellow sun filled the sparkling blue sky. I started in one of my favorite places, the Meadow in Delaware Park and, in a routine that began to mark every day, I began taking photos, dozens of them. I shot the bright sun rising over the golf course, the emerging yellow leaves on the Meadow's three majestic willow trees, crocuses, mustard flowers, dog woods, and cherry blossoms. I captured silvery clouds and fantastic, multicolored light shows as the sun set on some my favorite places: the burnished red brick of Lafayette High School, the statue of General Bidwell at Colonial Circle, the former synagogue on Richmond and Connecticut, and the tower of the First Presbyterian Church at Symphony Circle. The best sunsets were at the foot of both Porter Avenue and Ferry Street. Here, where I could listen to the sounds of the rushing river, see the huge lake and the distant Canadian shore and feel the towering presence of the Peace Bridge, I found solace in a world that seemed suddenly to have gone wrong. My sadness was lifting and I could sense my deep, hollow pain being gradually transformed.

"You've got to start a Facebook page," my friend Ryan Gallivan said. Ryan is an adored Shoshone baseball coach, a child of the West Side with a passionate love for Buffalo. "Share your photos," he said. "Encourage others to do the same." Believe me," he said with the acquired wisdom of a life-long coach, "you'll be amazed at the response." His idea was to create a Facebook page that would function as kind of a community "family album," a place where the people of Buffalo could share images of the places that they loved. By focussing on and sharing the beauty in our midst we sensed that our project could help transform our communal pain into communal healing. Ryan and I called the Facebook page, "Picture this: Views from the home front, Buffalo, NY"

Ryan was right. The response was immediate. Our site was flooded with wonderful photos from people all over the city, posting detailed shots of homes, storefronts and churches, the rushing waters of the Niagara River and the Falls; of roses and the fabulous cherry blossoms at the Japanese Gardens; and most of all, extraordinary photos of sunsets everywhere. By the end of April, our Facebook page had close to one thousand friends and over 10,000 "hits." Ryan and I had touched a powerful nerve, a deep and latent desire by hundreds of people of Buffalo to share their love of their city at a time when we all needed it the most. As people trained their cameras on the places in the city that they loved, as they looked closely at the flowers, the sunsets, the magnificent parks and the fantastic architectural details which surround us, their connections to the city were renewed, strengthened, and restored. As April morphed into May, we prayed that Buffalo might soon be back from what Governor Cuomo had called "one hundred days of hell" and that the city of my heart, like my own, was beginning to heal.

But then, on May 30, five days after the murder of George Floyd in Minneapolis, the seething anger felt in cities across the nation burst onto the streets of Buffalo. The protests had begun quietly on Saturday, May 30 in the late afternoon when demonstrators of all ages, races, colors and creeds, almost all of them wearing protective face masks, almost all of them carrying homemade signs, and chanting "I can't breathe" and "No justice, no peace," filled the square in front of City Hall. While most of the protestors dispersed by 8:00 pm, many remained gathered around the McKinley Monument. Concerned about tips that the federal court house was a planned target, about a dozen US marshals were placed there to guard it.

As dusk began to fall, the tension increased. Bottles were thrown, vandals sprayed graffiti on the McKinley Monument and someone hurled a flaming object through a window at City Hall. Other protestors urged people to stay peaceful. "Stop it," a young African-American man shouted. "Why would you hurt your city?" Buffalo police in riot gear now joined the fray, forming a line across Delaware Avenue. Now, finally, as it turned dark, the few dozen remaining protesters began a circuitous (and sometimes violent) route that took them up Niagara Street to Elmwood, Grant and other streets on the West Side.

What happened that night was a sickening coda to what had been a peaceful and uplifting public demonstration. Businesses were vandalized. The windows of small, family-owned shops, some owned by immigrant families, were broken, their bewildered owners wondered what, coming in the wake of the closing enforced by the pandemic, they had done to deserve this. Though heartened by the efforts of dozens of volunteers who showed up on Sunday morning to help these small business owners to repair their businesses, what, many wondered what could happen next.

Mayor Brown, Buffalo's first African-American mayor, offered some hope even as he walked a very fine line. How could he represent the anger of his African-American political base and also take a firm stand for law and order? Confronted by this challenge, Brown adapted a subtle yet effective strategy that blended a passionate defense of the aggrieved peaceful protesters, with an assertive call for law and order. Brown's healing rhetoric and his eagerness, along with Police Commissioner Byron Lockwood, to "take a knee" with protesters in Niagara Square, were effective.

A set-back to the long hoped-for harmony occurred when on June 4, 2020, police officers from the Buffalo Police Department pushed 75-year-old peace activist Martin Gugino to the ground at a Niagara Square protest. While the Gugino event sparked outrage, passions did begin to cool following the imposition of a week-long 8 pm curfew. On June 5, at about 7 pm, 250 men and women from the University of Buffalo's Jacobs School of Medicine and Biomedical Sciences marched slowly down Main Street to Niagara Square. They were "white coats for black lives" and as they took a knee in somber silence, the whole community took note. Two days later, over 120 more "white coats for black lives," this time members of the staff at the Erie County Medical Center knelt silently together in the parking lot for 8 minutes and 46 seconds to honor the memory of George Floyd. And on June 9, 400 to 500 Buffalo teachers filled Niagara Square, still more evidence of the growing community-wide demonstration of support for racial justice.

Could it be that Buffalo's long legacy of inequality was in the process of healing and transformation? Was it possible that, as Federal District Judge John T. Curtin had long ago hoped, Buffalo might just become a beacon of pluralism for cities across the country? Could we really overcome the twin viruses that plagued us through the terrible Spring of 2020? Anything seemed possible to me when on June 13th, *The News* published a photographic "Salute to Seniors," a magnificent portfolio of portraits that staff photographer Mark Mulville had taken of more than 2,000 high school seniors all over Western New York. There was Niagara Falls senior Zayvon Sewell, a broad smile on his face, his favorite chess board held high above his head. Amherst High School senior Benjamin Mekinulov, standing tall, looking up into the sky, his cello held firmly in both of his hands. Cleveland Hill High School senior Aque'lah Douglas, happily balancing a basketball on the index finger of her right hand. Southwestern High School senior Jordan Smith, standing in front of a bright red fire truck and wearing the uniform of the fire fighter he hopes someday to be. Lewiston-Porter High School senior Gabriel Steiner, proudly carrying on his shoulder, his large, brass bass saxophone. Maryvale High School senior Rosa Vu, photographed joyously playing her violin. Niagara Falls senior Zachary Brydges, dressed in his catcher's uniform, his baseball bat in hand.

The faces of the high school seniors that Mulville had shot were happy and full of hope. They, like the rest of us, had gone through a horrifically challenging time and yet here they were, in Mulville's photos, reaching out, showing us that we, the people of Buffalo, would be alright. When, on July 12, at the delayed opening game of the Hertel North Buffalo Youth Baseball League at Shoshone Park, my grandson Max took the mound for the North Buffalo Blaze, I knew that they would.

Acknowledgements

It was **Ryan Gallivan** who encouraged me to pursue the healing work of creating our Facebook page "Picture this: Views from the homefront." It is a must see portfolio of hundreds of photographs taken during the high point of the pandemic of the places that people love in the city that they love.

See also **Sharon Cantillon**'s remarkable collection of portraits of health care workers in *The Buffalo News* on April 15, 2020 and Mark Mulville's portraits of high school seniors in the June 13th, 2020 edition of *The Buffalo News*.

Afterword

Me and Jeremiah

Following the destruction of Solomon's Temple in around 600 BC, the Jews of Judea were uprooted from their ancient homeland and exiled to Babylonia. While some of them mourned in despair, others saw an opportunity in what history refers to as "the Babylonian Captivity." Among them was the Prophet Jeremiah who, in a plea that changed history, urged his people to commit themselves to the new land in which they found themselves. Here's what he said and here, at some level, is what I heard during the years of my life in Buffalo:

"Build houses and settle down," he wrote. "Plant gardens and eat what they produce. Marry and have sons and daughters; find wives for your sons and give your daughters in marriage, so that they too may have sons and daughters. Increase in number there; do not decrease. Also, seek the peace and prosperity of the city to which I have carried you into exile. Pray to the Lord for it, because if it prospers, you too will prosper. (Jer. 29:5–7)

Jeremiah was right. Embrace your new home. Unravel its past, improve its present, plan for its future. Jump in, get dirty. Live, learn, love. Over the course of the more than half century that I have lived in Buffalo, my faith in Jeremiah's advice has been generously realized and abundantly fulfilled. My commitment to this place, to Buffalo, has led not only to my own personal transformation but to the transformation of the city itself.

Jeremiah's advice has worked for me and its worked for my children and grand children. They too – Charlotte, Eli and Max; Charlie, Lydia and Jonathan, who now lives in Brooklyn – have deep and lasting ties that bind them to Buffalo, a place where they know that, like me, they will never be alone. Buffalo is the city of their hearts as it is the city of mine.

Gratitude

Thanks to the book production team

Irene Sipos, David Levine, Karen Brady – book editors

Pauline Goulah, Linda Prinzi – book designers

Michael Morgulis – cover art

Brian Meyer, Western New York Wares – book distribution

Ralph Salerno, Keller Brothers – printer

Marti Gorman – advisor

Tim Bohen – publishing experience and expertise

Index

A

Adelphia Communications, 138
Adeyollah, Sabu, 125
African-American Heritage Corridor. 78–79
Agassiz Circle, 18, 65–66
Albright-Knox Art Gallery, 21, 90, 130, 159
Ali, Mugali, 156
Allen, John, 114
All Saints Parish, 96
Anderson, David, 116
Anderson Gallery, 71
Angie, Joanna, 107–109, 111, 124
Anthony, Jack, 98
Appleby, Rodney, 125
Arena, Sam, 162
Arlen, Harold, 78
Arluck, Samuel, 78
Arnone, James, 219
Aronoff, Jason, 71
Arthur, George, 77–79, 81, 92
Assumption Church, 36–37, 158

B

Bagel Jay's, 22
Bailey-Delavan, 18, 43
Baird Foundation, 137
Banham, Mary, 49
Banham, Reyner, 48–50, 71
Bannon, Anthony, 29
Barton, Maeve, 219
Basie, Count, 154
Bass Pro, 138–143
Baugh, Florence, 95
Bay Beach, Ontario, 187
Bazelon, Pat, 51, 71, 104
Beecher, Tom, 219
Belanger, Keith, 130
Belle Watlings running club, 59, 96
Bennett, Lewis J., 215–216
Berkoff, Saul, 23
Bethel A.M.E. church, 153
Bethlehem Steel, 16, 51, 55
Beyer, Bruce, 29
Billoni, Mike, 116
Bingham, Robert, 82
Bissonette, Fr. Joseph, 95
Black Rock, 17, 33–41, 45, 56, 77, 79–80, 86, 149, 157–158, 212
Black Rock Business Mens' Association, 37
Black Rock Historic Photo Project, 39
Black Rock Savings and Loan Association, 35–36
Black Student Union, 53
Blessed Trinity RC Church, 52, 95
Blizzard of 1977, 67, 69
Blue Bird Bus Company, 46
Blum, Bette, 59
Bohen, Tim, 193, 202, 203, , 206, 209
Bondi, Karima, 19, 55, 163
Bon Ton, The, 78
Botticelli, Vincent, 16
Bozer, Joan, 61–62, 64–66, 73
Brady, Karen, 45–46, 70
Breen, Michael, 168
Britzzalaro, Pat, 203
Broadway Market, 24, 45
Broderick Park, 151
Brown, Byron W., 139, 152, 168, 214–215, 219, 222, 229
Brown, William Wells, 91
Buffalo Academy of the Visual and Performing Arts, 153
Buffalo Architectural Guidebook 50

Buffalo Arts Studio, 107, 109, 124
Buffalo Athletic Club, 96
Buffalo Bills, 109–110
Buffalo Bisons, 153
Buffalo and Erie County Public Library, 26, 44, 62,83,124
Buffalo Creek Reservation, 82–84
Buffalo Fire Department, 191, 200–201, 208, 218
Buffalo Friends of Olmsted Parks, 61
Buffalo Garden Walk, 15, 197, 198
Buffalo Green Fund, The, 59
Buffalo and Erie County Historical Society, 44, 90
Buffalo Irish Center, 188, 190, 206
Buffalo Irish Genealogical Society, 190
Buffalo Jewish Family Services, 178
Buffalo Maritime Center, 222
Buffalo Nine, The, 2
Buffalo Olmsted Parks Conservancy , 15, 62, 65, 73
Buffalo Philharmonic Athletic Club, 59, 90, 96
Buffalo Philharmonic Orchestra, 21, 29, 57, 67
Buffalo Place, 113
Buffalo River, 198
Buffalo Science Museum, 90
Buffalo Slow-Roll , 15, 152
Rockwell Hall, 29
Buffalo Teachers Federation, 222
Buffalo Zoo, 60–61
Burchfield Penney Art Center, 29
Burgos, Ephraim, 126
Burke, Brendan, 217, 219
Burke, Christopher, 219
Burke, Mary Pat, 219
Burney, Jay, 63–65, 73
Burstein, Dr. Gale, 221, 226
Butera, Sal, 162

C

Caci, Joe, 162
Cala, Elena, 163
Callahan, Tom, 189
Calumet Building, 97, 103–111, 115–116, 120, 123, 132
Calumet Institute, The, 156
Calvaneso, Steve, 122
Canalside, 15, 137, 143, 147, 161
Canna, Ange, 111
Canna, Russ, 111
Cannon Design, 130, 134
Cantillon, Sharon, 227, 231
Capitano, Peter, 162
Cappas, Alberto, 53–54, 72, 86
Carmelite Monastery, 218
Carmina, Steve, 110
Carney, Joy, 203
Castle, "Bunny", 27–28
Catanzaro, Michael, 201
Cavanaugh, Megan Beecher, 219
Cazenovia Park, 195, 199, 205
Celtic Angels, 190
Central Park United Methodist Church, 217
Central Park, 5, 7–8, 53, 56, 66, 211–218
Central Park Homeowners Association, 217
CEPA Gallery, 67, 99, 114
Channel 17, WNED-TV 40
Checkers Running Club, 59
Chelowa, Susan, 157–158
Citizens for Common Sense 129, 131
City on the Edge, 20–21, 31, 56, 58, 100, 126, 134, 161
City on the Lake, 53, 54, 56, 74, 94, 97, 187
City Hall, 110, 125, 214, 219, 228–229
City Honors School, 141–143, 157, 176, 187, 217
Clarkson, Max, 49, 62, 71
Clarkson, Will, 49–50, 71
Clay, LaVerne, 111

Club Moonglow , 153
Cohen, Gary, 185–186
Cohen, Harold, 48–50, 70–71, 113
Cohen, Michael, 186
Cohn, Ann Joyce Holland, 183
Coit House, 62
Cold Spring, 40
Coles, Robert T., 28–29
Collins, Chris, 221
Collins, Max, 168
Collins, Mike, 40
Collins, Teddy, 168
Colonial Circle, Buffalo, 59
Colored Musicians Club ,78, 114, 153
Colpoys, Matty, 201
Columbia Market, 161
Commercial Slip, 137, 147, 161
Community Development Act of 1974, 51–52
Coniglio, Angelo, 162, 169
Cooper, Evelyn, 95
Corcoran, Danny, 208
Corcoran, Jack, 208
Corcoran, Meg, 120, 124, 168
Cornplanter Tract, 82, 84
Corrin, Patty, 121, 125
Costa, Michele, 141–142
Costantini, Allen, 54
Cottage Street Collective, 69
Coughlin, Jim, 203
Coyle, Jack, 193, 207
Crangle, Joe, 29
Crann, Tom, 115
Creative Associates, 67
Cronin, Jeannie, 194
Cronin, Peggy, 194–196, 200, 202–203, 205–206
Crowley, Kathleen, 194, 208
Cruz, Carlos Villaneuva, 168
Crystal Beach, 17, 166, 188
Cunningham, Kathy, 197
Cuomo, Gov. Andrew, 221, 223, 228
Cuomo, Mario, 135
Curry, Donna, 197
Curtin, John T., 64, 89–98, 116, 150, 187, 198, 230

D

D'Aloisio, Nick, 118
Daniels, Marva, 95
Dan Montgomery, 24, 78
Dargavel, Dennis, 194, 207
Darwin D. Martin House, 46,50
Daughters of Erin, 190
DeBeer, Ian, 168
Dee, Tom, 167
Degenhart, Mary, 33–34
Degenhart, Mikey, 36, 41
Delavan-Grider, 18
Delaware Avenue Jewish Center, 179, 180
Delaware District, 17, 28, 58, 176, 212
Delaware Park, 28, 30, 33–34, 39, 56–58, 60–62, 96–97, 154, 185, 213, 227
Delaware Park Shakespeare Festival, 67
Delaware Park Shortway, 58
Delaware Park Steering Committee (58–60, 62, 64, 73
Delaware Plaza,, 21–22
Delmonte, Jeanette, 169
Delmonte, Ralph, 169
Dexter's Pharmacy, 28
Dickman, Bob, 186
DiFranco, Ani, 114–115
DiLeo, Joe, 160–163, 166
DiTondo, Sebastiano, 79
Dole, Jim "Doler," 202
Donnelly, Bill, 72
Donnelly, Mike, 72
Donnelly, Tom, 72
Donovan, Jeanne, 125
Donovan Building, 57
Douglas, Aque'lah, 230
Dow, Peter, 29, 167, 222

Doyle, Bobby, 191–192, 208
Doyle, Jack, 192
Doyle, Vincent, 95

E

E. Ferry Street, 45, 152–154
Ederer, Lucy, 169
Electric District, 131
Elkin, Saul, 58, 67, 72
Ellicott District, 77–79, 86
Elmwood Avenue Festival of the Arts, 15
Elmwood Village, 15, 27, 151
Emerson Vocational High School, 24
Empire State College SUNY, 79, 81, 84–85, 88
Empire State Development Corporation, 137
Erie Basin Marina, 96
Erie Canal, 33–36, 41, 90, 135, 147, 161
Erie Canal Harbor Development Corporation (ECHDC), 138–140, 143, 147, 167, 222
Erie County Savings Bank, 20, 62
Esmonde, Donn, 136, 140, 143–144
Evans, Frank G. Dr., 28
Evans, Walker, 90
Evans, Willie, 24, 26

F

Fahey, Chris, 208
Falkenstein, Ed, 181
Farrell, Peggy, 109, 114
Favor, Macy, 125
Fenian Raid, 47
Fenians of the Gaelic Athletic Association, 190
Ferrer, Riccardo, 126
Ferry Street Corridor Project, The, 150, 152–154, 222
Fillmore-Leroy, Buffalo, 52
First Presbyterian Church, 227
First Ward, 22, 40, 45, 47, 52, 91, 96, 193, 195, 203–204, 224
Fisherman's Wharf, 100, 103
Fitzgerald, Barb, 194
Five Corners, 217
FLARE – Fillmore Leroy Area Residents , 52
Fleron, Lou Jean, 29
Floyd, George, 228
Foglia, Angela, 22
Fort Erie, 59
Forum, The, 27–28
Foss, Lukas, 21, 29
Foster Hall, 52
Fox, Austin, 63,70
Franklin & Chippewa, 100, 102
Friedman, Catherine, 211
Friedman, Janice, 179
Friedman, Milton, 57
Friends of the Buffalo Story, The 147, 152, 167
Friends of the School of Architecture, 50
Frisch, Michael D., 41
Fruit Belt, 18, 39, 40, 45, 127

G

Gaelic Youth Choir, 190
Gall, Kathy, 203
Gallivan, David, 86
Gallivan, Ryan, 219, 227–228, 230
Gallo, Laura Corrin, 219
Gallo, Lucille, 212, 218
Gallo, Patrick, 111, 168, 212–213
Gallo family, 218–219
Gambini, Bert, 125
Ganci, Rick Sr., 219
Gannon, Grace, 194, 208
Gannon, Jeannie, 208
Gardner, Irene, 81
Gaston, Doug "Trigger," 125
Geiger, Rich, 130
Genesee-Moselle, 18
Gerber, David, 136
Giambra, Joe, 160, 163–166, 168,226
Giambra, Joel, 131, 139

Gilbert, Don, 186
Gilmartin, Pat, 168
Giacobbe, Frank, 162
Gioia, Anne, 197
Gioia, Richard, 168
Golden Cup, The, 222
Golden Tee Golf Club 60
Goldfarb, Norman, 27
Goldman, Barbara, 5, 7, 12, 173
Goldman, Charlie, 6, 35, 44–45, 70, 96, 111, 116–117, 121–122, 150, 157–158, 168, 172–174, 176–178, 212–214
Goldman, Charlotte, 213
Goldman, Kitty, 14, 46, 176–177, 211, 219
Goldman, Kitty Friedman, 186
Goldman, Lydia, 158, 176–178, 187–188, 212–214, 218, 223
Goldman, Mark, 45, 62, 116
Goldman, Megan, 213
Goldman, Tillie, 5–8, 13
Goldman, Tony, 5, 7, 18–19, 99–100, 103–105, 108, 112, 118, 120, 124, 130, 141–142, 156–159, 173
Goldstein, Rose, 179
Goman, Stone Horse Lone, 148–149
Gomes, Jimmy, 125
Gordon, Barrett, 150–151, 168
Gordon, Cricket, 211, 219
Gorman, Marti, 224
Gotham Antique Warehouse, 36
Governor's Inn, 26
Grant-Amherst, 43
Graphic Controls, 49, 71
Great Arrow Building, 69
Greenberg, Heschel, 184
Greenberg, Steven, 186
Greene, Finley, 61
Griffin, James D, 61, 86–87, 96, 113
Griffin, Richard E., 29, 95, 98
Gross, Alan, 57–59
Grosvenor Collection, 44
Guaranty Building, 74
Gugino, Martin, 229
Gurary, Nosan, 184

H

Hallwalls, 99
Halpern, Steve, 144, 154–155, 184–186
Hamlin Park, 40
Harrington, Mike, 225
Hawley, Jesse, 148
Hayes, Matt, 203
Hayes Hall, 45, 49, 51
Healy, Dan, 40
Hello World Restaurant, 27, 74
Heneghan, Mary, 190, 192, 206
Heneghan, Tom Jr., 206
Hertel North Buffalo Youth Baseball League, 217–218
Higgins, Brian M., 137, 140, 145, 189, 194, 207–208
Higgins, Daniel J., 29, 207
Hill, Lorna, 114
Hochfield, Marilyn, 98
Hoffman, Monte, 29
Hogan, Josephine, 117, 120
Holly Farms, 111, 156
Holtz, Carol, 95
Holy Cross Cemetery, 203–204
Holy Family RC Church, 195–196, 206
Hornung, John, 219
Hotel Buffalo, 20
Hotel Worth, 20
Hoyt, Carol, 26–28, 43
Hoyt, "Sam", 167
Hoyt, William B., 26–28, 56, 58, 60
Hoyt Lake, 185
Humboldt Parkway, 18, 22, 28–29, 65
Huntington, Richard, 100
Hurley, Maureen, 139

I

Ingalls, Don, 222
Inner Harbor, 134, 137–138
Irene K. Gardner Pedestrian Bridge, 81
Irish Classical Theater Company, 108, 117–118, 122, 164, 222
Irish Republican Army, 204
Irving Collective, The, 86
Islamorada, Florida, 138

J

Jacobs, Jane, 9–11, 13, 20, 111, 130–131, 157
Jamie Moses Band, The, 109
Jay, David, 98
Jewish Community Center (JCC), 22–23, 26, 57
Jewish Federation of Greater Buffalo, 181
John, Thomas, 82–84
Jordan, Joe, 59
Just Buffalo Literary Center, 67, 74, 99, 108

K

Kahn, Joan, 59
Kaiser, Margaret, 168
Kaisertown, Buffalo, 40
Kam, Charlie, 188, 208
Kam, Diane, 188, 208
Kam, Kristin, 187–188
Kane, David, 108–109, 114
Kane, James, 197
Kane, Pat, 192
Katz, Lenny, 186
Keane, Bill "Puff," 199, 208
Keane, Dick, 193, 199
Keane, Jim, 191, 193, 199–200, 209
Keane, Katy, 191
Keane, Margaret, 191, 200, 208
Keane, Meg, 191
Keane, Mike, 199
Keane, Neal, 199
Keil, Angelica, 85
Kelleher, Barbara Fitzpatrick, 208
Kelleher, Mary Annunciata, 194
Kensington Expressway, 18, 28, 45, 56
Kent, Fred, 11, 61, 141–144, 157
Kerns, Rev. Walter, 52, 95
Kinzua Dam, 82
Kirst, Sean, 45
Kleinhans Music Hall, 59
Kornmehl's Kosher Meat Market, 23
Kowsky, Frank, 50
Krakowiak, Walter, 35–37
Kregal, Jesse, 57–59, 72
Ku Klux Klan, 101
Kunz, Mary, 125

L

LaChiusa, Chuck, 47
Lalley, Kevin, 203
La Luna , 56, 123–125
Lampe, David, 61
Lampe, Ruth, 61
Landmarks Society of the Niagara Frontier, 62, 64
Lane, Jeffrey Paul, 117
Lange, Neil, 186
Langer, Eli, 215–217
Langer, Jonathan, 89, 213
Langer, Max, 6, 214, 216–217, 230
Langer, Rob, 215
Langer, Susan, 178
Larkin Soap Company, 49
LaRussa, Charlie, 100–105, 108, 124
LaSalle Park, 96
Lasher, Terry, 50
Latona, Laura, 168
LaVoie, Franklin, 115, 219
Leader, Elizabeth, 215
Leaf, James, 148, 168
Lehman, Bob O., 40
Lehner, Marissa, 168

Leone, Charlie, 36, 39
Levick, Irving, 29
Levine, Murray, 185, 226
Licata Plumbing, 111
Lickfeld, Jim, 201
Lindemann, Edna, 29
Lindsay, John, 9, 11–12, 61, 144
Linwood Historic District, 152
Lippes, Joel, 112
Lipsey, Stan, 116
Little Harlem, The, 24–26, 153
Lockwood, Bonnie Kane, 198, 200, 208
Lockwood, Byron, 229
LoGiacono, Peter, 169
Lonergan, Edward K., 204
Lovejoy, 17
Lower Manhattan Expressway, 8–9
Lower West Side, 54, 127, 160, 163, 165–166
Lower West Side Resources and Development Corporation, 55
Lunenfeld, Marvin, 115
Lynch, Kevin, 9–11

M

M. Wile, 16
MacCameron, Bob, 87
Madison, Joe, 125
Magavern, Bill, 62
Maggio, Tony, 162
Maggiore, Sal, 162
Maher, Dennis, 141
Mahoney, Kevin, 219
Mahoney, Maeve, 22
Maiman, David, 186
Maiman, Ginger, 186
Maio, Mark, 88
Makowski, Stanley, 58
Malliaris, Stavros, 112
Marine Midland Bank, 63
Marine Midland Tower, 87
Market Arcade, 113
"Mark Goldman's Rubberneck Bus Tour of Buffalo," 45–47
Masiello, Anthony, 131–132, 134–138
Masling, Joe, 185
Massey, Chuck, 150, 168, 222
Mastman's Deli, 23
McCartney, Susan, 65, 74, 111, 144
McDonnell, Tommy, 192, 198
McEwen, Billy, 114
McGrath, Margaret, 206, 209
McKendry, Dave, 219
McKinley Monument, 228
McKinley Parkway, 198
McMahon, Bridget, 202
McMahon, John E., 204
Meadow, The, 57–58, 60–61, 96
Media Studies, 67
Mekinulov, Benjamin, 230
Meldrum, Michael, 114
Mendell, Mark, 130, 134
Menza, Don "Red", 163
Merino, Lou, 163
Merla, Richie, 163
Meter Building, 48
Michigan Street, 24, 45, 152–154
Michigan Street Baptist Church, 78
Mikhashoff, Yvar, 115
Miles, Marshall, 78
Mintz, Rabbi Shay, 179
Montague, John, 137, 148, 222
Montague, Julian, 168
Montana, John, 46–47, 89
Montefiore Club, 172–173
Montgomery, Ann, 24–26, 78
Montgomery, Dan, 24–25, 78
Morgulis, Michael, 69–70, 74, 108
Morris, Don, 219
Morris, Johnny, 138
Morris, Johnny Jr., 139
Moses, Jamie, 109, 114, 124–125

Moxley, Henry, 78
Moynihan, Daniel P., 61, 64–65
Mulville, Mark, 230
Murphy, Michael G., 223
Murray, Joseph T., 93, 95-97, 98, 116, 187
Murray, Karen Lickfeld, 198, 201–203, 205, 209
Muscarella's Pastry Shop, 19, 160
Mutual Rowing Club , 205

N

Nagle, Teddy, 193
Nardin Academy, 151
Neri, Martha, 73
New Buffalo Graphics, 69
New Chippewa Hotel, 102
New York State Department of Transportation (NYSDOT), 57–58
New York State Thruway (NYS Thruway), 35–36, 56, 80–81, 163
Niagara Falls, 59, 230
Niagara Frontier Transportation Agency, 152
Niagara Movement, 92
Niagara Parkway, 59
Niagara River, 35–36, 38–39, 45, 55, 59, 80–81, 91, 141, 151, 185, 212, 228
Niagara Square, 63, 67, 214, 229–230
Nietzsche's, 114
Niland, Bridget, 222
North Buffalo, 18, 22, 52, 57, 95, 176, 181, 185, 188, 211–218
Northern Irish Aid (NORAID), 192
Norton Union, 53
Noto, Sam, 163
Nussbaumer, John, 129–130, 144

O

O'Brien, Charlie, 193
Offerman, Frank, 153
Offerman Stadium, 45, 153–154, 168, 222–223
Ohio Street Bridge, 96, 142
Olivenzia, Chito, 125
Olmsted, Frederick Law, 15, 18, 62, 199, 215
Olmsted Conservancy, 65, 199
Olmsted Parks, 58
O'Neil, Mary Alice, 200–201
O'Neill, Chris, 108–109, 114, 117–119, 123, 164
O'Neill, Josephine, 108–109, 117–119, 123, 125, 164
O'Neill, Kevin, 191
O'Neill, Lara, 117–119, 123, 164
O'Neill, Mary Alice, 209
O'Neill, Vincent, 107, 109, 117–119, 123, 125, 164, 222
Osterreicher, Mickey, 29
Otowega Club, 216
Ott, Debora, 70, 74, 108
Otto, John, 203
Outer Circle Orchestra, 114
Outer Harbor, 15
Overdorf, Gene, 203–204, 209
Overdorf, Peggy, 203
Ozarin, Bess, 179–181
Ozarin, Sylvia, 179–181

P

Pace, Jim, 209
Parkside Community Association, 29, 61, 95, 98
Parkside Lodge, 61
Parkside Lutheran Church, 216
Pataki, George, 134–138
Patti, Larry, 178
Paul Robeson Theater, 114
Paulus, Greg, 225
Peace Bridge, 48, 59, 188, 227
Perez, Francisco ("Frankie,") 53–56, 72,125
Perry, Clayton, 168
Pfeiffer Theater, 117
Pidyon Ha'ben, 172, 174
Pine Grill, The, 24, 26, 28, 78

Pirakas, Joe, 95
Pitts, James, 86
Pizarro, Jose, 53–54, 72
Poloncarz, Mark, 225–226
Popper, Lilli, 180
Popper, Otto, 23, 180
Precious, Tom, 224
Preservation Coalition, 65, 74, 111–112, 136, 144
Price, Arlene, 72
Price, William D., 51–53, 95
Project for Public Spaces , 61
Prudential Building, 46, 51, 63–65, 116
Pucho Olivencia's Puerto Rican American Community Organization, 55
Puerto Rican and Hispanic Heritage Parade, 15
Puerto Rican-Chicano Coordinating Committee, 55–56
Puerto Rican Organization for Dignity, Elevation and Responsibility (PODER), 53–54

Q

Qadir, Abdul Rachman, 125
Quinan, Jack, 50
Quinn, Larry, 86, 139
Quinones, Frankie, 126

R

Ranalli, Steve, 167
Randall, Jack, 116
Randall, John, 50, 63–66, 73–74
Rawson, Stratton, 115
Red Jacket, 83, 91, 97, 192
Red Jacket Parkway, 199
Redmond, Dan Jr., 209
Redmond, Dan Sr., 209
Reilly, Margaret, 192
Republic Steel, 16, 22
Reville, Eugene, 93, 95-97, 98, 187
Ricco, Joe, 154
Rich, Bob, 138–139
Rich, Mindy, 138–139
Richardson, Mozella, 95
Rigas Family, 138
Rince Na Tiarna Irish Dancers, 190, 191, 206
Ring Road, 57–60, 96
Ritz, Joe, 19
Rivera, Wendell, 126
Riverside, 17, 97
Riverside Park, 81
Rizzo, Sal, 161
Rodriguez, Casimiro "Caz," 53, 72
Rodriguez, Ramon, 125
Rodriquez, "JaJo", 126
Rogliano, Joseph S., 219
Rogovin, Milton, 55, 163
Root Building, 23
Rose Garden, 58
Rosen, Samantha, 223
Rossman, Sophia, 179
Rubino, Joe, 114
Ruins, 147, 148–149, 161
Ryan, Joe, 52–53
Ryan, Eileen, 72
Ryan, Marge, 196–202, 208

S

Sachs, Diana, 115
Salvatore, Russell, 162
Santasiero's Restaurant, 37
Sapienza, Vicky, 27, 74
Sarsnett, George C., 78
Scahill, Joan, 206
Scajaquada Creek Expressway, 45, 57, 60, 72
Scalabrini, Giovanni Battista, 166
Scamacca, Sam, 165
Scanlon, Amanda, 202
Scanlon, Chris, 192, 202–203
Scanlon, Kara, 203
Scanlon, Mark, 202
Schiller, Harvey, 22

Schmand, Mike, 219
School of Irish Culture and Language, 190
Schuele Paint Company), 111
Schuper House, 37
Schuta, Terry, 198, 200
Schwartz, Rosie, 6, 127–144, 173
Schwendler, Norm, 59
Sebastian, Joe, 162
Sedita, Frank, 19
Seneca-Babcock, 43
Seneca Chief, 137
Seneca Nation, 134, 148
Sewell, Zayvon, 230
Shakespeare Hill, 58, 72
Shanahan, Chris, 203
Shanor Electric, 111
Shatzel, Dave, 112
Shea's Theater, 46, 113
Sheehan, Liz, 219
Shelgren, Olaf "Bill," 62–63, 73
Shoshone Park, 15, 217-218, 230
Silvestri, Phil, 110
Simon, Jeff, 125
Sipos, David, 125
Skretney, William M., 136–137, 139
Skylon International Marathon, The, 59–60, 72
Smith, Rick, 142–143
Smukler, Phyllis, 179
Soldiers Place, 59
South Buffalo Alive, 15
Spanish Speaking Political Caucus, 55
Spirit of Buffalo Study Group, 66
SS Canadiana, 17
St. Agatha's RC Church 195–196
St. Ambrose RC Church, 95, 196
St. Anthony of Padua RC Church, 161–162, 166
St. Brigid's RC Church, 40
St. Francis Xavier RC Church, 35–37
St. John's RC Church, 192
St. John the Evangelist RC Church, 195, 199
St. Joseph RC Church, 91
St. Lawrence Seaway, 16, 90, 187
St. Louis RC Church 63, 73
St. Lucy's Parish, 22, 79, 80, 82, 160, 166
St. Lucy's Society, 79
St. Margaret's RC Church, 23, 217–218
St. Mark Parish, 52, 95, 217–219
St. Martin's RC Church, 195–196
St. Patrick's Day, 197
St. Patrick's RC Church, 222, 225
St. Paul's Episcopal Church, 85,91
St. Rose of Lima RC Church, 95, 217–219
St. Teresa's RC Church, 45 95, 187, 190, 195, 196, 198
St. Thomas Aquinas RC Church, 195–198, 202-204
Stan and The Ravens, 114–115
Stanton, Msgr. Willian, 95
Stern, Trudy, 74
Stieglitz, David, 63–65, 73, 86
Stitt, Jackie, 222
Stitt, Larry, 222
Studio Arena Theater, 113
Sullivan, Dennis, 208
Sullivan, Louis, 50, 63
Sullivan, Ray, 208
Sullivan, Terry, 115
Sullivan's Raid, 83
Sultz, Irv, 22
Swift, Tim, 60
Symphony Circle, Buffalo, 59
Szczygiel, Peggy, 206

T

Talbert, Mary, 91–92, 97
Tan, Sandra, 225
Tanzella, Joe, 79–82
Tasca, Peter, 169
Temple Beth Abraham, 177
Temple Beth El, 182

Temple Beth Zion, 172, 182, 184
Texidor, Juan, 126
Theater District Association, 113, 125, 127
Theater Loft, 114
Theater of Youth, 113
Theater Place, 86, 113
Them Jazzbeards 108, 114
Third Room, The, 122, 124–125
Thomas, Michael Tilson, 29
Tielman, Tim, 47, 51, 63, 65, 74, 111, 116, 129, 136–137, 139–142, 144, 147
Timon, Bishop John, 91, 97
Tinney, Al, 114, 125
Tobin, Nancy, 74
Tonawanda Reservation, 82
Tralfamadore , 115, 121
Trio, Jimmy Gomes, 114
Twentieth Century Club, 49

U

Unitarian Universalist Church, 29
University District, 51
Utzig, Jack, 33–35, 37, 39

V

Vendome, 24
Viola, Ralph, 109–110
Virginia Street Festival, 55
Vitello, Andy, 114
Volker, Tracy, 168

W

Wahl, Erica, 114
Walker, Sherman, 78
Wallace, Anthony F. C., 83–84
Waltz, Mary, 81
Wantuch, Brian, 141–142
Warfe, Don, 112
War of 1812, 38, 83
Warren Spahn Way, 199
Wash Project, The, 150–151, 168
Waszkielewicz, Tony, 201
Weimer, Rev. John, 95
Weinrib, Harry, 178, 186
Weissman, Karla, 186
Werrick, John, 125
Westinghouse Electric, 84–85
Westminster Presbyterian Church, 211
West Side Arterial, 56
Whitman, Marilyn, 186
Whitman, Walt, 40
Williams, Cy, 199
Williams, Olive, 62
Win, Zaw, 150, 168
Witherspoon, Reggie, 225
Wood, Scott, 167
Wright, Frank Lloyd, 46, 50, 74, 112
Wright, Lydia Dr., 28, 48, 70, 96

Y

Young, Perry, 106–107

Z

Zeligman, Max, 179
Ziskind, Semyon, 179
Zisquit, Daria, 174
Zisquit, Donald, 174–177, 184, 186
Zisquit, Linda, 174–176, 186